FROM A TO B
A CARTOON GUIDE
TO GETTING AROUND BY BIKE

DAVE WALKER

BLOOMSBURY SPORT

LONDON · OXFORD · NEW YORK · NEW DELHI · SYDNEY

BLOOMSBURY SPORT
Bloomsbury Publishing Plc
50 Bedford Square, London, WC1B 3DP, UK
29 Earlsfort Terrace, Dublin 2, Ireland

BLOOMSBURY, BLOOMSBURY SPORT and the Diana logo are trademarks of Bloomsbury Publishing Plc

First published in Great Britain 2021

Copyright © Dave Walker, 2021

Dave Walker has asserted his right under the Copyright, Designs and Patents Act, 1988,
to be identified as Author of this work

All rights reserved. No part of this publication may be reproduced or transmitted in any form or by any means,
electronic or mechanical, including photocopying, recording, or any information storage or retrieval system,
without prior permission in writing from the publishers

A catalogue record for this book is available from the British Library

Library of Congress Cataloguing-in-Publication data has been applied for

ISBN: HB: 978-14729-7613-0; eBook: 978-14729-7615-4

2 4 6 8 10 9 7 5 3 1

Printed in China by RRD Asia Printing Solutions Limited

To find out more about our authors and books visit www.bloomsbury.com and sign up for our newsletters

CONTENTS

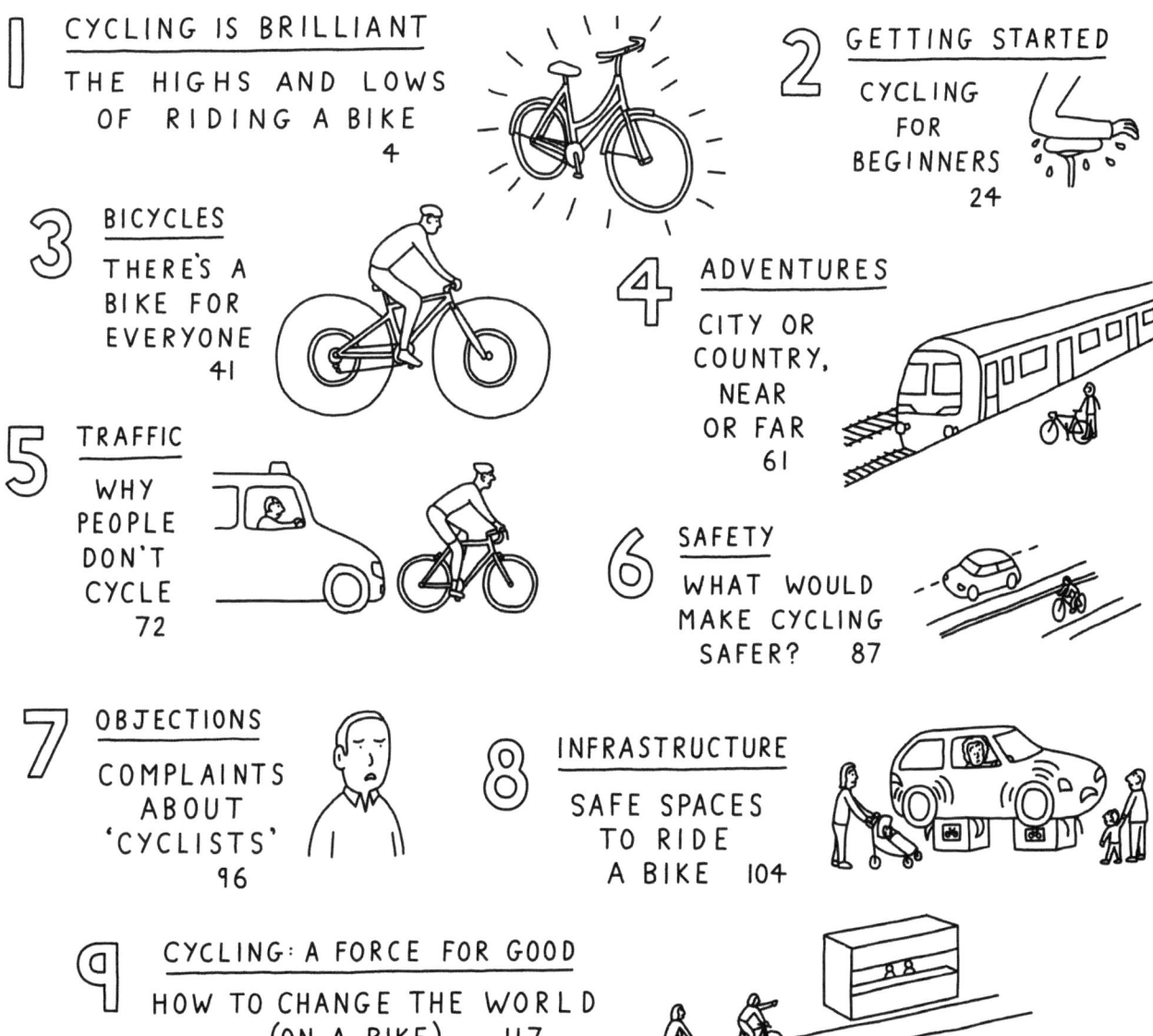

1 CYCLING IS BRILLIANT
THE HIGHS AND LOWS OF RIDING A BIKE 4

2 GETTING STARTED
CYCLING FOR BEGINNERS 24

3 BICYCLES
THERE'S A BIKE FOR EVERYONE 41

4 ADVENTURES
CITY OR COUNTRY, NEAR OR FAR 61

5 TRAFFIC
WHY PEOPLE DON'T CYCLE 72

6 SAFETY
WHAT WOULD MAKE CYCLING SAFER? 87

7 OBJECTIONS
COMPLAINTS ABOUT 'CYCLISTS' 96

8 INFRASTRUCTURE
SAFE SPACES TO RIDE A BIKE 104

9 CYCLING: A FORCE FOR GOOD
HOW TO CHANGE THE WORLD (ON A BIKE) 117

CHAPTER 1

CYCLING IS BRILLIANT
THE HIGHS AND LOWS OF RIDING A BIKE

INTRODUCTION

HELLO AND WELCOME. THIS IS A BOOK ABOUT GOING...

FROM
A
[DOWNS]
[UPS]
[VARIOUS COMPLICATIONS WE WILL DEAL WITH IN LATER CHAPTERS]
TO
B

BY BICYCLE

(OR ANOTHER KIND OF CYCLE WITH A DIFFERENT NUMBER OF WHEELS) →

1.
3.
5.

IF YOU ARE MORE INTERESTED IN THE SPORT AND RACING SIDE OF CYCLING YOU WILL MOST CERTAINLY STILL ENJOY THIS BOOK

WE JUST ASK THAT YOU CONDUCT YOUR RACING ON AN UPRIGHT DUTCH BICYCLE FOR THE DURATION

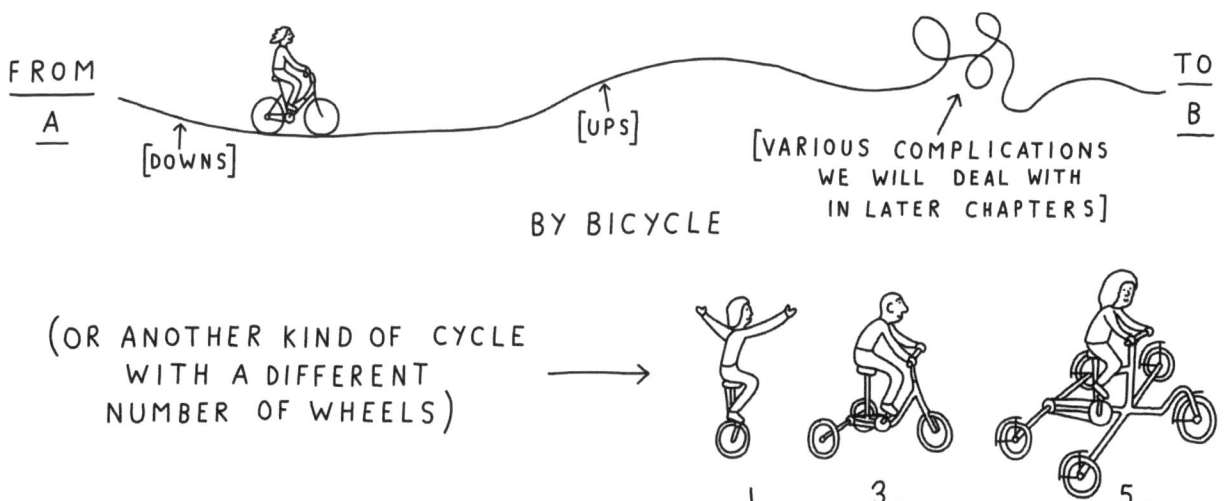

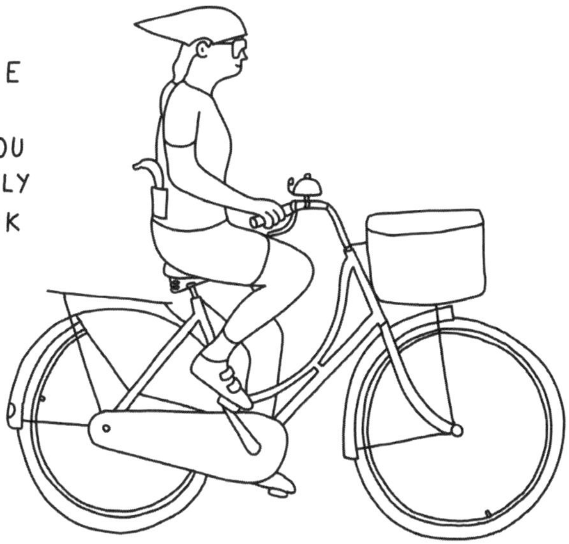

IN THIS BOOK

INTRODUCTORY REMARKS (CONTINUED)

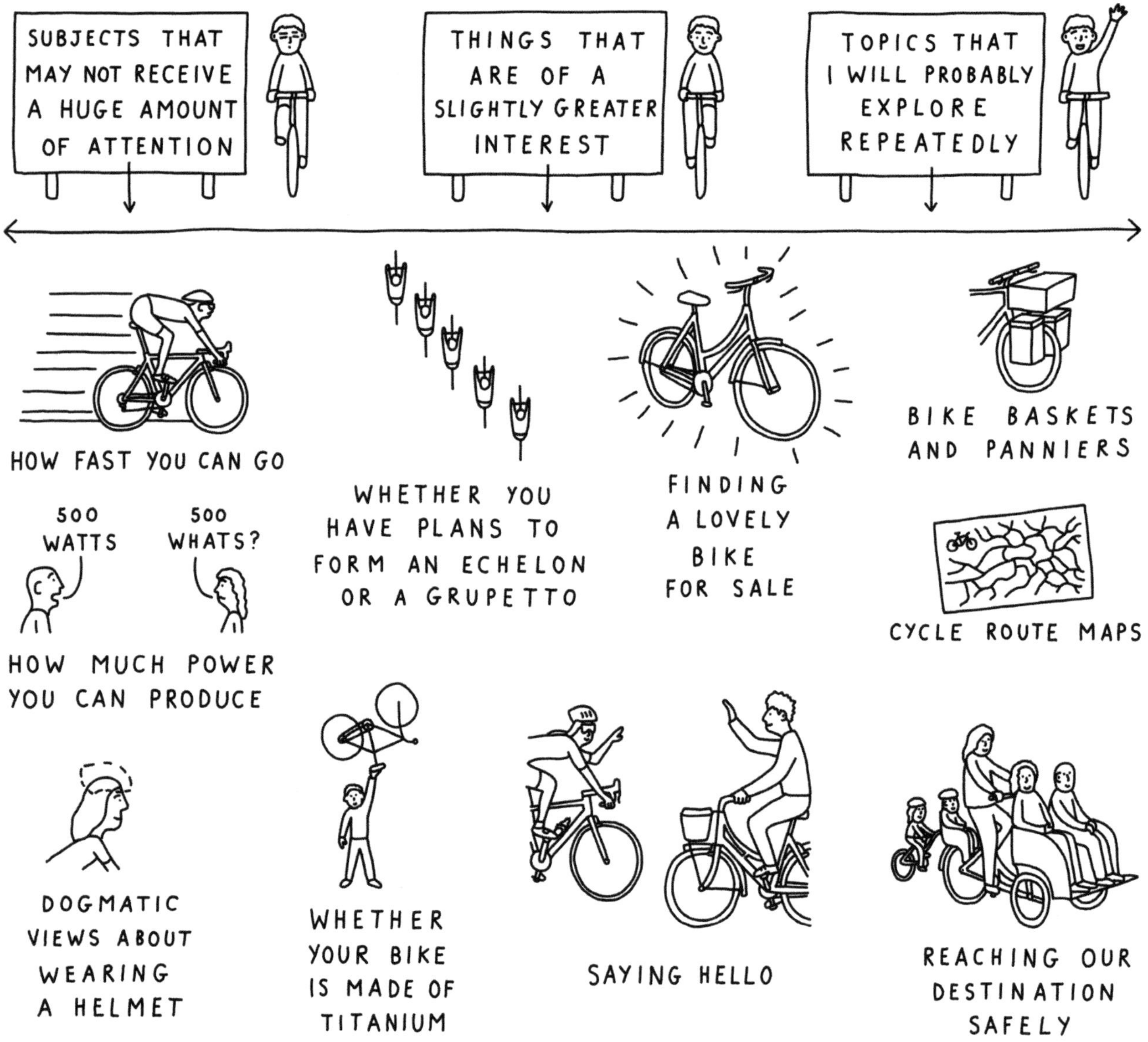
SUBJECTS THAT MAY NOT RECEIVE A HUGE AMOUNT OF ATTENTION
THINGS THAT ARE OF A SLIGHTLY GREATER INTEREST
TOPICS THAT I WILL PROBABLY EXPLORE REPEATEDLY
HOW FAST YOU CAN GO
500 WATTS
500 WHATS?
HOW MUCH POWER YOU CAN PRODUCE
DOGMATIC VIEWS ABOUT WEARING A HELMET
WHETHER YOU HAVE PLANS TO FORM AN ECHELON OR A GRUPETTO
WHETHER YOUR BIKE IS MADE OF TITANIUM
FINDING A LOVELY BIKE FOR SALE
SAYING HELLO
BIKE BASKETS AND PANNIERS
CYCLE ROUTE MAPS
REACHING OUR DESTINATION SAFELY

FROM A TO B

THE ADVANTAGES OF TRAVELLING BY BICYCLE

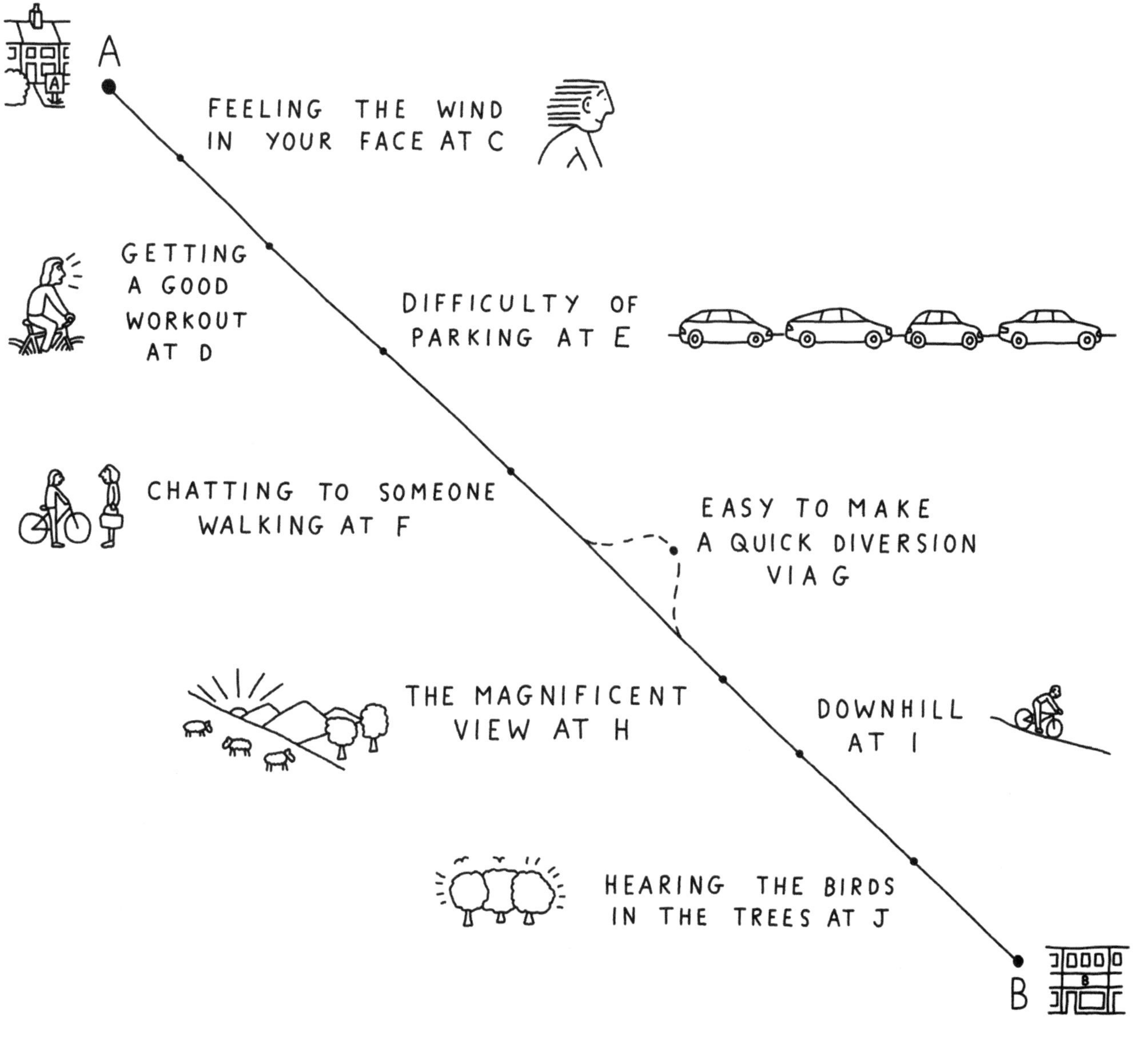
A
FEELING THE WIND IN YOUR FACE AT C
GETTING A GOOD WORKOUT AT D
DIFFICULTY OF PARKING AT E
CHATTING TO SOMEONE WALKING AT F
EASY TO MAKE A QUICK DIVERSION VIA G
THE MAGNIFICENT VIEW AT H
DOWNHILL AT I
HEARING THE BIRDS IN THE TREES AT J
B

MULTI-TASKING

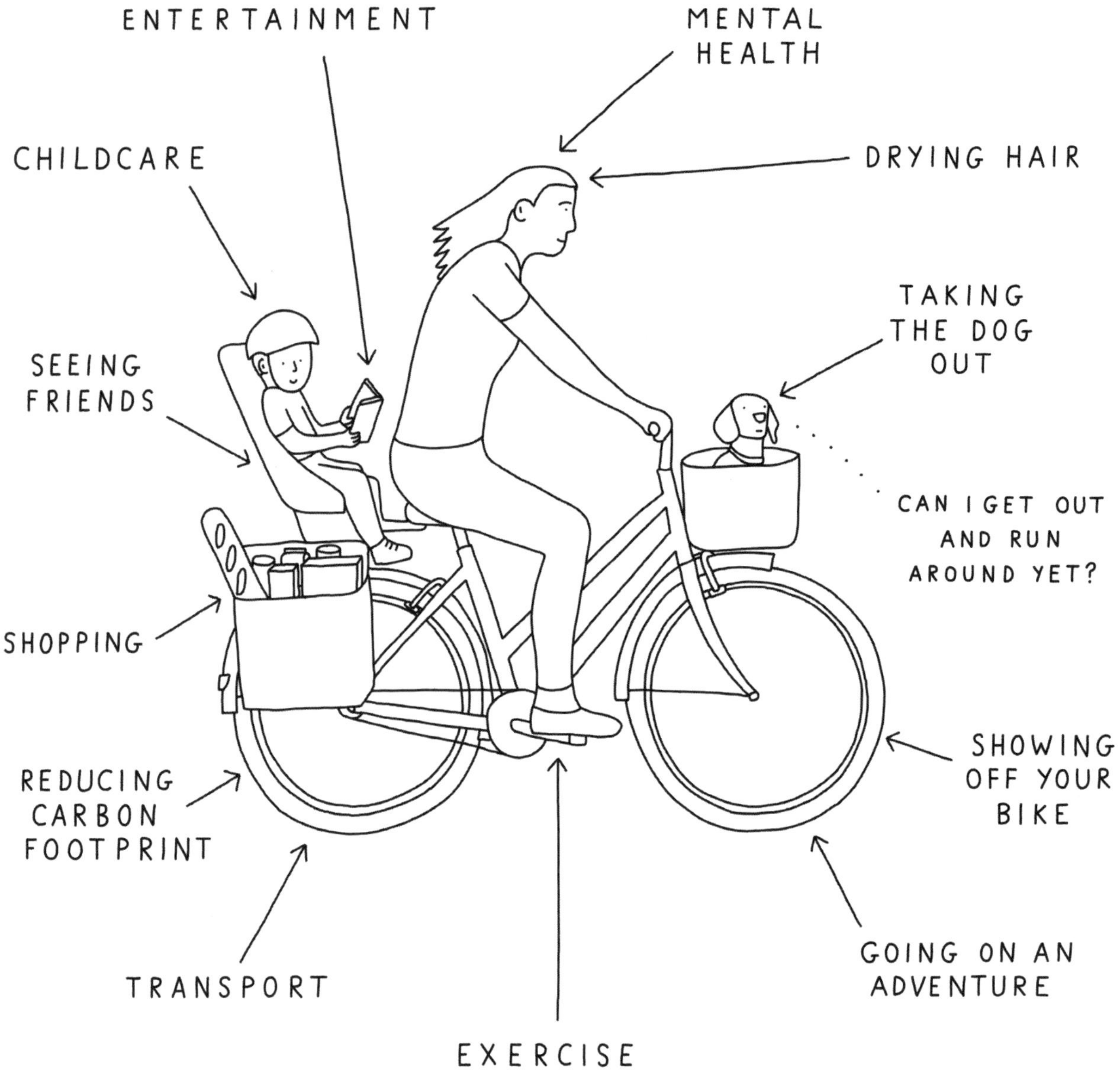
ENTERTAINMENT
MENTAL HEALTH
CHILDCARE
DRYING HAIR
TAKING THE DOG OUT
SEEING FRIENDS
CAN I GET OUT AND RUN AROUND YET?
SHOPPING
SHOWING OFF YOUR BIKE
REDUCING CARBON FOOTPRINT
GOING ON AN ADVENTURE
TRANSPORT
EXERCISE

WHAT I'M THINKING ABOUT

WHEN I'M RIDING MY BIKE

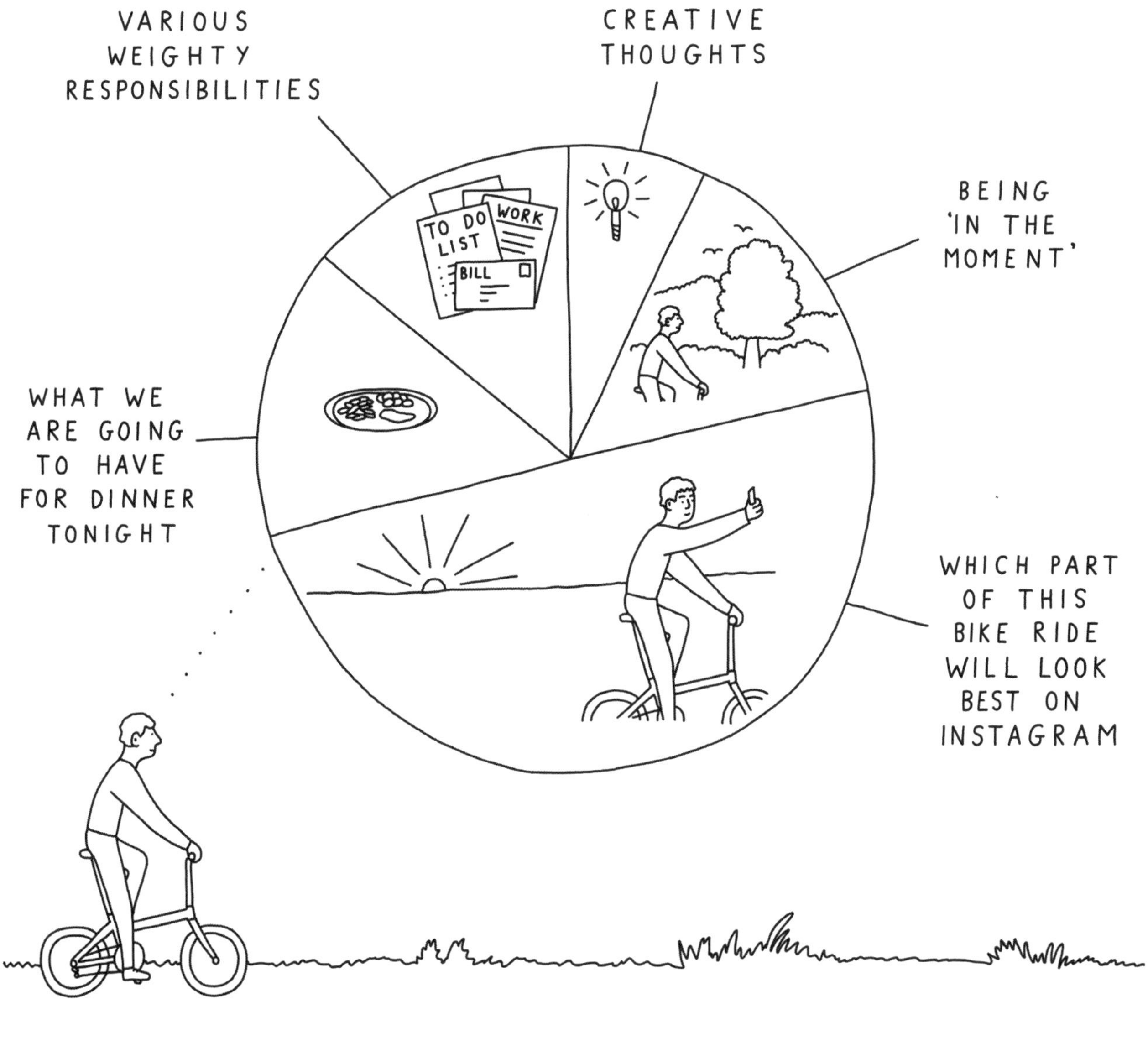
VARIOUS WEIGHTY RESPONSIBILITIES
CREATIVE THOUGHTS
BEING 'IN THE MOMENT'
WHAT WE ARE GOING TO HAVE FOR DINNER TONIGHT
WHICH PART OF THIS BIKE RIDE WILL LOOK BEST ON INSTAGRAM
TO DO LIST
WORK
BILL

FRIENDS
TO RIDE YOUR BIKE WITH

STYLISH JAMES

CONFIDENT EVA

HIGHLY-PREPARED ASIM

MECHANICAL AMY

SPEEDY SARAH

NAVIGATIONAL ZOE

CONVERSATIONAL MARIO

LEISURELY CLARA

WOBBLY PHIL

FAMILY CYCLING

CYCLING WITH CHILDREN

ON YOUR BIKE

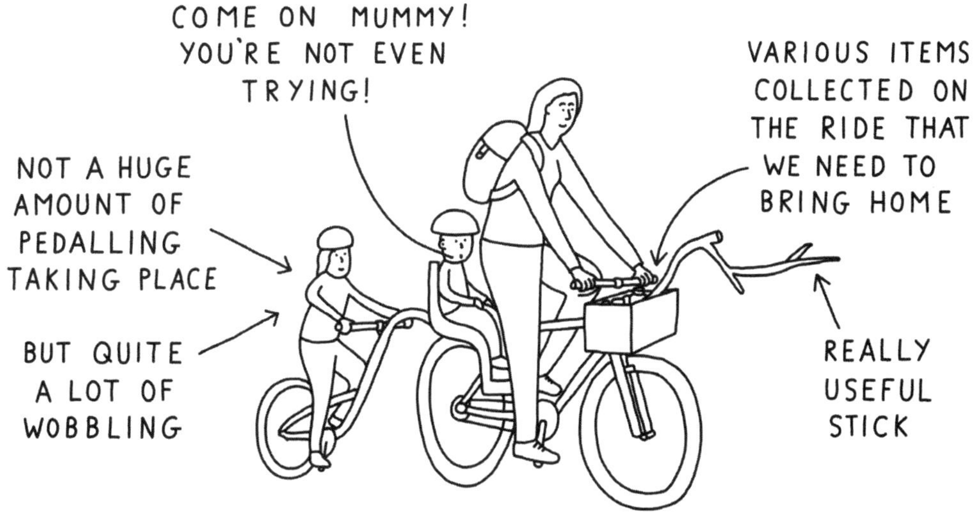
COME ON MUMMY! YOU'RE NOT EVEN TRYING!
NOT A HUGE AMOUNT OF PEDALLING TAKING PLACE
BUT QUITE A LOT OF WOBBLING
VARIOUS ITEMS COLLECTED ON THE RIDE THAT WE NEED TO BRING HOME
REALLY USEFUL STICK

ON THEIR OWN BIKES

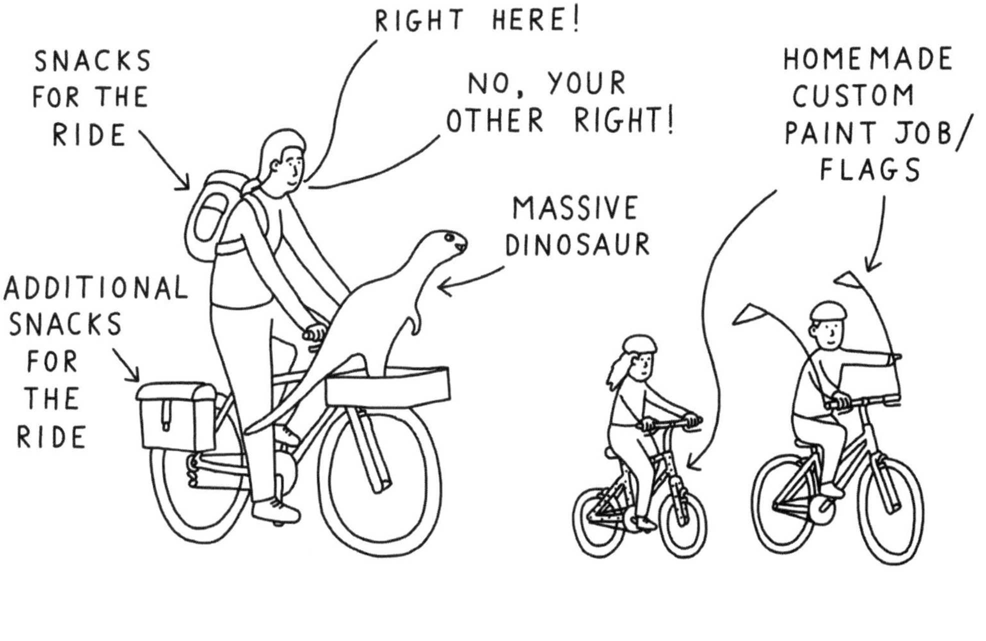
RIGHT HERE!
NO, YOUR OTHER RIGHT!
SNACKS FOR THE RIDE
HOMEMADE CUSTOM PAINT JOB/ FLAGS
MASSIVE DINOSAUR
ADDITIONAL SNACKS FOR THE RIDE

COMMUTING
BY BIKE

NO NEED TO BE CRAMMED IN WITH OTHER COMMUTERS

YOU KNOW HOW LONG YOUR JOURNEY WILL TAKE

A WAY TO FIT EXERCISE INTO YOUR DAILY ROUTINE

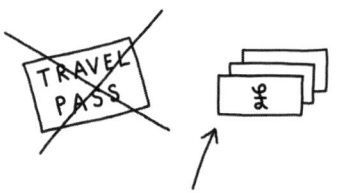

MONEY SAVED WHILE COMMUTING

(LATER SPENT ON NEW BIKE)

IT SAVES YOU MONEY

AT WORK

HOW TO RECOGNISE CO-WORKERS WHO COMMUTE BY BIKE

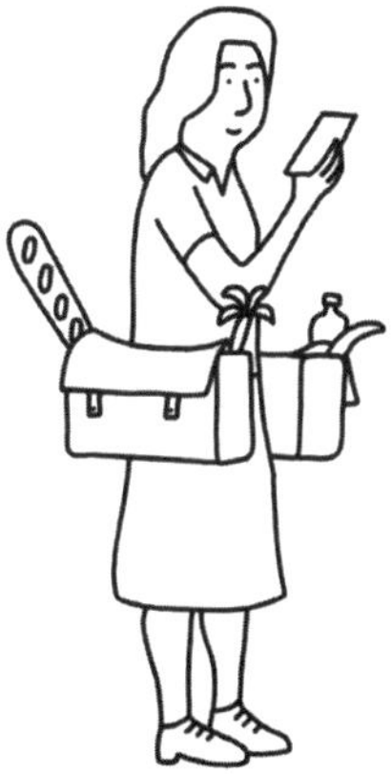

USE PANNIERS INSTEAD OF A LUNCH BOX

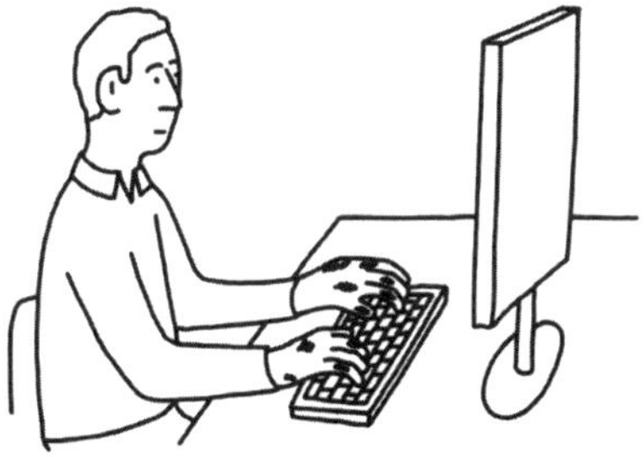

OIL-STAINED HANDS

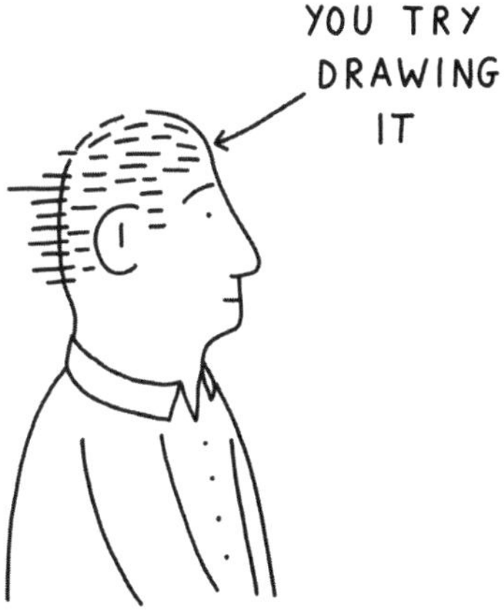
YOU TRY DRAWING IT

HAIR SIMULTANEOUSLY FLATTENED AND WINDSWEPT

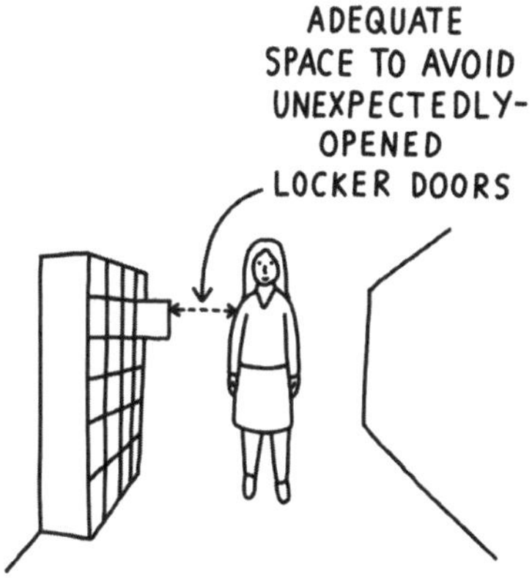
ADEQUATE SPACE TO AVOID UNEXPECTEDLY-OPENED LOCKER DOORS

'TAKING THE LANE' IN THE CORRIDOR

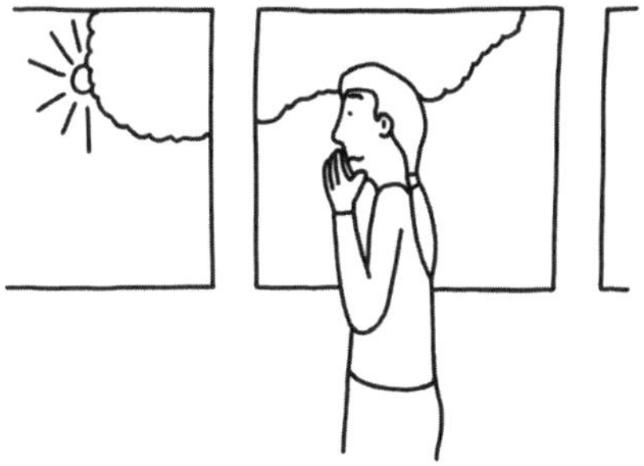

NERVOUSLY LOOKING OUT OF THE WINDOW AT THE WEATHER

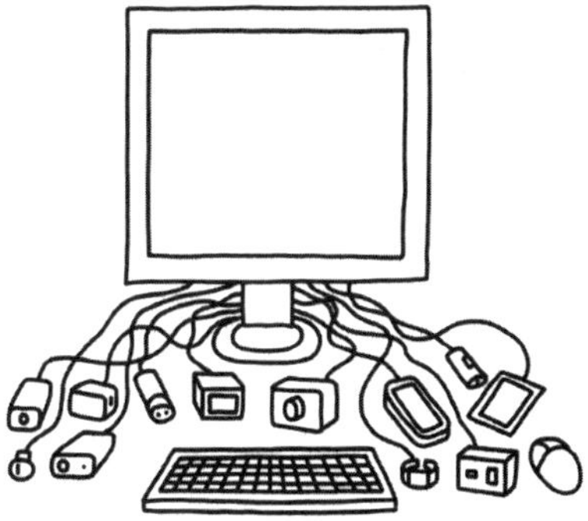

DEVICES RECHARGING ALL OVER DESK

SHOPPING BY BIKE

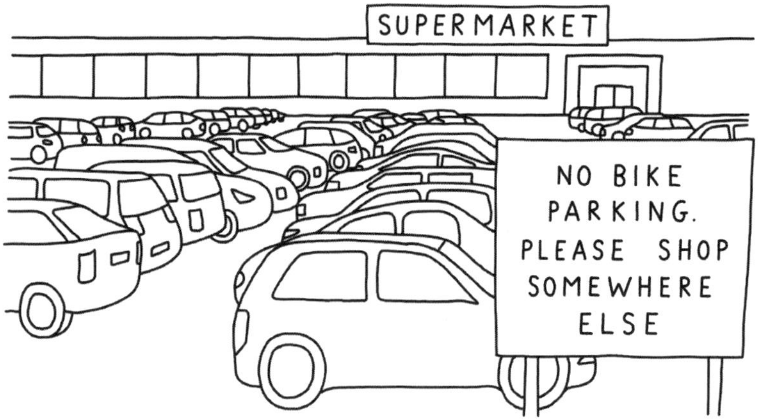
SUPERMARKET
NO BIKE PARKING. PLEASE SHOP SOMEWHERE ELSE

CHOOSE WHERE TO SHOP

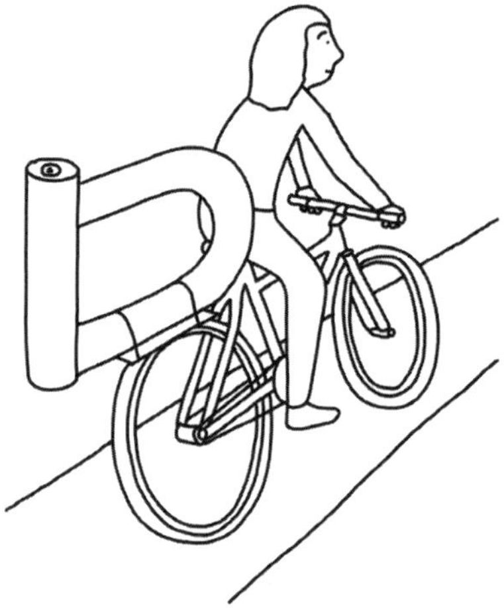

BRING A GOOD LOCK

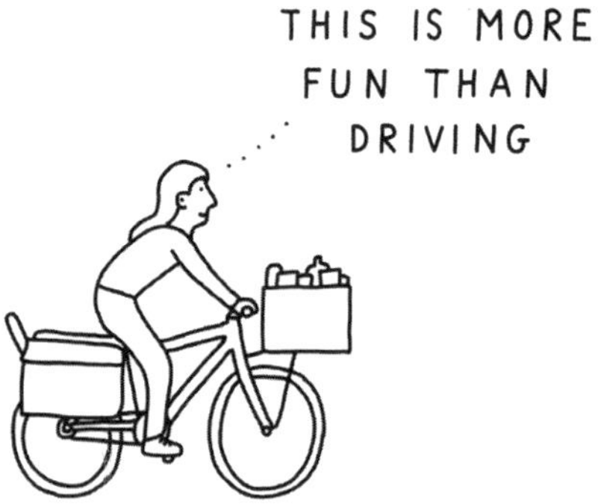
THIS IS MORE FUN THAN DRIVING

SET YOUR BIKE UP WITH SOME PANNIERS OR A BOX / BASKET

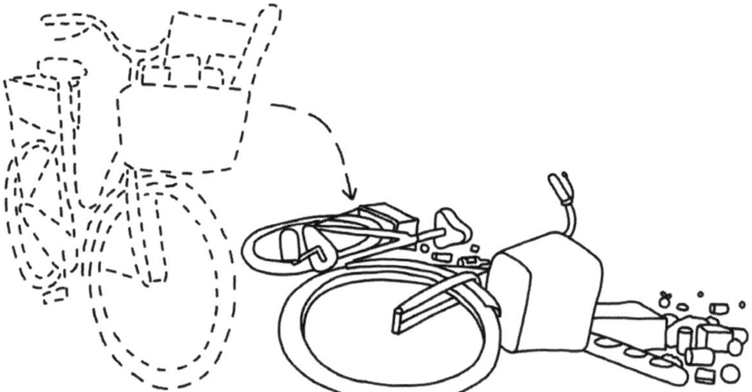

BUT ALSO WORK ON YOUR BALANCE

ROMANCE

ON A BIKE

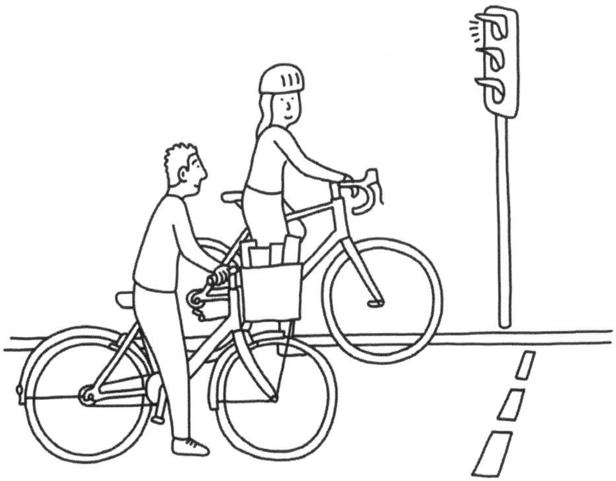

TRAFFIC LIGHT GLANCE

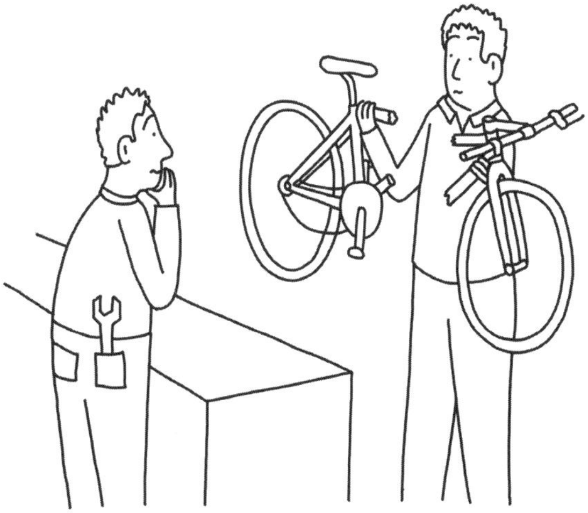

BIKE SHOP MEETING

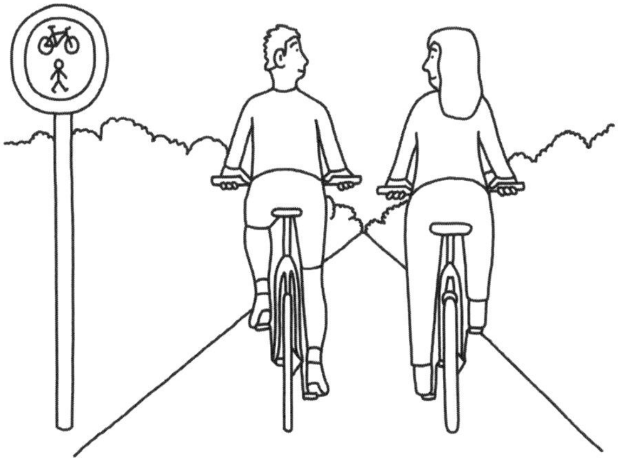

SHARED-USE PATH DATE

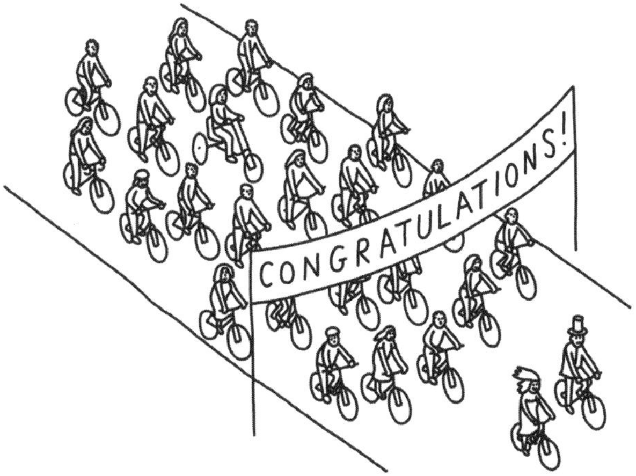
CONGRATULATIONS!

PELOTON WEDDING

HILLS
MOTIVATIONAL SENTIMENTS

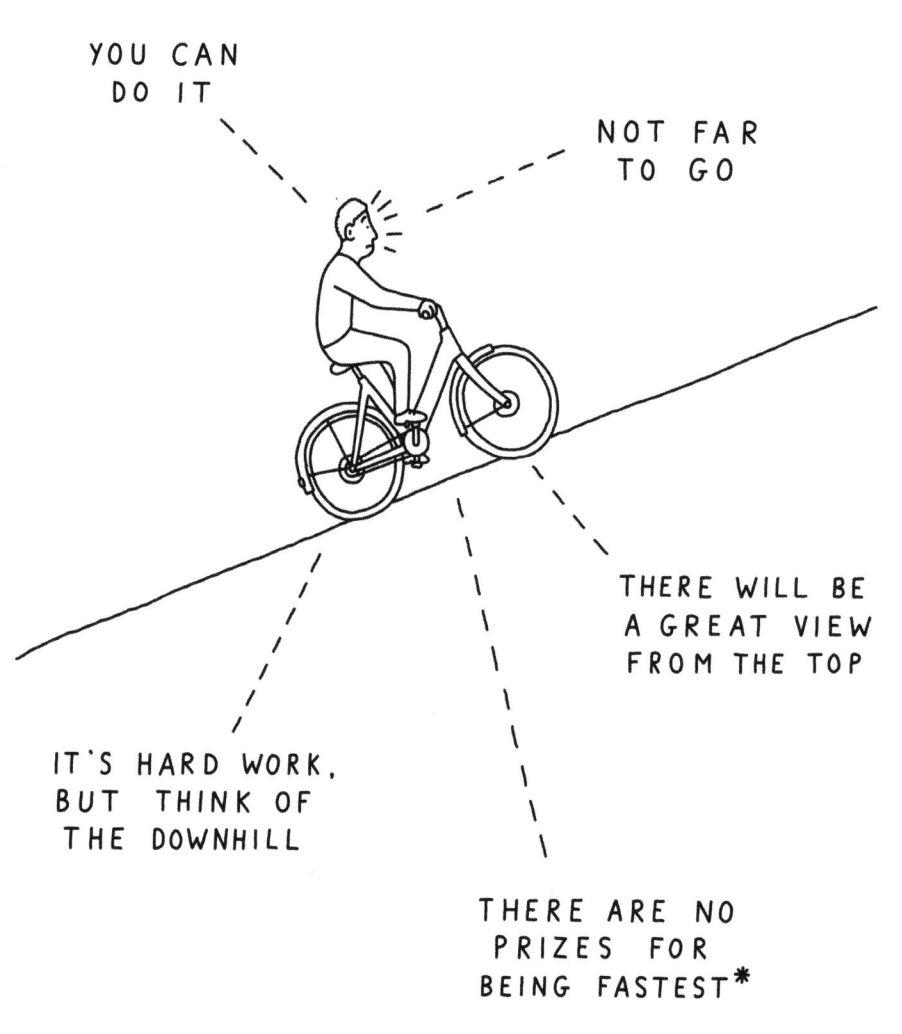

YOU CAN DO IT

NOT FAR TO GO

THERE WILL BE A GREAT VIEW FROM THE TOP

IT'S HARD WORK, BUT THINK OF THE DOWNHILL

THERE ARE NO PRIZES FOR BEING FASTEST*

*SOMETIMES THERE ARE PRIZES FOR BEING FASTEST

NOT-QUITE-SO-MOTIVATIONAL SENTIMENTS, SHOULD YOU REQUIRE THEM

HAVE YOU THOUGHT ABOUT CHANGING DOWN A GEAR?

HOW ABOUT GETTING AN E-BIKE?

A FEW YEARS AGO, YOU'D HAVE MANAGED THIS WITH NO PROBLEM AT ALL

PUNCTURES

TWELVE TERRIBLE THINGS THAT CAN CAUSE THEM

HEDGE TRIMMINGS

ATTEMPT TO FIX PREVIOUS PUNCTURE

POTHOLE

INFLATION ISSUES

DRAWING PIN

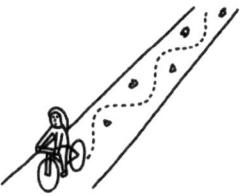

GLASS FROM UNSWEPT CYCLE PATH

BRAKES RUBBING ON TYRE

TINY FLINT

SABOTAGE

STINGER

WORN OUT TYRES FROM SHEER QUANTITY OF MILES

PITCHFORK FROM ANTI-CYCLE ROUTE COLUMNIST

YOUR BIKE
WHY IT SEEMS TO BE BROKEN

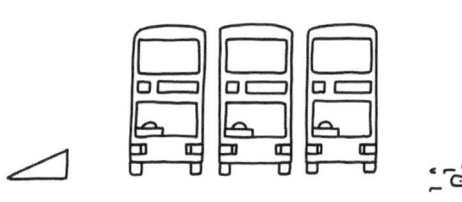

A JUMP WAS ATTEMPTED

OFFERING TOO MANY LIFTS

OVERZEALOUS CLEANING

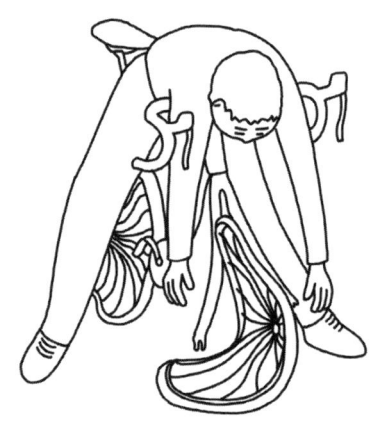

GENERAL WEAR AND TEAR

THE CYCLE MECHANIC

TODAY'S CUSTOMERS

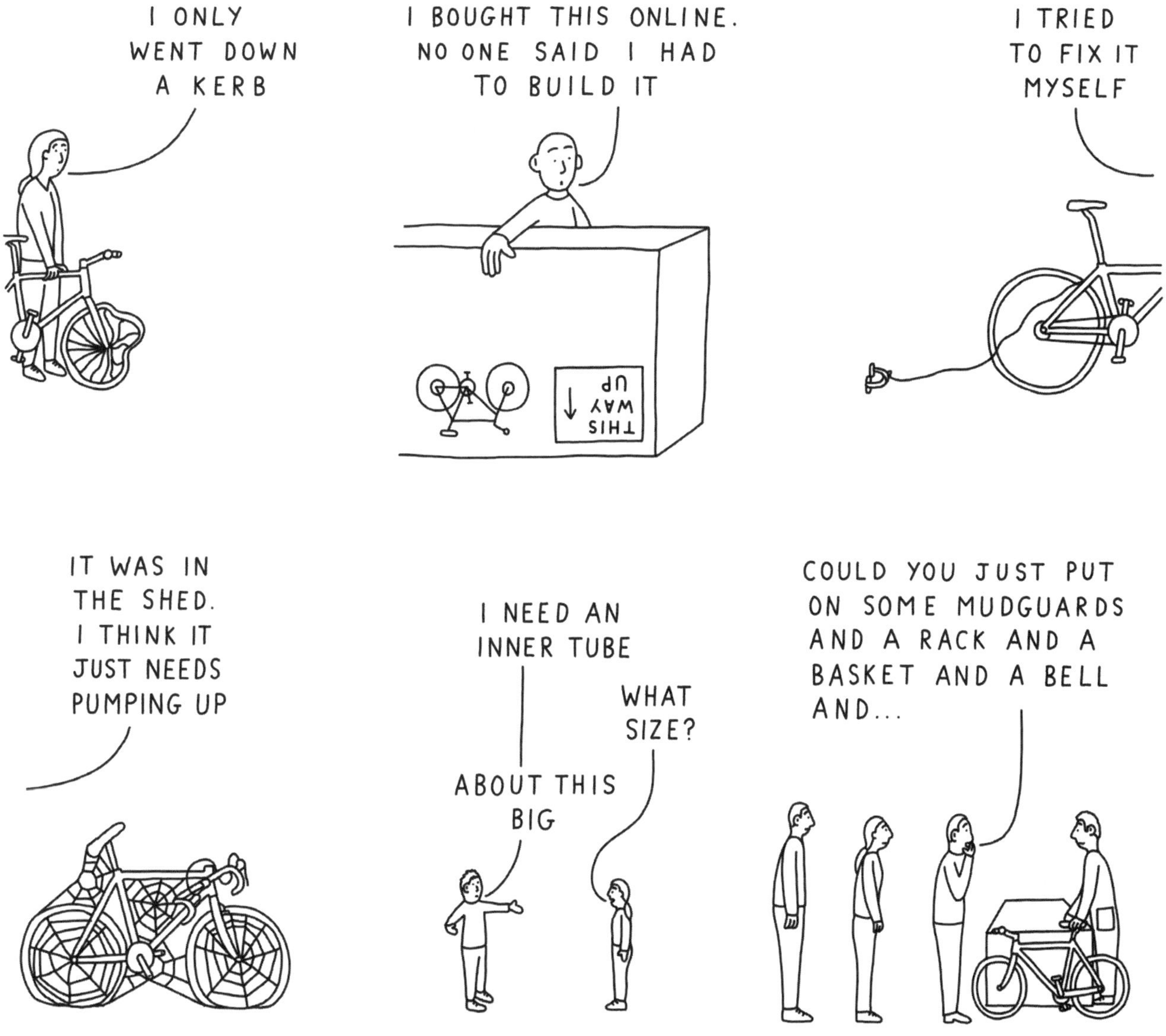

I ONLY WENT DOWN A KERB
I BOUGHT THIS ONLINE. NO ONE SAID I HAD TO BUILD IT
THIS WAY UP
I TRIED TO FIX IT MYSELF
IT WAS IN THE SHED. I THINK IT JUST NEEDS PUMPING UP
I NEED AN INNER TUBE
WHAT SIZE?
ABOUT THIS BIG
COULD YOU JUST PUT ON SOME MUDGUARDS AND A RACK AND A BASKET AND A BELL AND...

HELMET-WEARERS

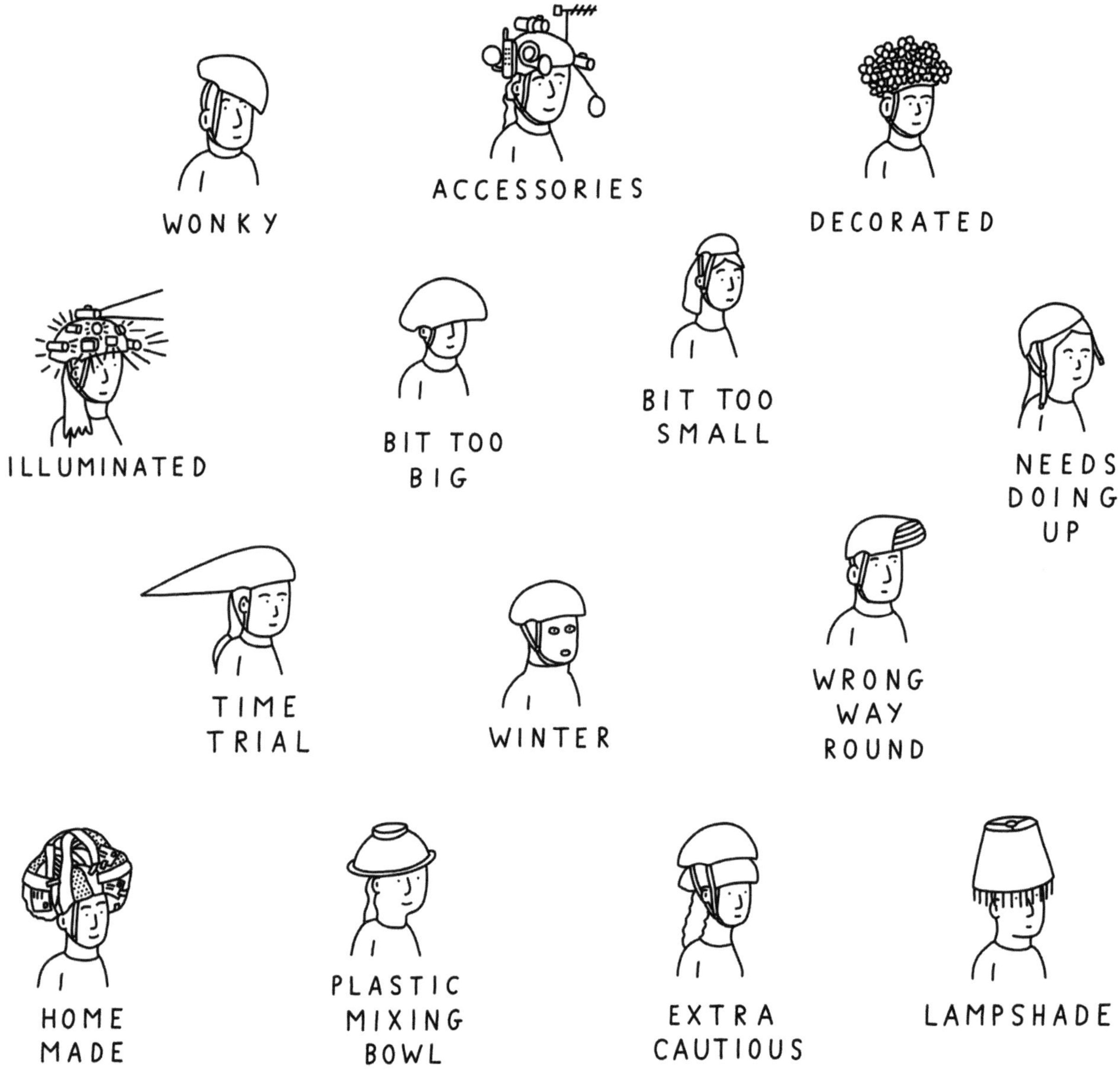
WONKY
ACCESSORIES
DECORATED
ILLUMINATED
BIT TOO BIG
BIT TOO SMALL
NEEDS DOING UP
TIME TRIAL
WINTER
WRONG WAY ROUND
HOME MADE
PLASTIC MIXING BOWL
EXTRA CAUTIOUS
LAMPSHADE

HOW SERIOUS ARE YOU?

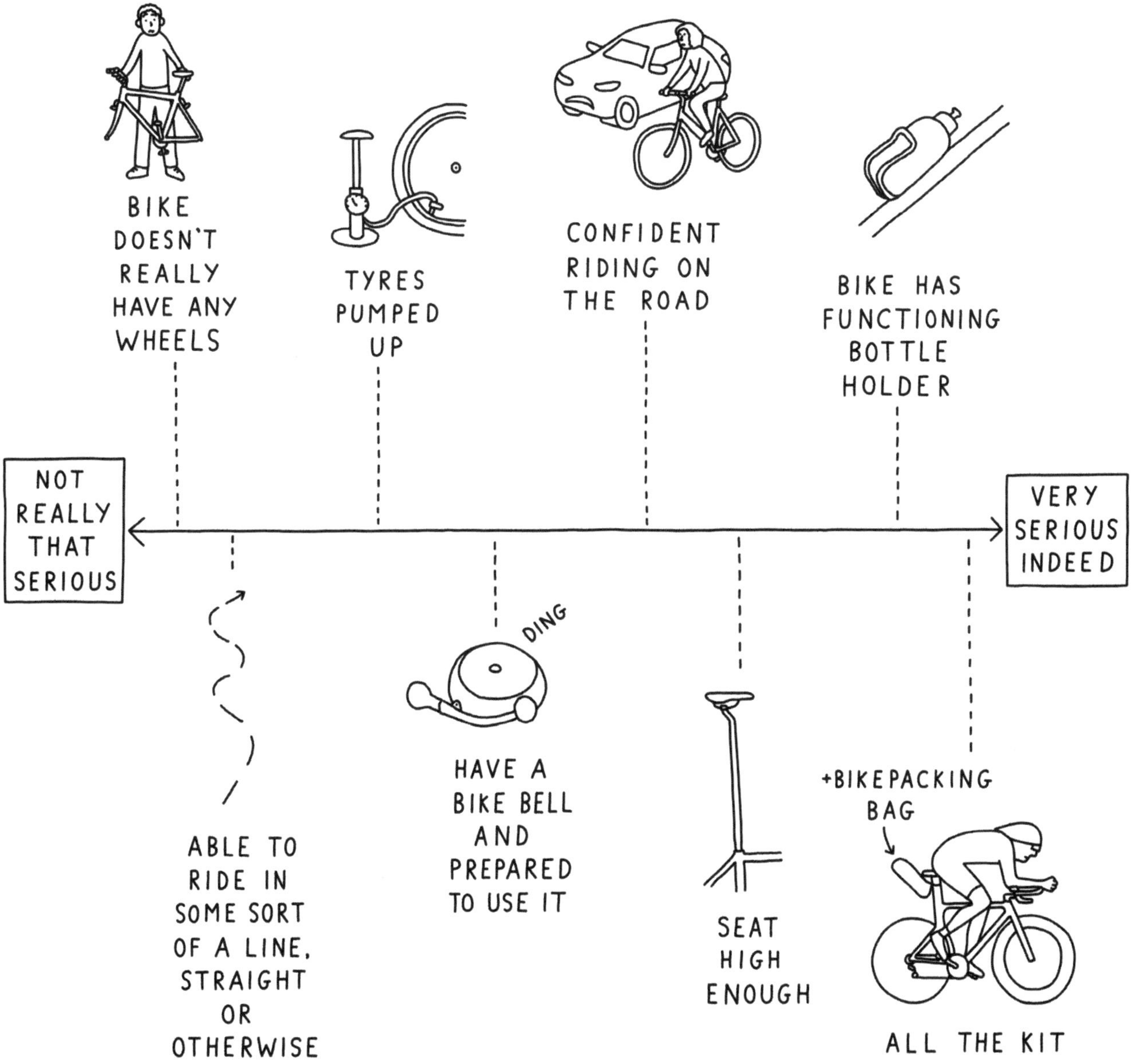
NOT REALLY THAT SERIOUS
VERY SERIOUS INDEED
BIKE DOESN'T REALLY HAVE ANY WHEELS
TYRES PUMPED UP
CONFIDENT RIDING ON THE ROAD
BIKE HAS FUNCTIONING BOTTLE HOLDER
ABLE TO RIDE IN SOME SORT OF A LINE, STRAIGHT OR OTHERWISE
DING
HAVE A BIKE BELL AND PREPARED TO USE IT
SEAT HIGH ENOUGH
+BIKEPACKING BAG
ALL THE KIT

THE EVOLUTION

OF A CYCLIST

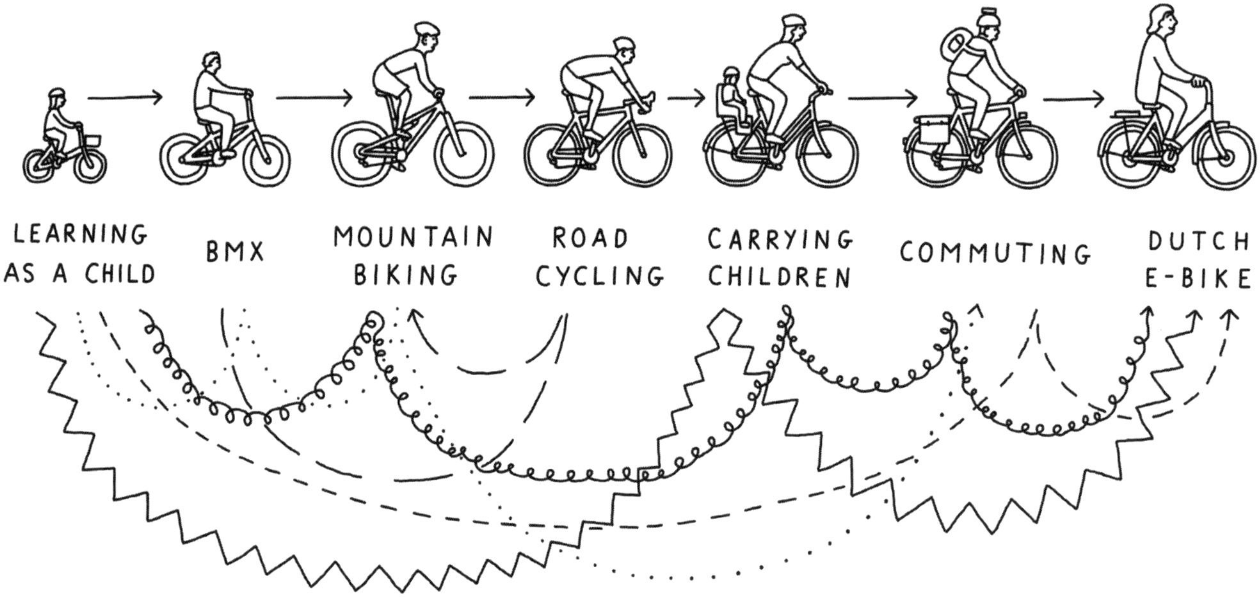

LEARNING AS A CHILD
BMX
MOUNTAIN BIKING
ROAD CYCLING
CARRYING CHILDREN
COMMUTING
DUTCH E-BIKE

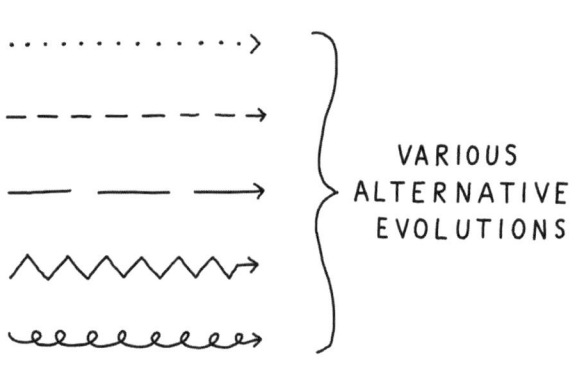

VARIOUS ALTERNATIVE EVOLUTIONS

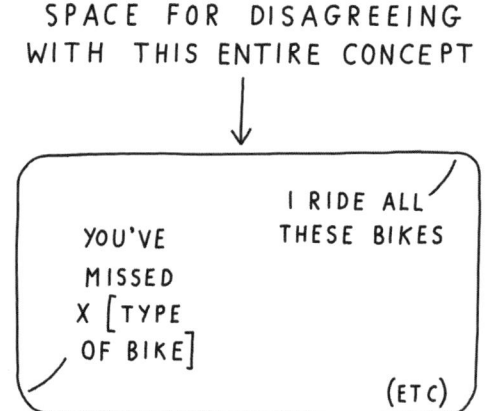

SPACE FOR DISAGREEING WITH THIS ENTIRE CONCEPT

I RIDE ALL THESE BIKES

YOU'VE MISSED X [TYPE OF BIKE]

(ETC)

WHY WE LOVE CYCLING

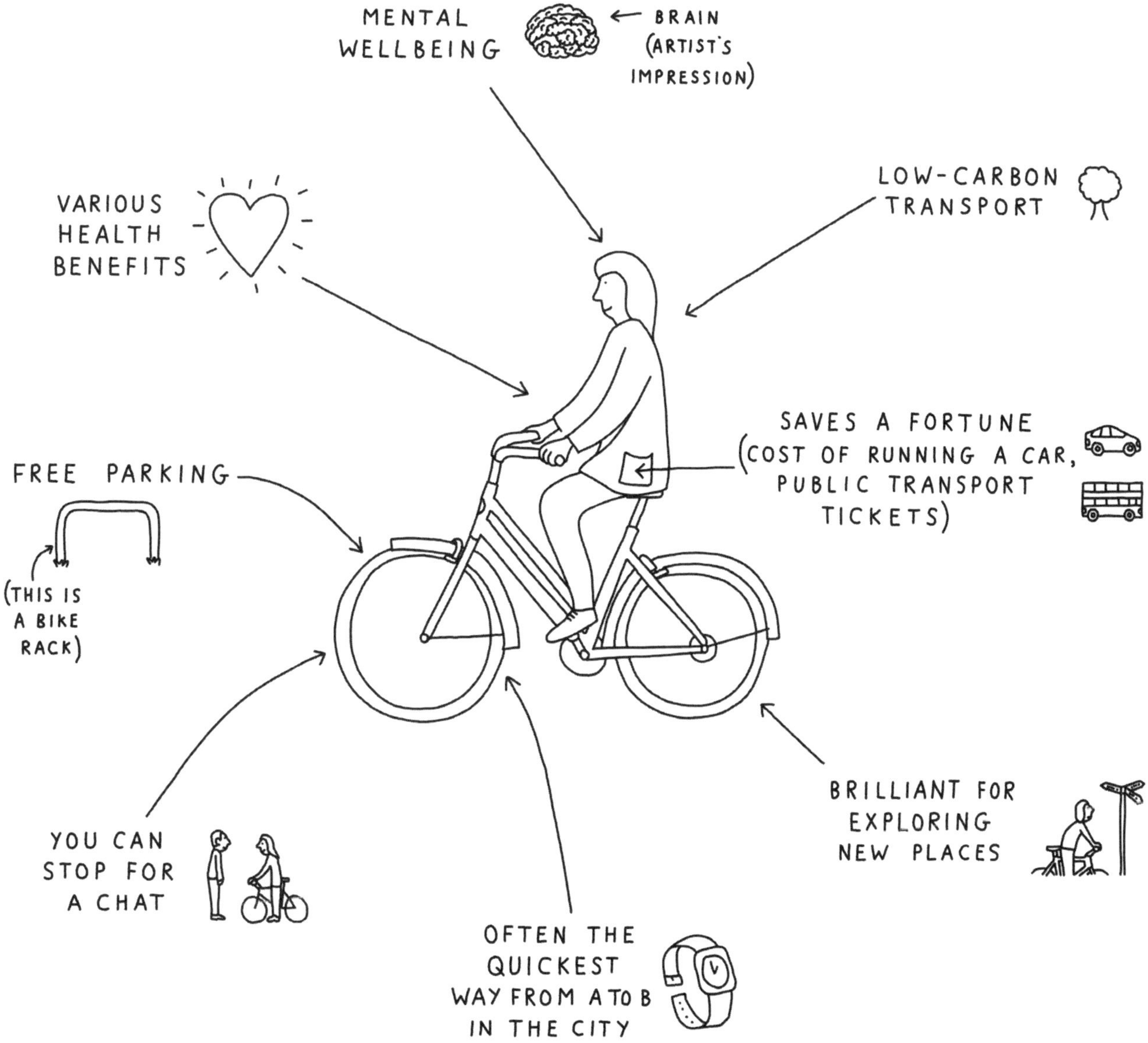

MENTAL WELLBEING
← BRAIN (ARTIST'S IMPRESSION)
LOW-CARBON TRANSPORT
VARIOUS HEALTH BENEFITS
SAVES A FORTUNE (COST OF RUNNING A CAR, PUBLIC TRANSPORT TICKETS)
FREE PARKING
(THIS IS A BIKE RACK)
BRILLIANT FOR EXPLORING NEW PLACES
YOU CAN STOP FOR A CHAT
OFTEN THE QUICKEST WAY FROM A TO B IN THE CITY

CHAPTER 2

GETTING STARTED
CYCLING FOR BEGINNERS

HOW TO RIDE A BIKE

SADDLE LOW TO START WITH
BRAKES WORK

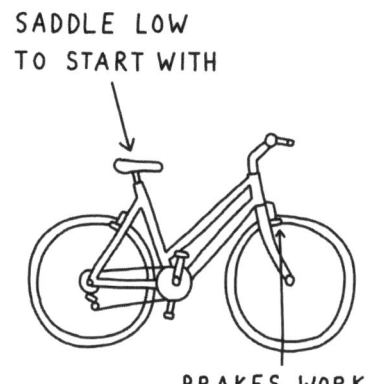

FIND A SERVICED BIKE THAT ISN'T TOO LARGE

TUMBLEWEED

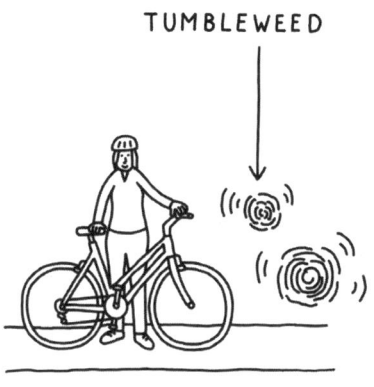

FIND A QUIET PLACE WITH NO TRAFFIC

PRACTISE THIS FOR A WHILE
HANDS ON THE BRAKES

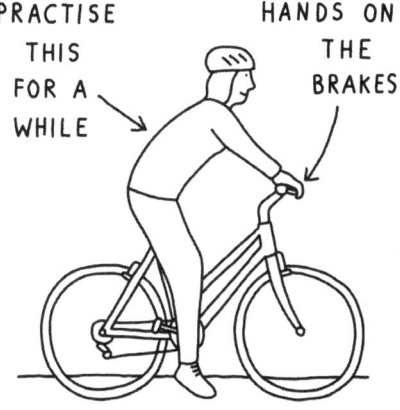

SIT ON THE BIKE, AND PUSH YOURSELF ALONG USING YOUR TOES

WHEN YOU ARE READY...

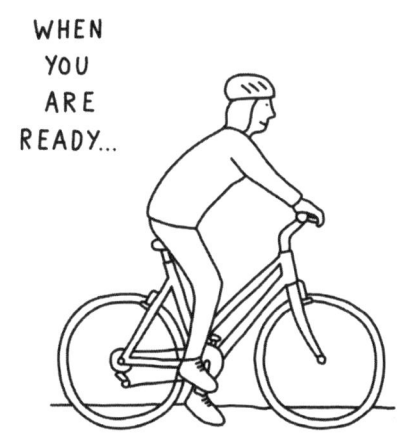

PUT ONE FOOT ON A PEDAL, AND PUSH YOURSELF ALONG WITH THE TOES OF THE OTHER FOOT

AGAIN, WHEN YOU ARE READY...

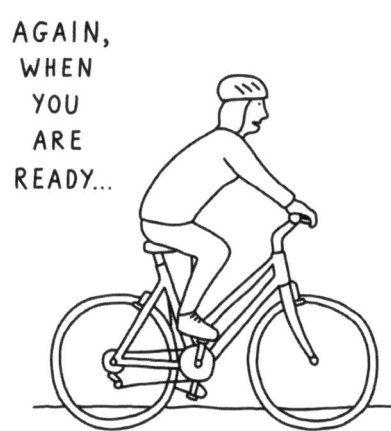

PUT YOUR OTHER FOOT ON THE OTHER PEDAL. AND GO!

OPTIONAL ADDITIONAL STAGE

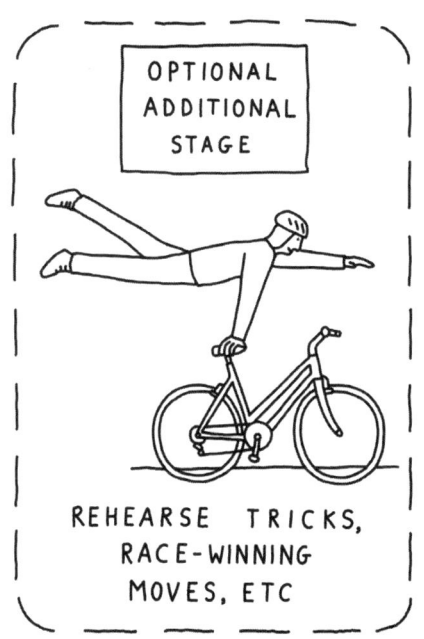

REHEARSE TRICKS, RACE-WINNING MOVES, ETC

THE BIKE SHOP

VISITING FOR THE FIRST TIME – A MAP

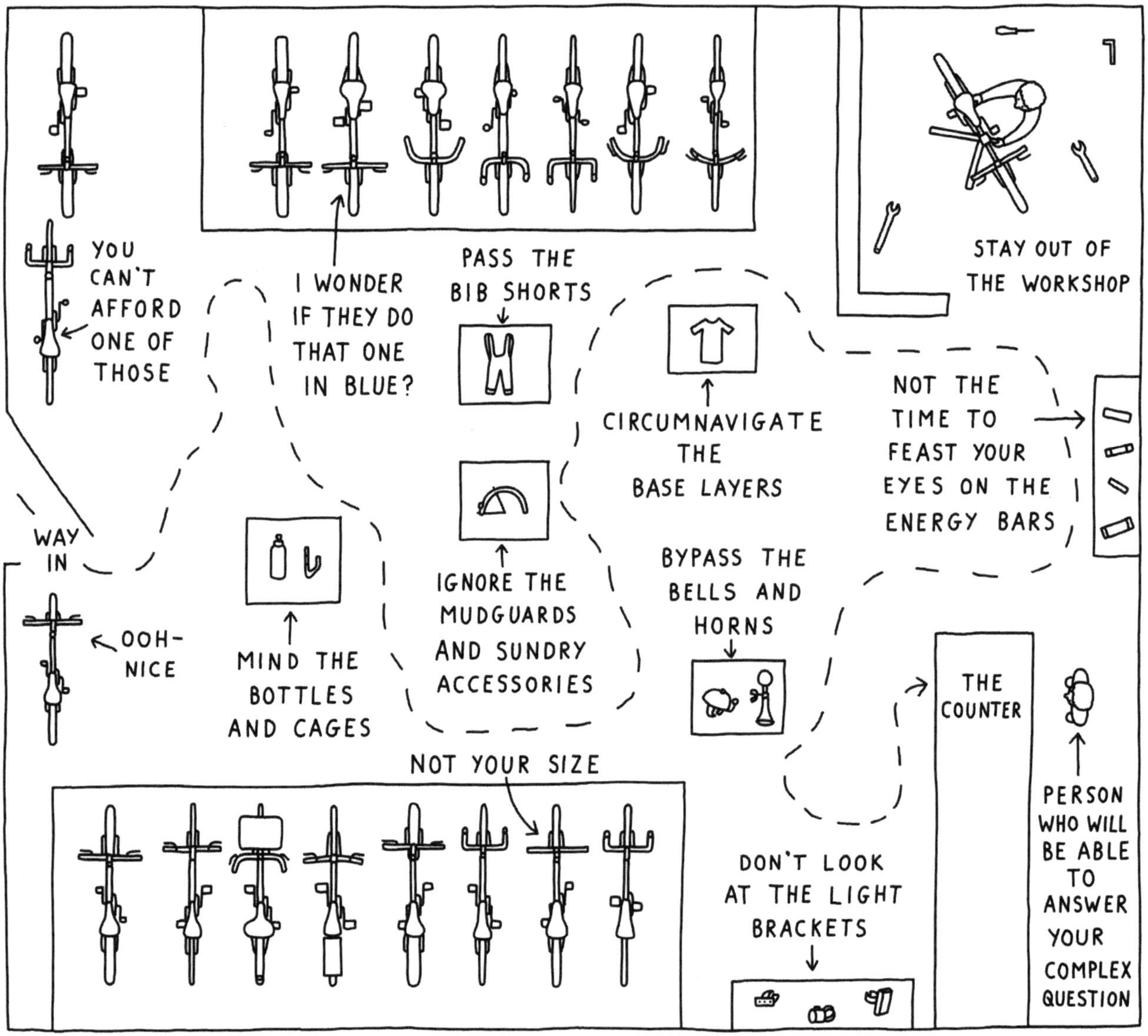

YOU CAN'T AFFORD ONE OF THOSE
I WONDER IF THEY DO THAT ONE IN BLUE?
PASS THE BIB SHORTS
CIRCUMNAVIGATE THE BASE LAYERS
STAY OUT OF THE WORKSHOP
NOT THE TIME TO FEAST YOUR EYES ON THE ENERGY BARS
WAY IN
OOH- NICE
MIND THE BOTTLES AND CAGES
IGNORE THE MUDGUARDS AND SUNDRY ACCESSORIES
BYPASS THE BELLS AND HORNS
THE COUNTER
PERSON WHO WILL BE ABLE TO ANSWER YOUR COMPLEX QUESTION
NOT YOUR SIZE
DON'T LOOK AT THE LIGHT BRACKETS

SECONDHAND BIKES
UNDERSTANDING THE ADVERTISEMENTS

'SHOULD POLISH UP OK'

'NOT SERVICED'

'IDEAL PROJECT'

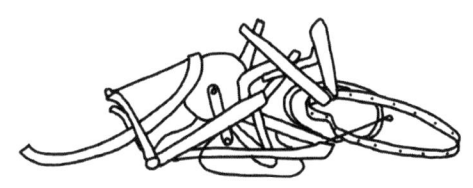

'TLC NEEDED'

CYCLING ON A BUDGET

SOME IDEAS FOR GETTING GOING WITHOUT SPENDING TOO MUCH MONEY

LOTS OF PEOPLE HAVE BIKES THEY DON'T USE IN THEIR GARAGES AND SHEDS

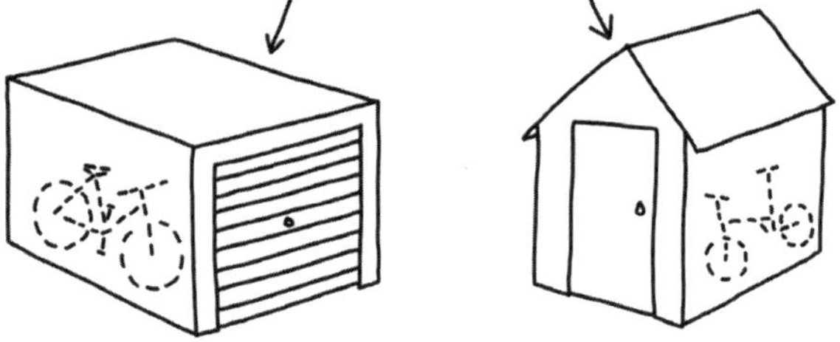

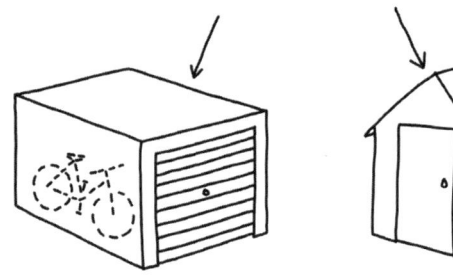

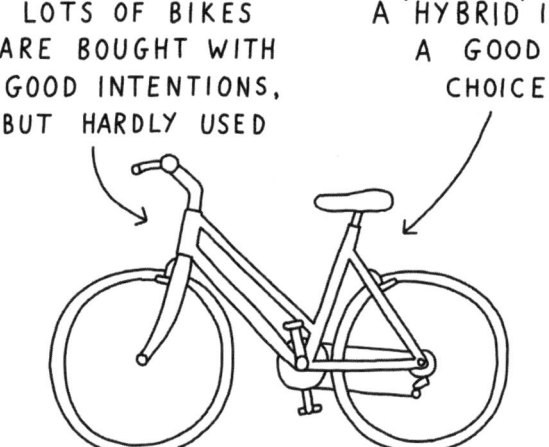

SEE WHETHER ANY OF YOUR FRIENDS OR FAMILY HAVE A BIKE THEY DON'T NEED

LOTS OF BIKES ARE BOUGHT WITH GOOD INTENTIONS, BUT HARDLY USED

A 'HYBRID' IS A GOOD CHOICE

YOU CAN GET A REALLY GOOD BIKE BY BUYING SECONDHAND

HEAVY

CHEAP FULL-SUSPENSION WORSE THAN NO SUSPENSION

WILL PROBABLY BREAK DOWN

HAS IT BEEN PROPERLY SET UP?

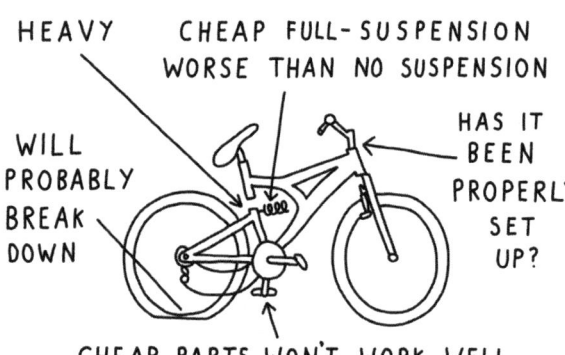

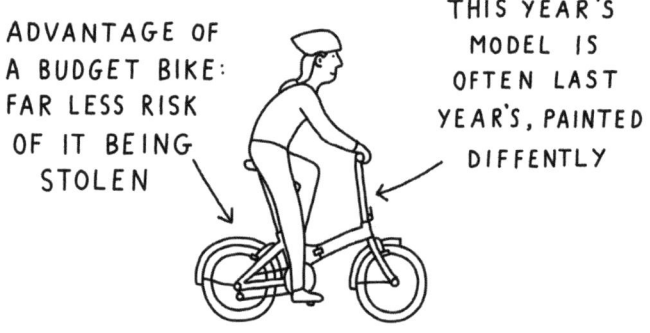

CHEAP PARTS WON'T WORK WELL

DON'T BUY A REALLY CHEAP NEW BIKE FROM THE INTERNET OR A NON-SPECIALIST SHOP

ADVANTAGE OF A BUDGET BIKE: FAR LESS RISK OF IT BEING STOLEN

THIS YEAR'S MODEL IS OFTEN LAST YEAR'S, PAINTED DIFFENTLY

YOU DON'T NEED ALL THE BELLS* AND WHISTLES TO ENJOY CYCLING

* YOU NEED ONE BELL

ACCESSORIES

TO BE ATTACHED AFTER A TRIP TO THE BIKE SHOP

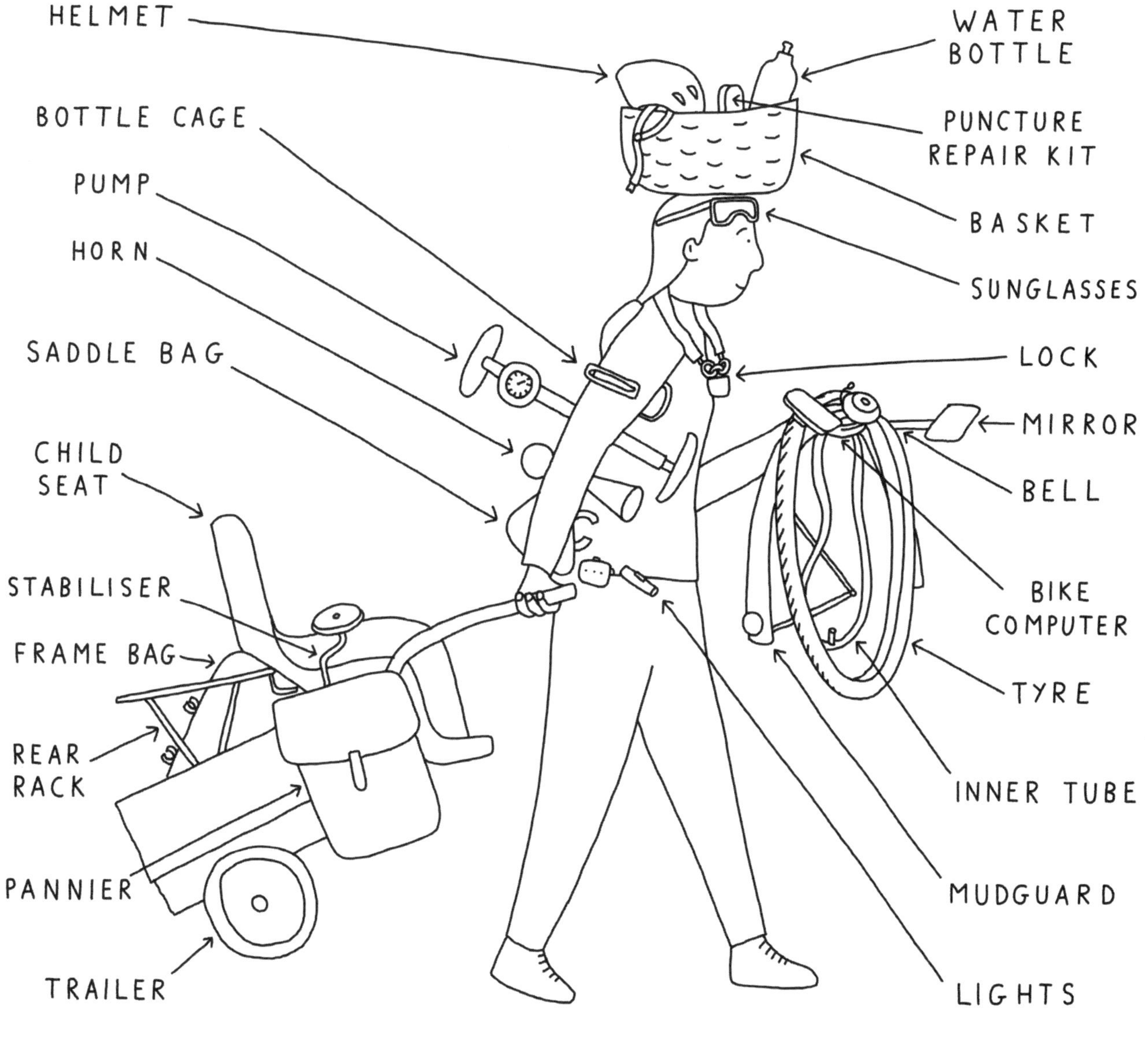
HELMET
BOTTLE CAGE
PUMP
HORN
SADDLE BAG
CHILD SEAT
STABILISER
FRAME BAG
REAR RACK
PANNIER
TRAILER
WATER BOTTLE
PUNCTURE REPAIR KIT
BASKET
SUNGLASSES
LOCK
MIRROR
BELL
BIKE COMPUTER
TYRE
INNER TUBE
MUDGUARD
LIGHTS

WHAT TO WEAR
WHEN YOU'RE CYCLING

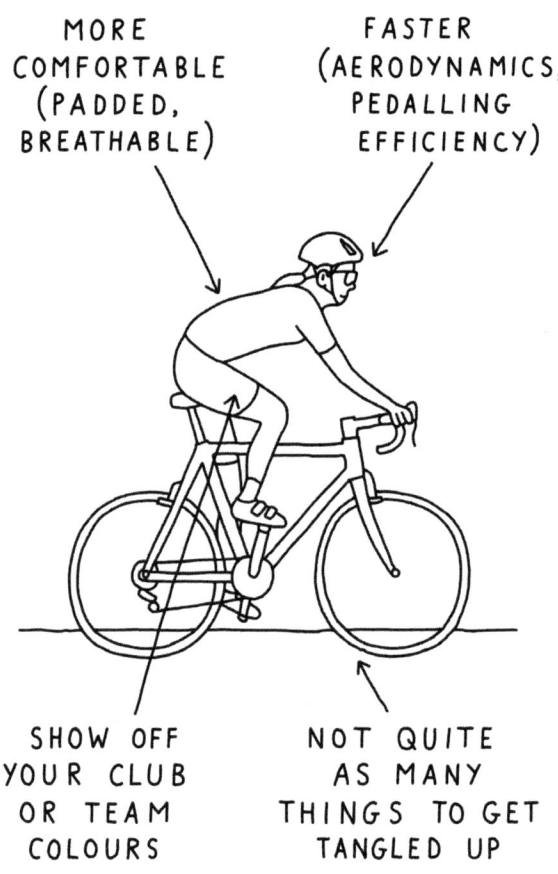

ORDINARY CLOTHES

- NO NEED TO CHANGE — FAFFING-AROUND REDUCED
- CAN JUST GET ON WITH YOUR DAY AFTER RIDING 
- SOME OF US DON'T FEEL COMFORTABLE IN LYCRA
- LOOKS A BIT LESS LIKE A ROBOT

SPECIAL KIT

- MORE COMFORTABLE (PADDED, BREATHABLE)
- FASTER (AERODYNAMICS, PEDALLING EFFICIENCY)
- SHOW OFF YOUR CLUB OR TEAM COLOURS
- NOT QUITE AS MANY THINGS TO GET TANGLED UP

SUMMARY OF THE SITUATION: THERE'S A PLACE FOR BOTH. WEAR WHAT YOU WANT, AND DON'T LET ANYONE TELL YOU YOU'VE GOT IT WRONG

WEARING A SKIRT
WHILST RIDING A BIKE

ISSUES:

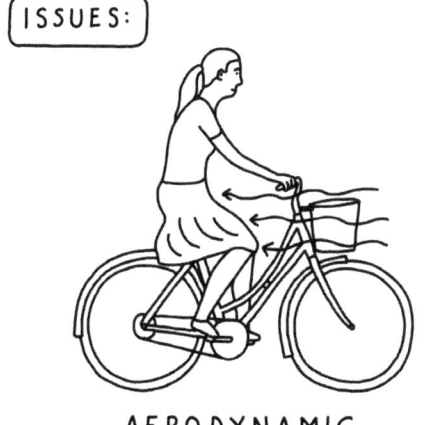

AERODYNAMIC CONCERNS

BILLOWING

GETTING CAUGHT UP IN THE MECHANISMS

A SIMPLE SOLUTION, STILL IN THE EARLY STAGES OF DEVELOPMENT →

POCKET — COIN — PEG — ELASTIC BAND — HOOK — PULLEY — BUNGEE — CLIP — WEIGHT — CORD

31

CLIPPING IN

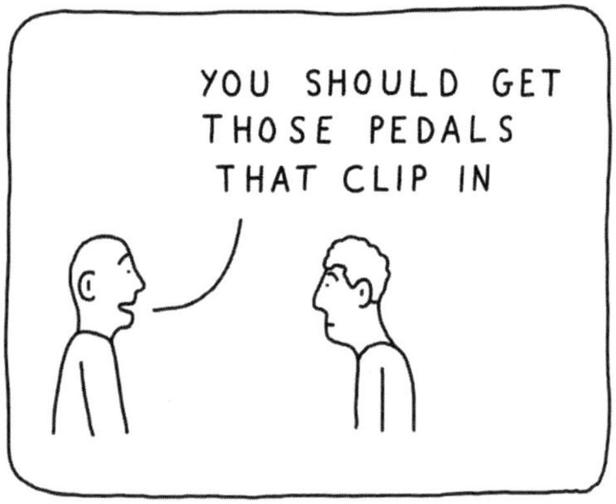
YOU SHOULD GET THOSE PEDALS THAT CLIP IN

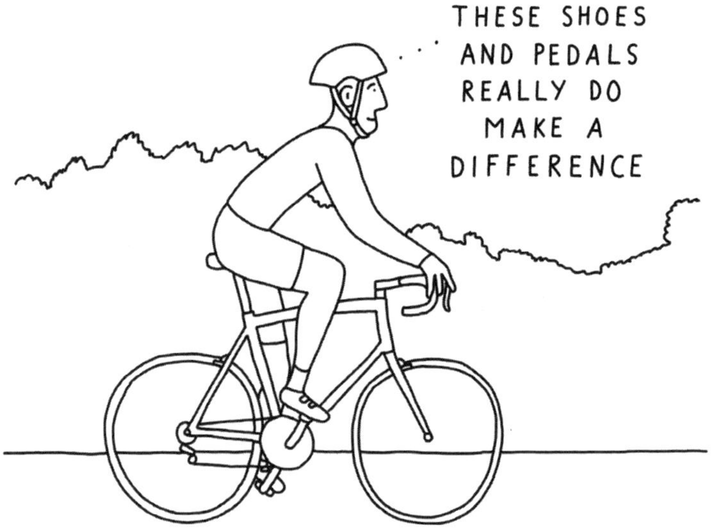
THESE SHOES AND PEDALS REALLY DO MAKE A DIFFERENCE

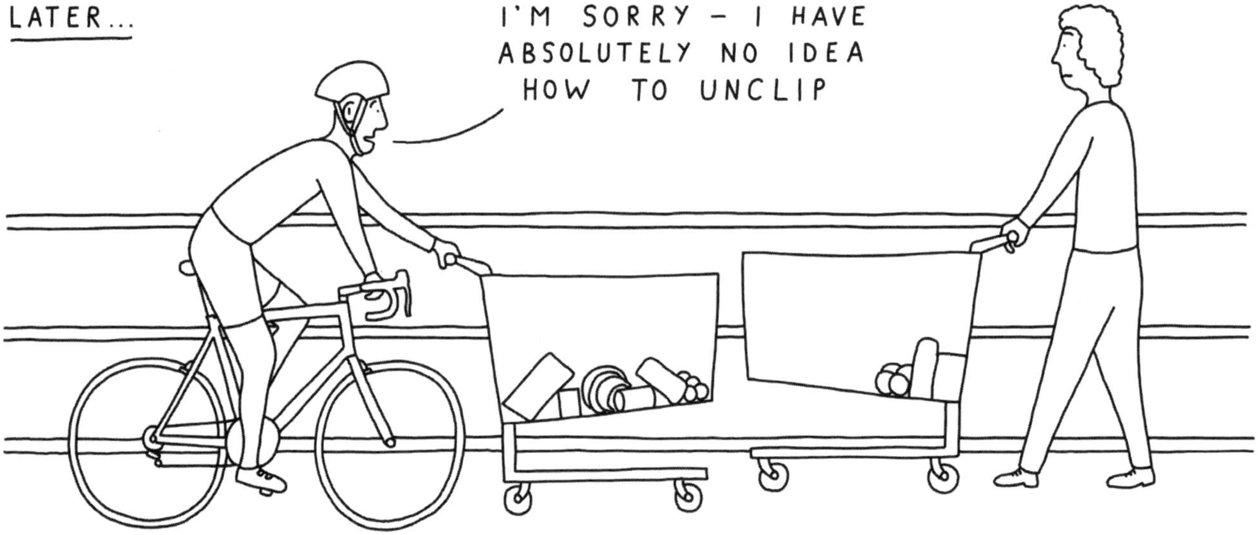
LATER...
I'M SORRY – I HAVE ABSOLUTELY NO IDEA HOW TO UNCLIP

ESSENTIAL THINGS TO TAKE
AND WHAT TO DO IF YOU FORGET THEM

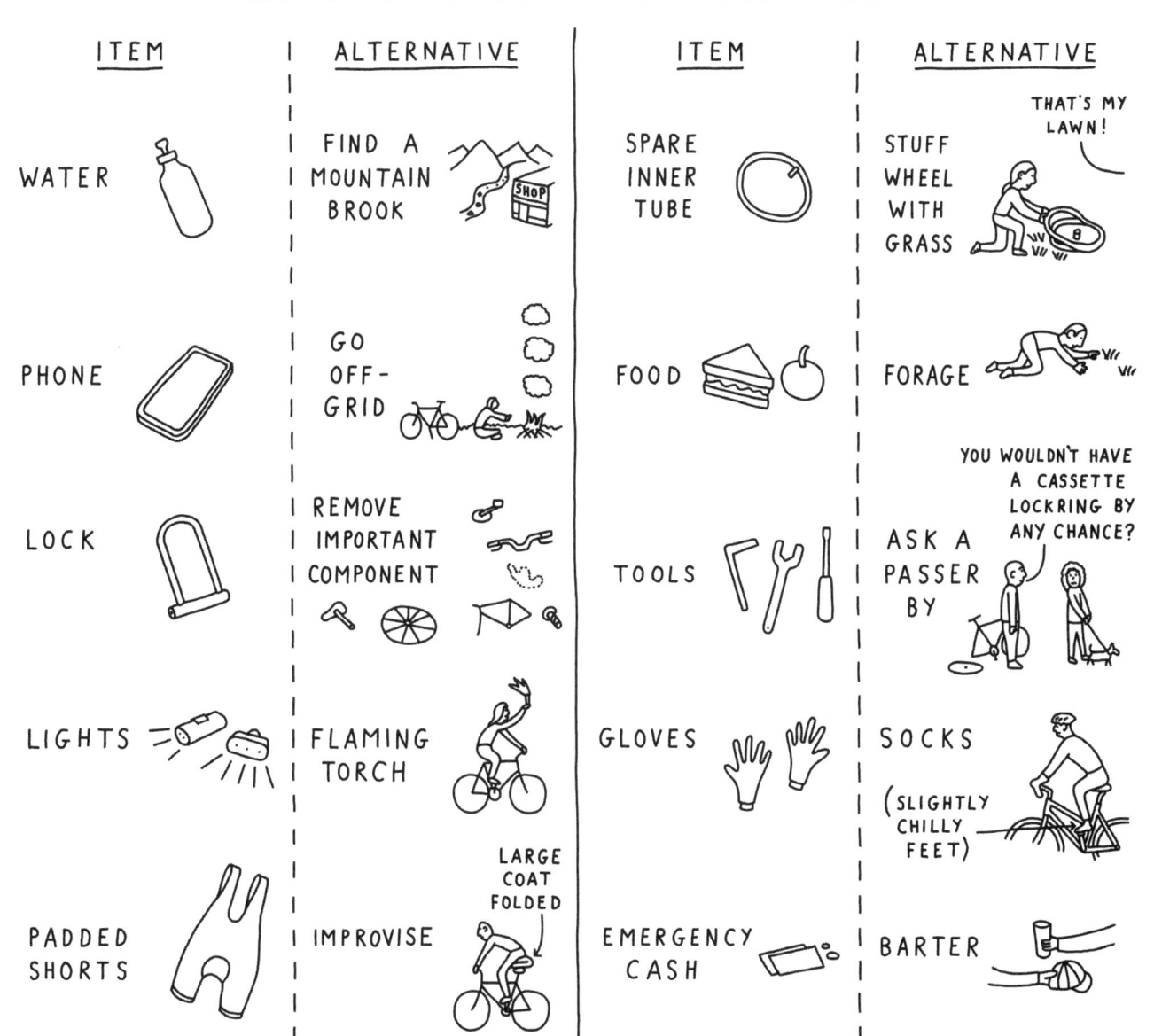

ITEM	ALTERNATIVE	ITEM	ALTERNATIVE
WATER	FIND A MOUNTAIN BROOK	SPARE INNER TUBE	STUFF WHEEL WITH GRASS ("THAT'S MY LAWN!")
PHONE	GO OFF-GRID	FOOD	FORAGE
LOCK	REMOVE IMPORTANT COMPONENT	TOOLS	ASK A PASSER BY ("YOU WOULDN'T HAVE A CASSETTE LOCKRING BY ANY CHANCE?")
LIGHTS	FLAMING TORCH	GLOVES	SOCKS (SLIGHTLY CHILLY FEET)
PADDED SHORTS	IMPROVISE (LARGE COAT FOLDED)	EMERGENCY CASH	BARTER

THE GUTTER

A BRIEF GUIDE

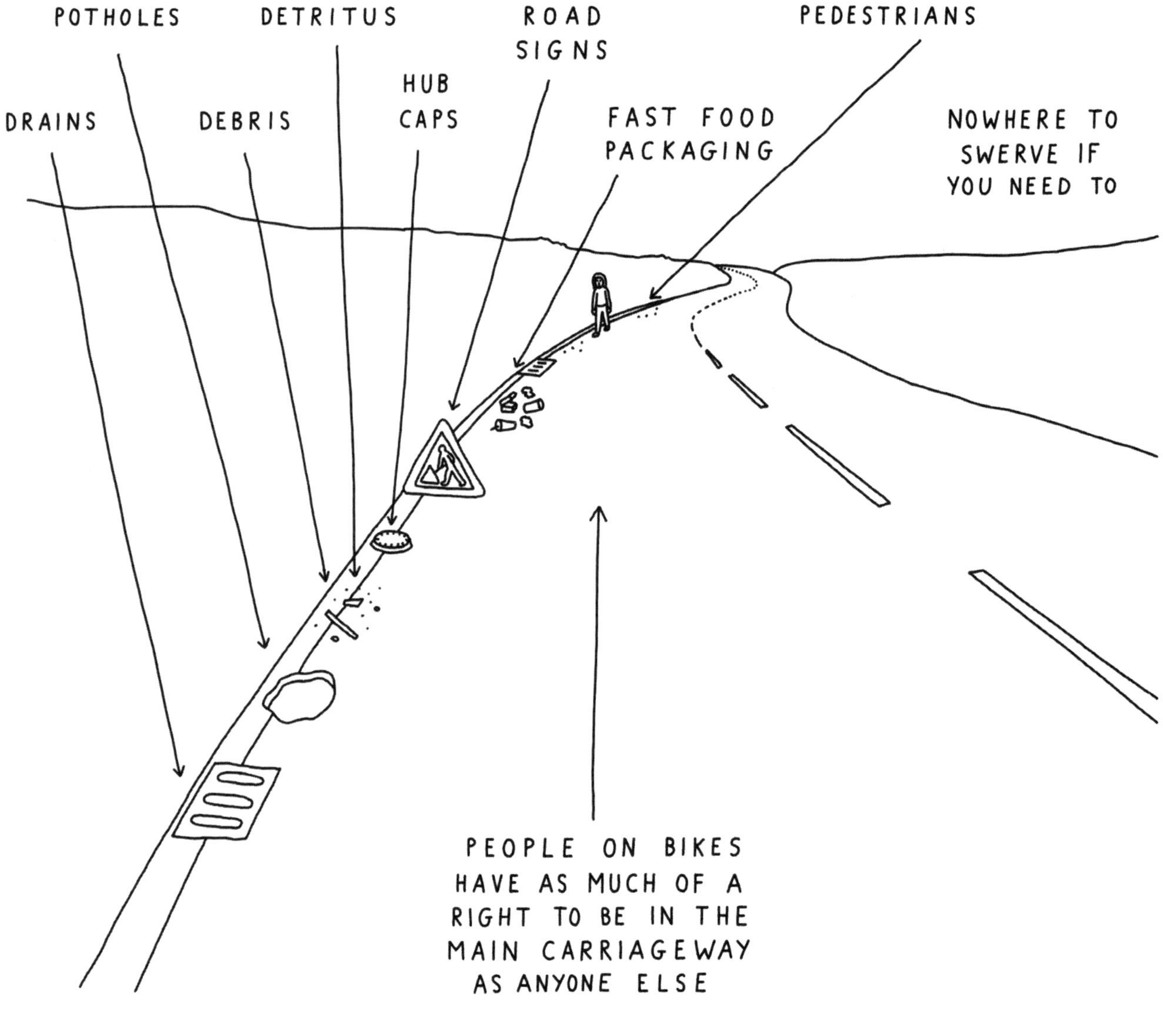
POTHOLES
DETRITUS
ROAD SIGNS
PEDESTRIANS
HUB CAPS
DRAINS
DEBRIS
FAST FOOD PACKAGING
NOWHERE TO SWERVE IF YOU NEED TO
PEOPLE ON BIKES HAVE AS MUCH OF A RIGHT TO BE IN THE MAIN CARRIAGEWAY AS ANYONE ELSE

LOCKING YOUR BIKE

BAD ──────────────────────────── GOOD

TO ITSELF	SIGNPOST	POLICE OFFICER	BIKE RACK
EVEN INCOMPETENT THIEF CAN JUST CARRY BIKE AWAY	POSSIBLE TO LIFT BIKE OVER SIGN	A WATCHED BIKE IS GOOD, BUT BEST TO LOCK TO SOMETHING IMMOVABLE	LOCK WITH SEVERAL LOCKS

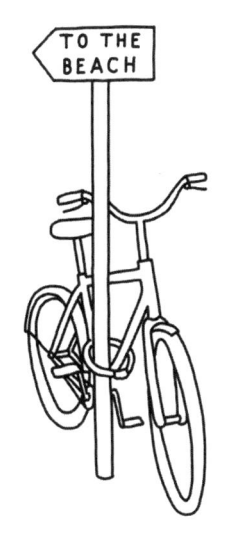

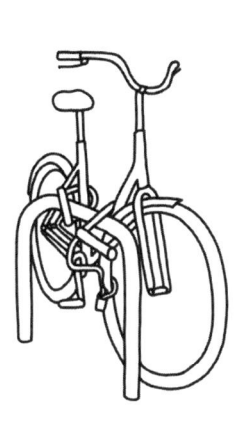

THE SADDLE
HOW TO KEEP IT DRY IN THE RAIN

SUPERMARKET BAG

APPLY SOME KIND OF PRODUCT

STAY ON YOUR BIKE

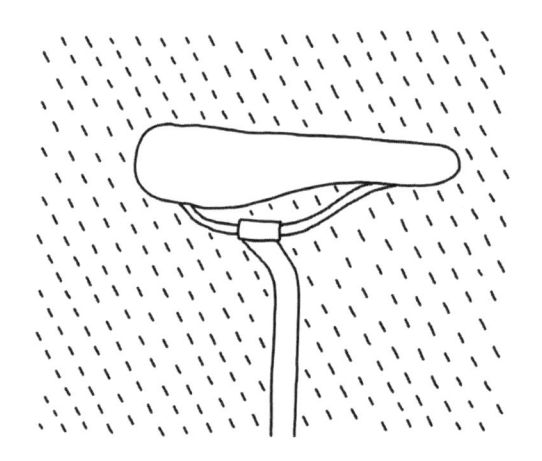

LEAVE BIKE IN SHED

EMPLOY AN ASSISTANT

HOPEFUL SLEEVE WIPE

THE SELF-DRAINING SADDLE

THE SOGGY BOTTOM

THE FITNESS DEVICE

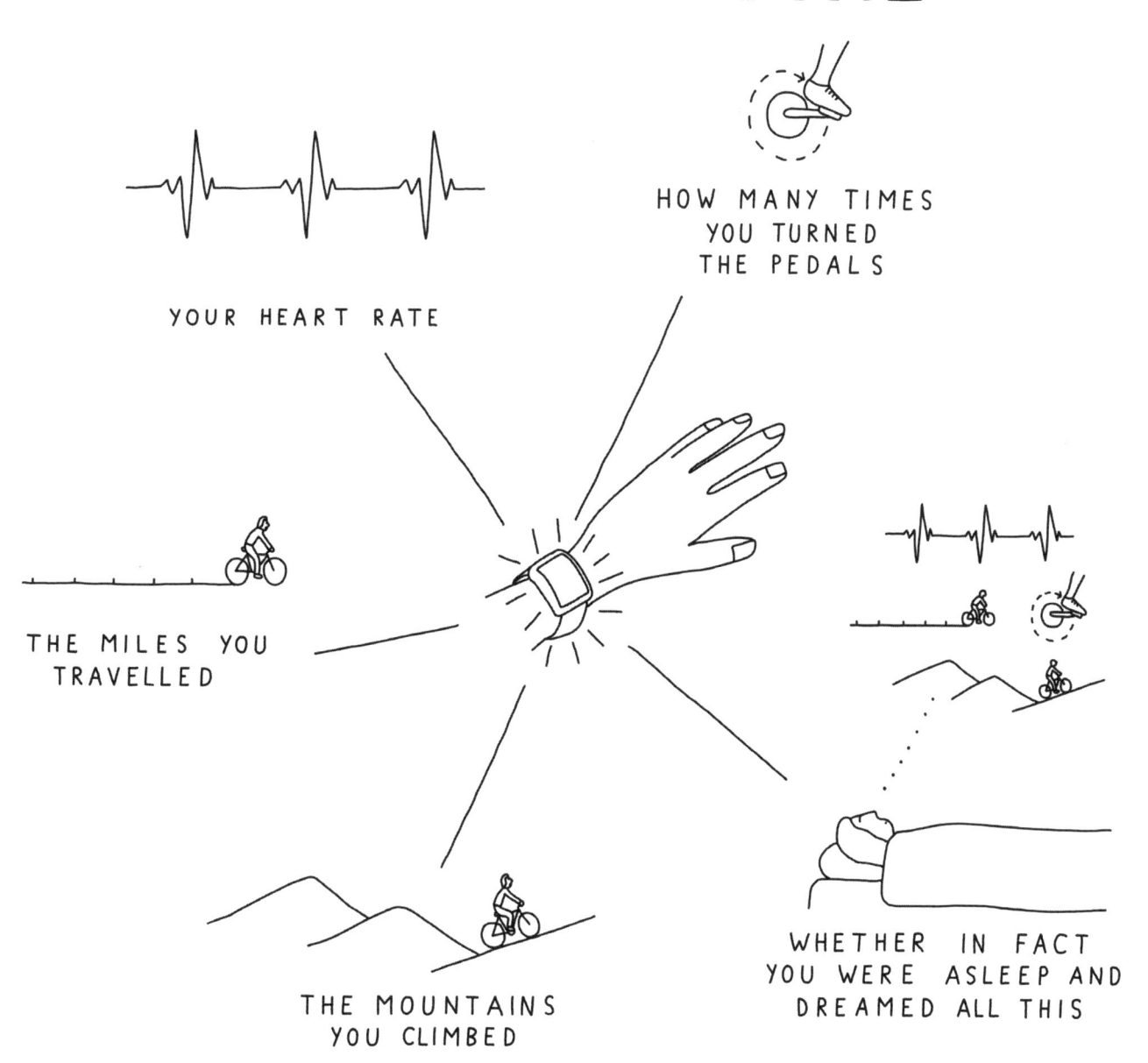

YOUR HEART RATE

HOW MANY TIMES YOU TURNED THE PEDALS

THE MILES YOU TRAVELLED

THE MOUNTAINS YOU CLIMBED

WHETHER IN FACT YOU WERE ASLEEP AND DREAMED ALL THIS

BIKE BELLS
REACTIONS FROM THE PUBLIC

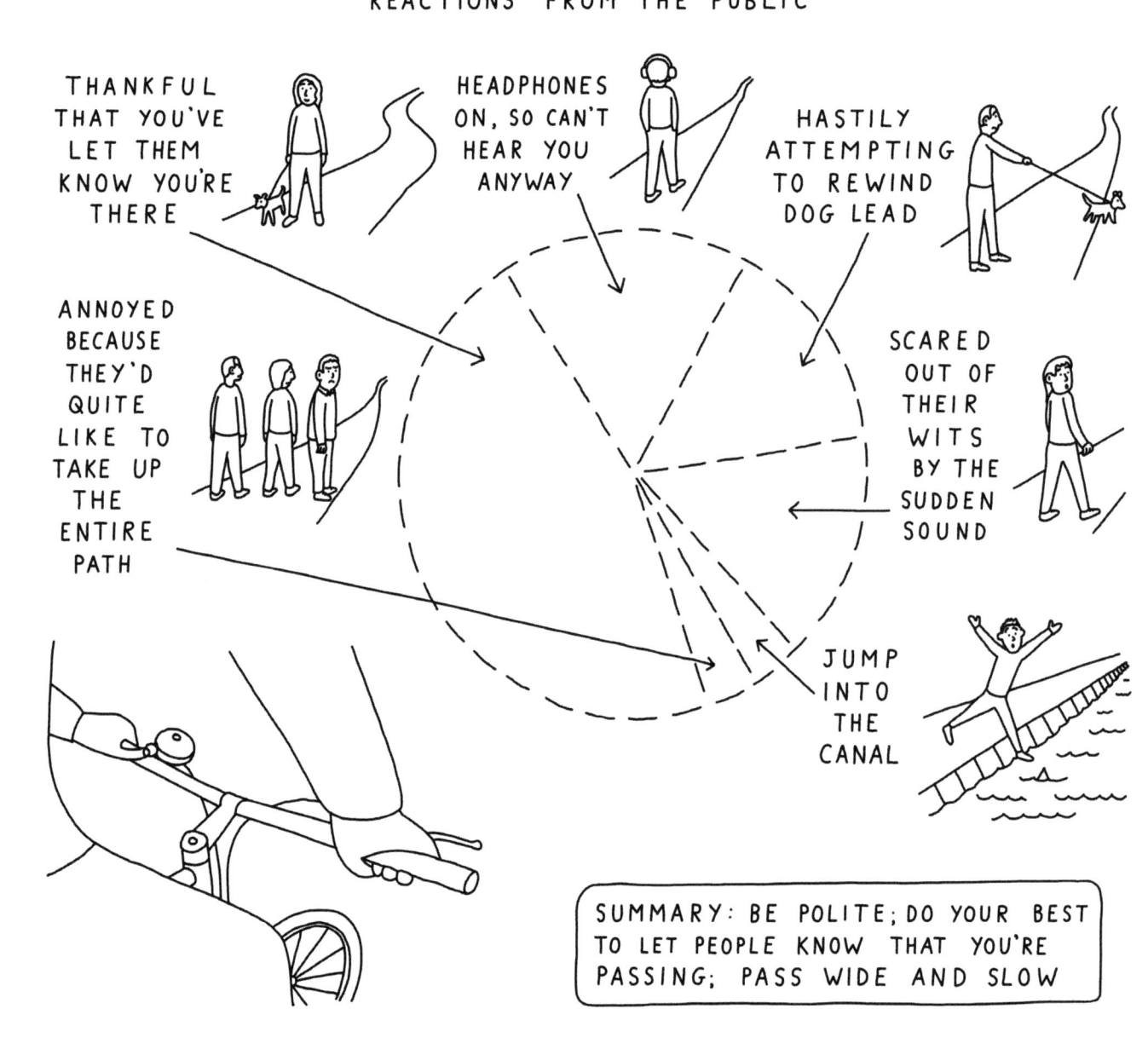

THANKFUL THAT YOU'VE LET THEM KNOW YOU'RE THERE

HEADPHONES ON, SO CAN'T HEAR YOU ANYWAY

HASTILY ATTEMPTING TO REWIND DOG LEAD

ANNOYED BECAUSE THEY'D QUITE LIKE TO TAKE UP THE ENTIRE PATH

SCARED OUT OF THEIR WITS BY THE SUDDEN SOUND

JUMP INTO THE CANAL

SUMMARY: BE POLITE; DO YOUR BEST TO LET PEOPLE KNOW THAT YOU'RE PASSING; PASS WIDE AND SLOW

BIKE PARKING
AT HOME

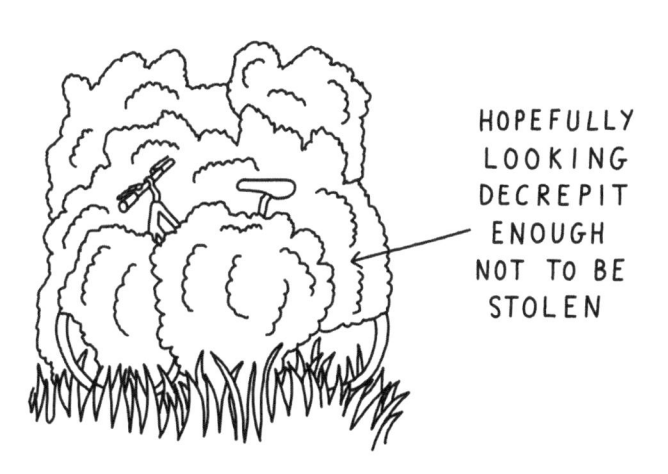

IN THE FRONT GARDEN, LETTING NATURE TAKE ITS COURSE

HOPEFULLY LOOKING DECREPIT ENOUGH NOT TO BE STOLEN

PLEASE CLAMBER CAREFULLY

THERE MIGHT BE ROOM FOR ANOTHER BIKE IN THE HALLWAY

CRAM ONE MORE INTO THE GARAGE

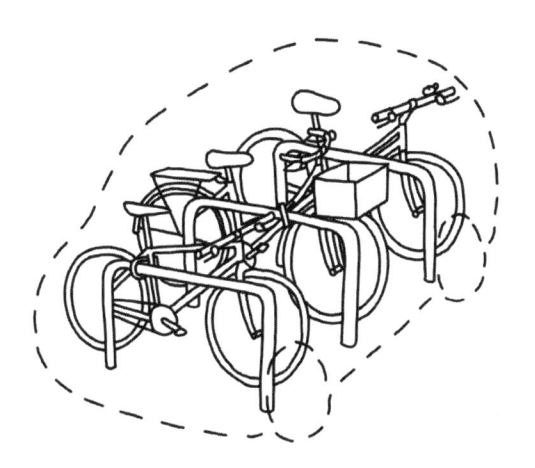

IN THE SPACE THE CAR USED TO OCCUPY

CAR VS BIKE

WHAT ARE THE COSTS?

CAR

- PAYING FOR THE CAR
- INSURANCE AND TAX 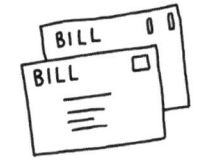
- FUEL 
- TYRES 
- MOT/SERVICING/REPAIRS 
- BREAKDOWN COVER 
- REPLACING THE COIL PACKS (NO IDEA WHAT THESE ARE)
- PAYING A LOT OF MONEY SO A MAN CAN PLUG IT INTO THE COMPUTER AND STILL NOT BE ABLE TO TELL YOU WHAT IS WRONG (TRUE STORY)

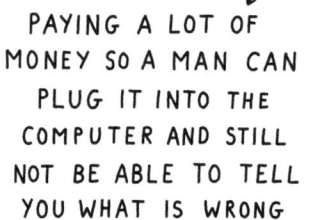

BIKE

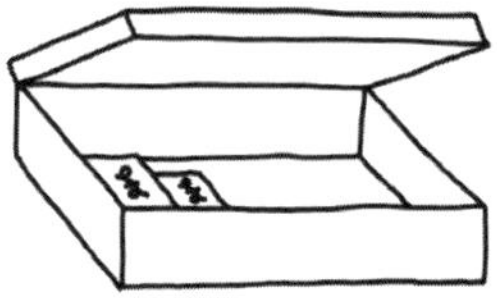

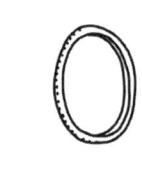

- PAYING FOR THE BIKE
- MAINTENANCE BY COMPETENT PERSON 
- TYRES
- OCCASIONAL BRAKE BLOCKS 
- ACCESSORIES THAT AREN'T STRICTLY NECESSARY 
- FUEL 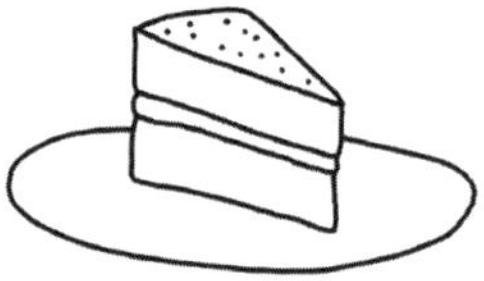
- MORE FUEL 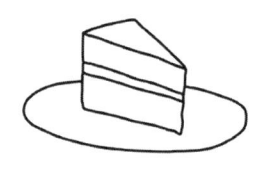
- [I'M JUST FILLING NOW]

CHAPTER 3

BICYCLES

THERE'S A BIKE FOR EVERYONE

THE BICYCLE
AN INTRODUCTION TO THE BASICS

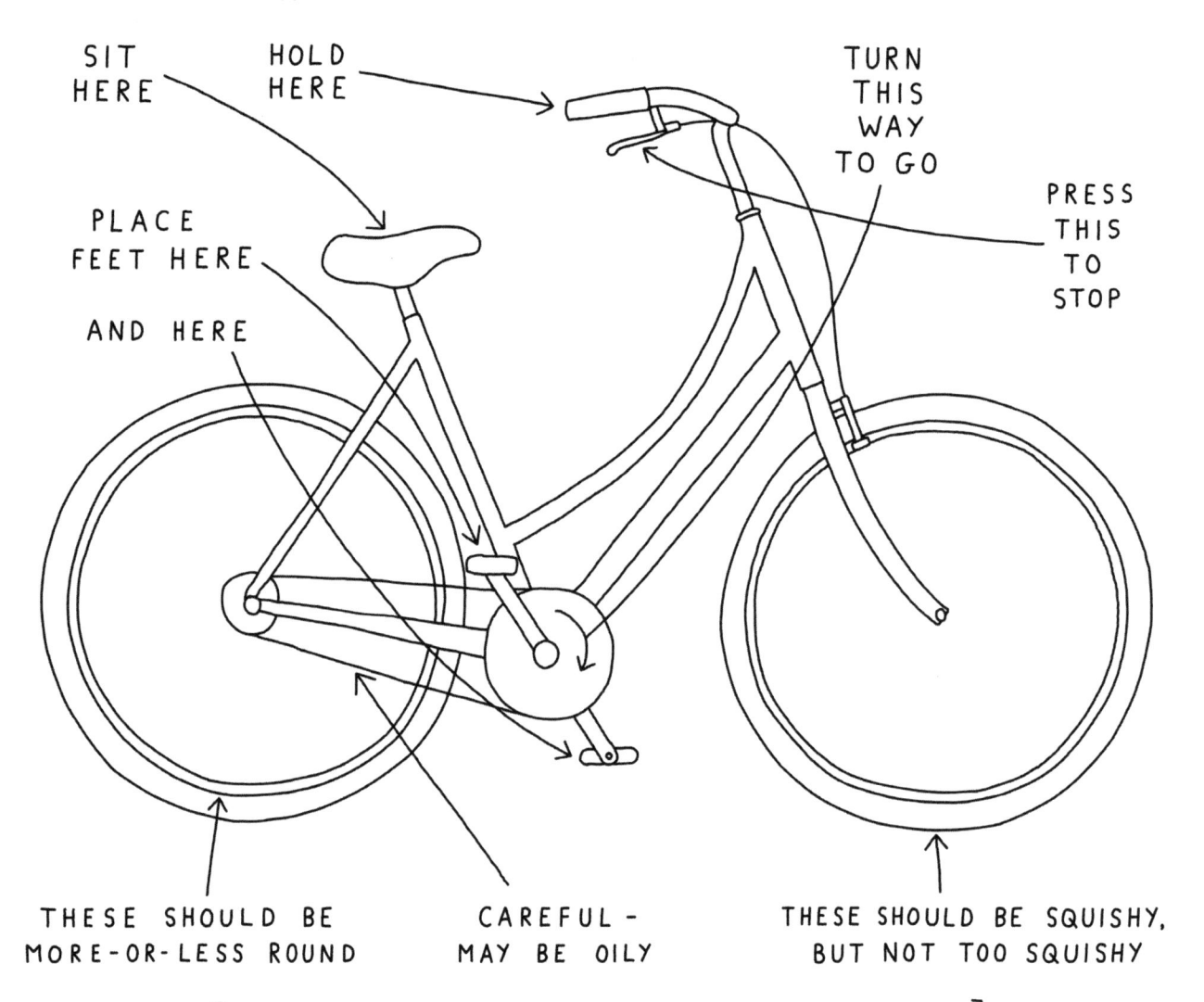

SIT HERE

HOLD HERE

TURN THIS WAY TO GO

PRESS THIS TO STOP

PLACE FEET HERE

AND HERE

THESE SHOULD BE MORE-OR-LESS ROUND

CAREFUL — MAY BE OILY

THESE SHOULD BE SQUISHY, BUT NOT TOO SQUISHY

[THERE ARE OTHER BITS TOO, BUT THEY ARE WELL BEYOND THE SCOPE OF CHAPTER THREE]

THERE'S A BIKE FOR EVERYONE
SIX DRAWINGS FOR THE PRICE OF ONE

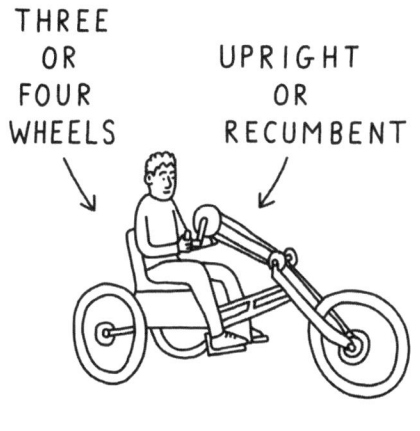

THREE OR FOUR WHEELS · UPRIGHT OR RECUMBENT

HAND CYCLE

TAKES AWAY THE NEED TO BALANCE

TRICYCLE

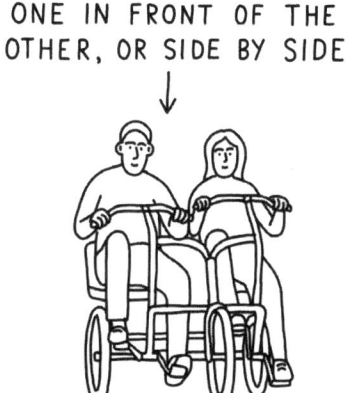

ONE IN FRONT OF THE OTHER, OR SIDE BY SIDE

TANDEM

WHEELCHAIR AND BIKE COMBINED

WHEELCHAIR CYCLE

EASIER TO GET ON AND OFF

LOW-STEP BIKE

FOR THOSE THAT STRUGGLE WITH THE USUAL LEANING-FORWARD POSITION

RECUMBENT

OTHER POSSIBILITIES: ELECTRIC-ASSIST, OR SOME COMBINATION OF THE CATEGORIES ABOVE

SUMMARY: AN EVEN GREATER VARIETY OF PEOPLE CAN NOW RIDE A BIKE

BUYING A BICYCLE
A VAGUE GUIDE TO THE DIFFERENT TYPES

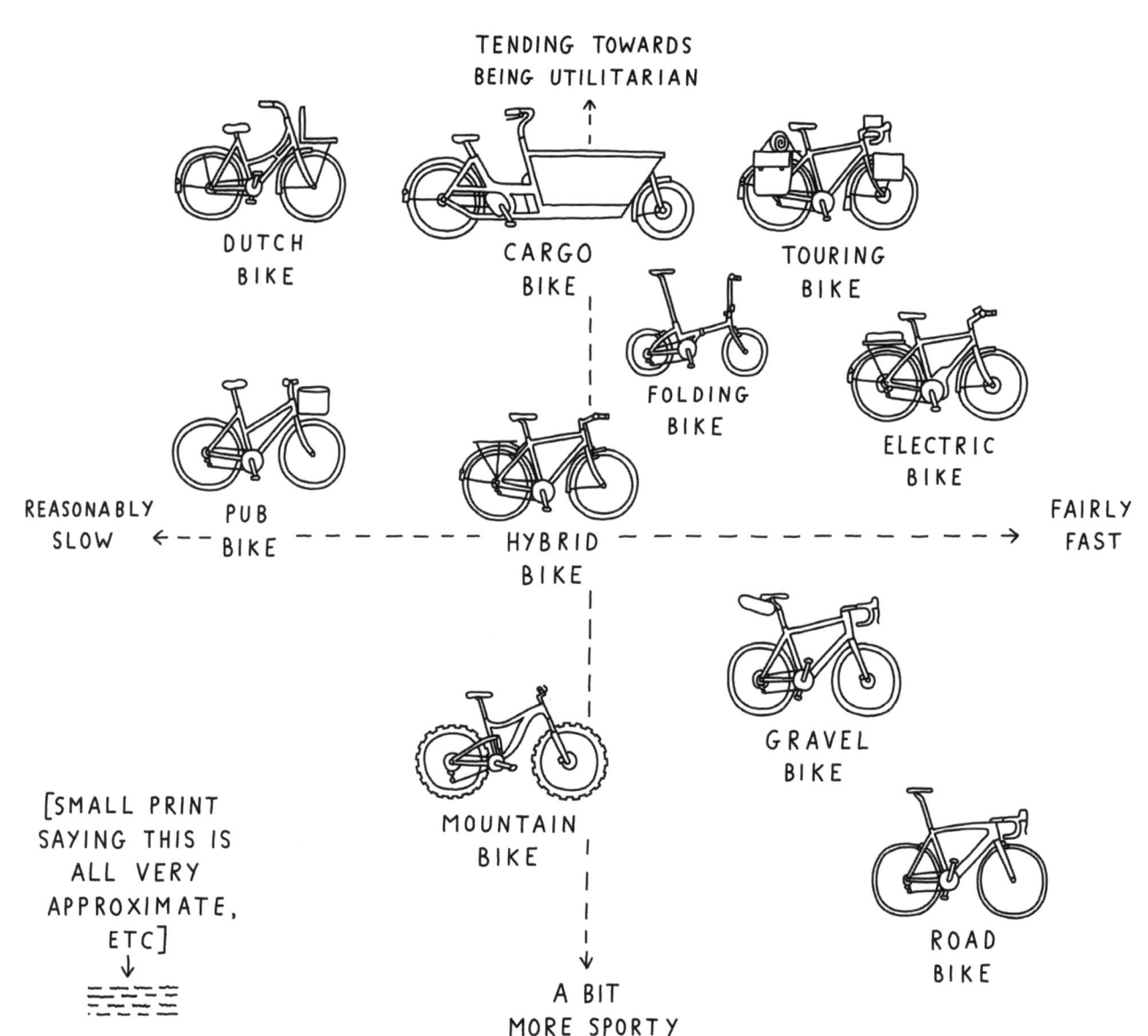

TENDING TOWARDS BEING UTILITARIAN ↑

DUTCH BIKE

CARGO BIKE

TOURING BIKE

FOLDING BIKE

ELECTRIC BIKE

REASONABLY SLOW ← PUB BIKE

HYBRID BIKE

→ FAIRLY FAST

MOUNTAIN BIKE

GRAVEL BIKE

ROAD BIKE

[SMALL PRINT SAYING THIS IS ALL VERY APPROXIMATE, ETC]
↓

↓ A BIT MORE SPORTY

THE DUTCH BIKE
OR TRADITIONAL BIKE

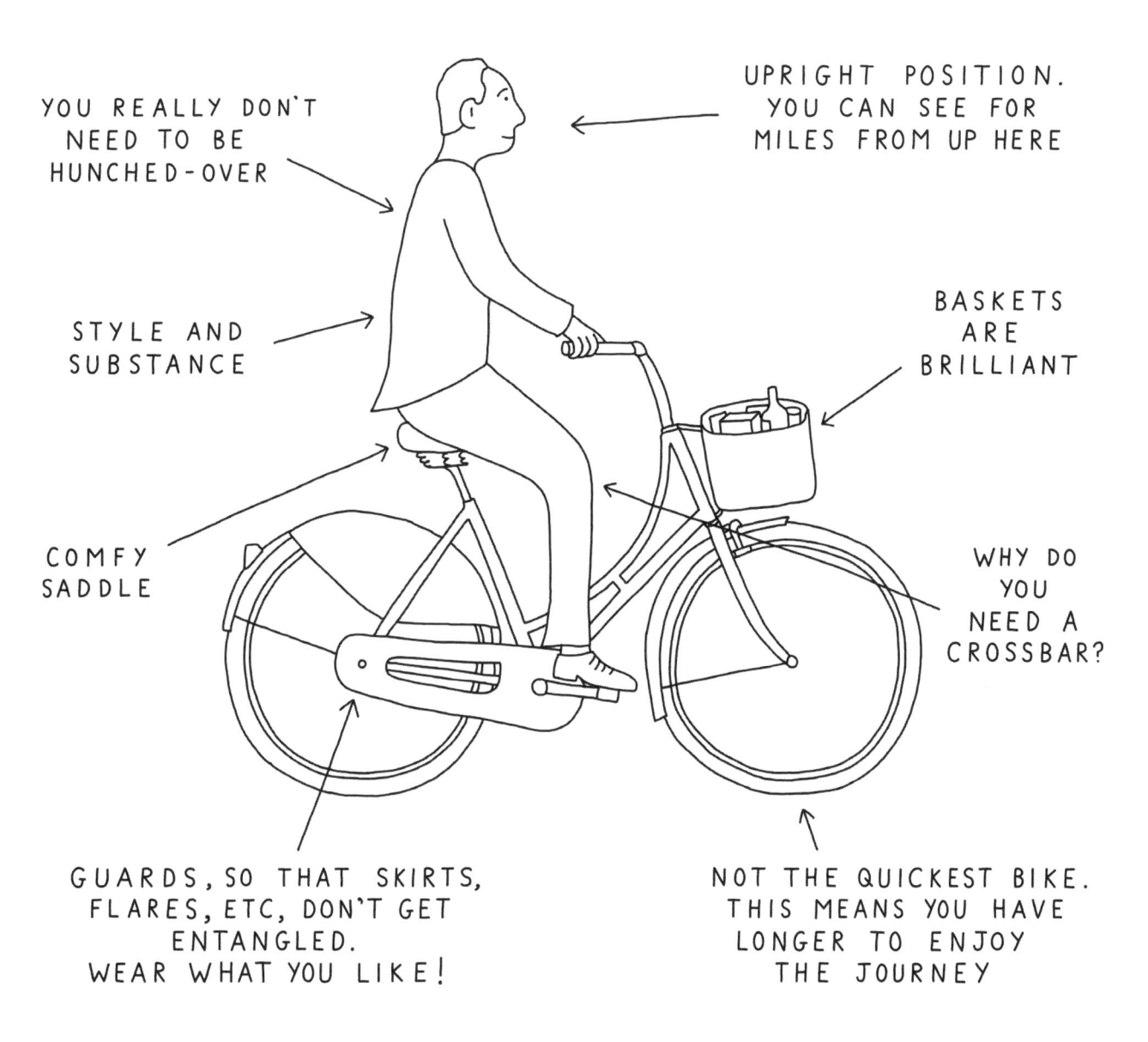

YOU REALLY DON'T NEED TO BE HUNCHED-OVER

UPRIGHT POSITION. YOU CAN SEE FOR MILES FROM UP HERE

STYLE AND SUBSTANCE

BASKETS ARE BRILLIANT

COMFY SADDLE

WHY DO YOU NEED A CROSSBAR?

GUARDS, SO THAT SKIRTS, FLARES, ETC, DON'T GET ENTANGLED. WEAR WHAT YOU LIKE!

NOT THE QUICKEST BIKE. THIS MEANS YOU HAVE LONGER TO ENJOY THE JOURNEY

THE HYBRID

THE RECOMMENDED ALL-ROUND BIKE
IF YOU CAN'T DECIDE

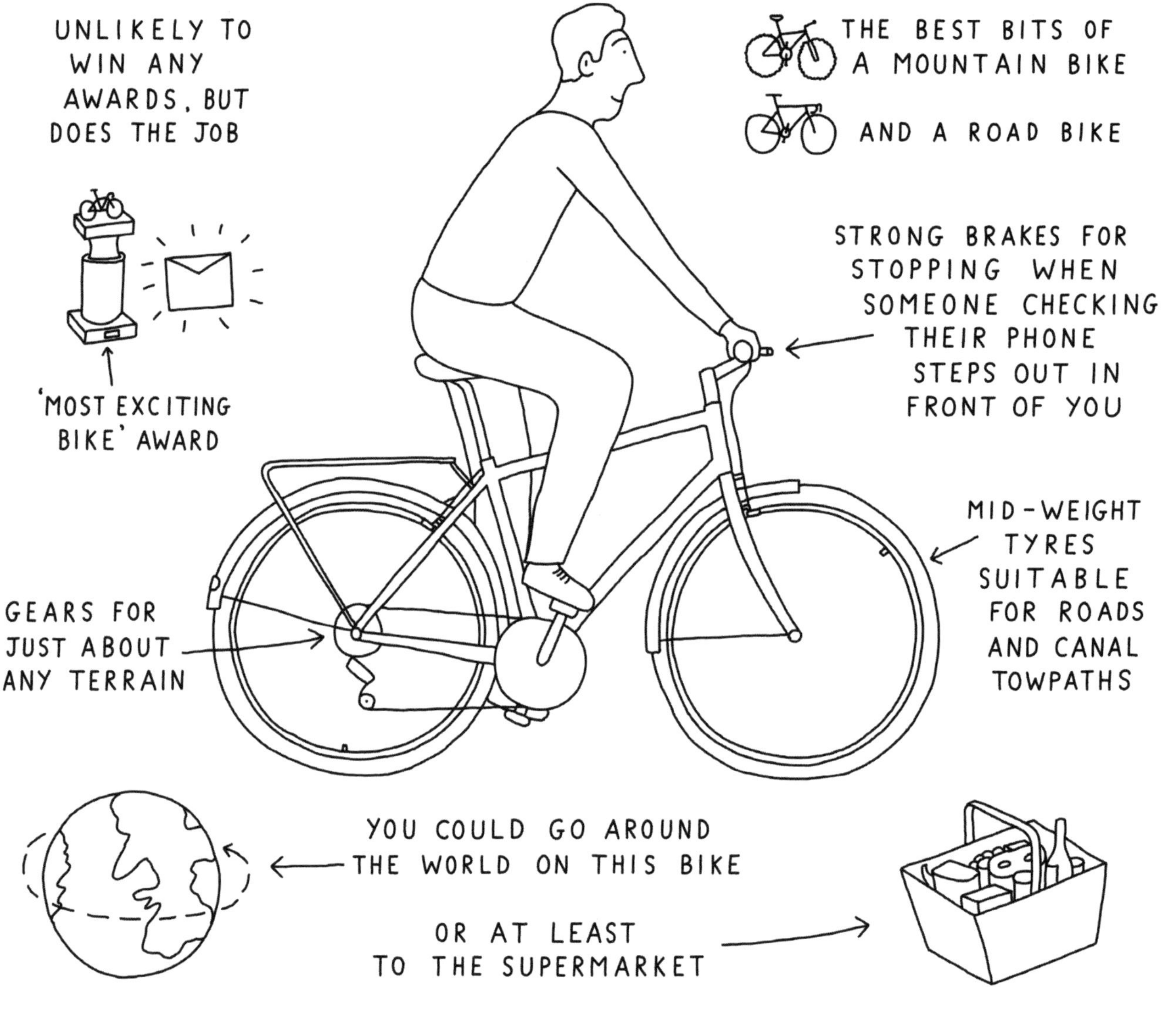
UNLIKELY TO WIN ANY AWARDS, BUT DOES THE JOB
'MOST EXCITING BIKE' AWARD
THE BEST BITS OF A MOUNTAIN BIKE
AND A ROAD BIKE
STRONG BRAKES FOR STOPPING WHEN SOMEONE CHECKING THEIR PHONE STEPS OUT IN FRONT OF YOU
GEARS FOR JUST ABOUT ANY TERRAIN
MID-WEIGHT TYRES SUITABLE FOR ROADS AND CANAL TOWPATHS
YOU COULD GO AROUND THE WORLD ON THIS BIKE
OR AT LEAST TO THE SUPERMARKET

THE ROAD BIKE
BUILT FOR SPEED

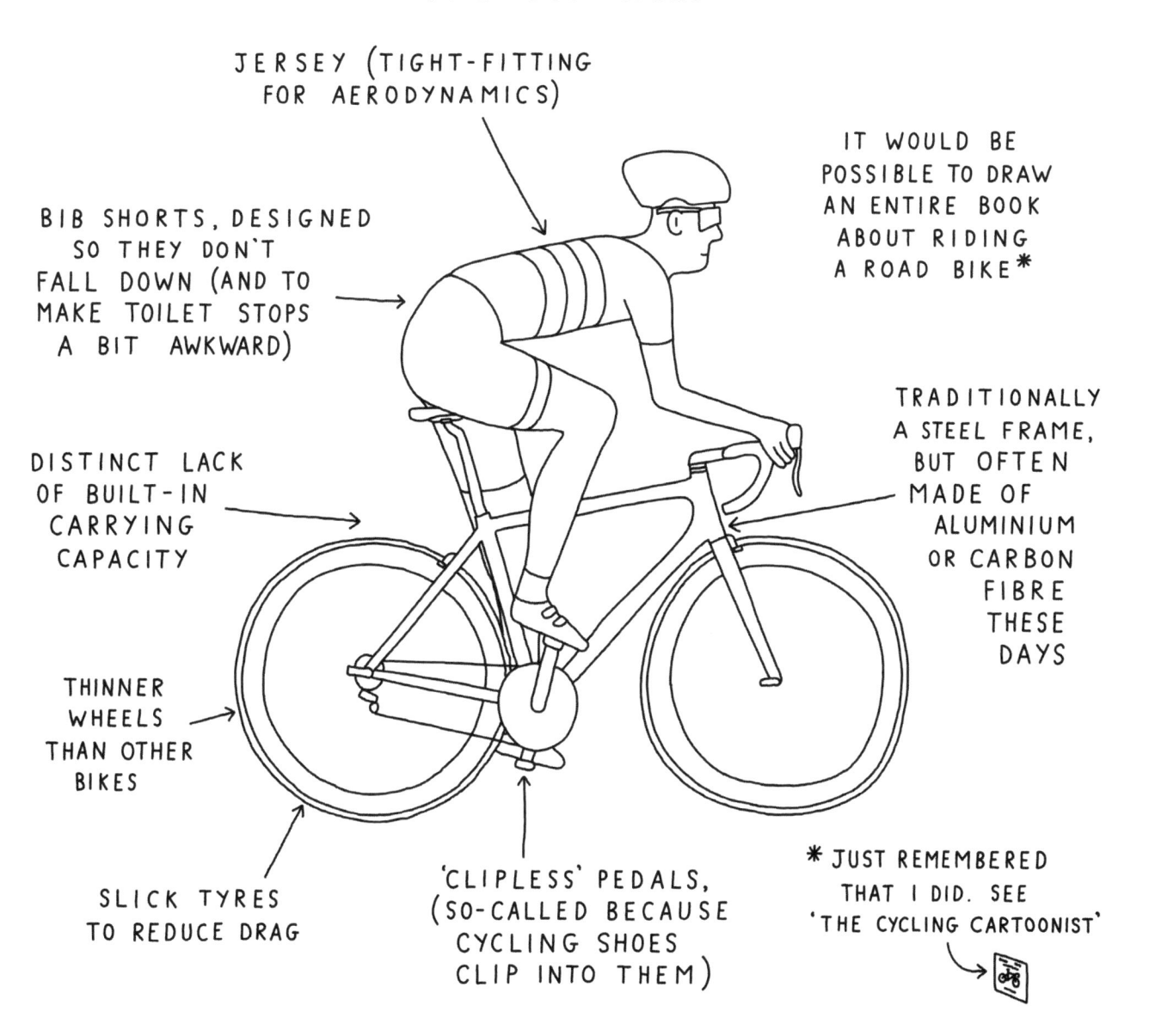

JERSEY (TIGHT-FITTING FOR AERODYNAMICS)

IT WOULD BE POSSIBLE TO DRAW AN ENTIRE BOOK ABOUT RIDING A ROAD BIKE*

BIB SHORTS, DESIGNED SO THEY DON'T FALL DOWN (AND TO MAKE TOILET STOPS A BIT AWKWARD)

TRADITIONALLY A STEEL FRAME, BUT OFTEN MADE OF ALUMINIUM OR CARBON FIBRE THESE DAYS

DISTINCT LACK OF BUILT-IN CARRYING CAPACITY

THINNER WHEELS THAN OTHER BIKES

SLICK TYRES TO REDUCE DRAG

'CLIPLESS' PEDALS, (SO-CALLED BECAUSE CYCLING SHOES CLIP INTO THEM)

* JUST REMEMBERED THAT I DID. SEE 'THE CYCLING CARTOONIST'

THE MOUNTAIN BIKE

FOR RIDING OFF-ROAD

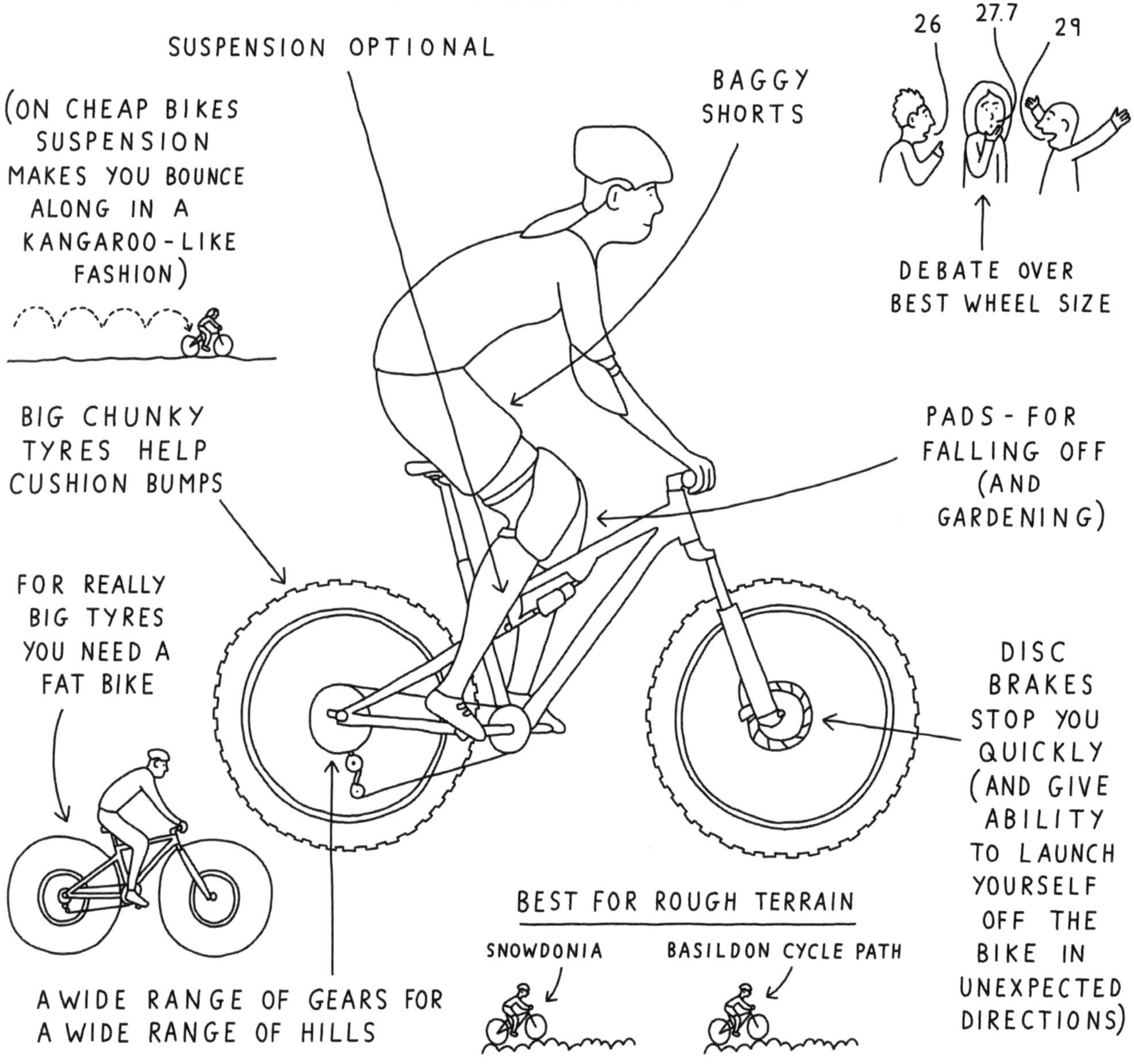
SUSPENSION OPTIONAL
(ON CHEAP BIKES SUSPENSION MAKES YOU BOUNCE ALONG IN A KANGAROO-LIKE FASHION)
BAGGY SHORTS
26
27.7
29
DEBATE OVER BEST WHEEL SIZE
BIG CHUNKY TYRES HELP CUSHION BUMPS
PADS - FOR FALLING OFF (AND GARDENING)
FOR REALLY BIG TYRES YOU NEED A FAT BIKE
DISC BRAKES STOP YOU QUICKLY (AND GIVE ABILITY TO LAUNCH YOURSELF OFF THE BIKE IN UNEXPECTED DIRECTIONS)
BEST FOR ROUGH TERRAIN
SNOWDONIA
BASILDON CYCLE PATH
A WIDE RANGE OF GEARS FOR A WIDE RANGE OF HILLS

THE FOLDING BIKE

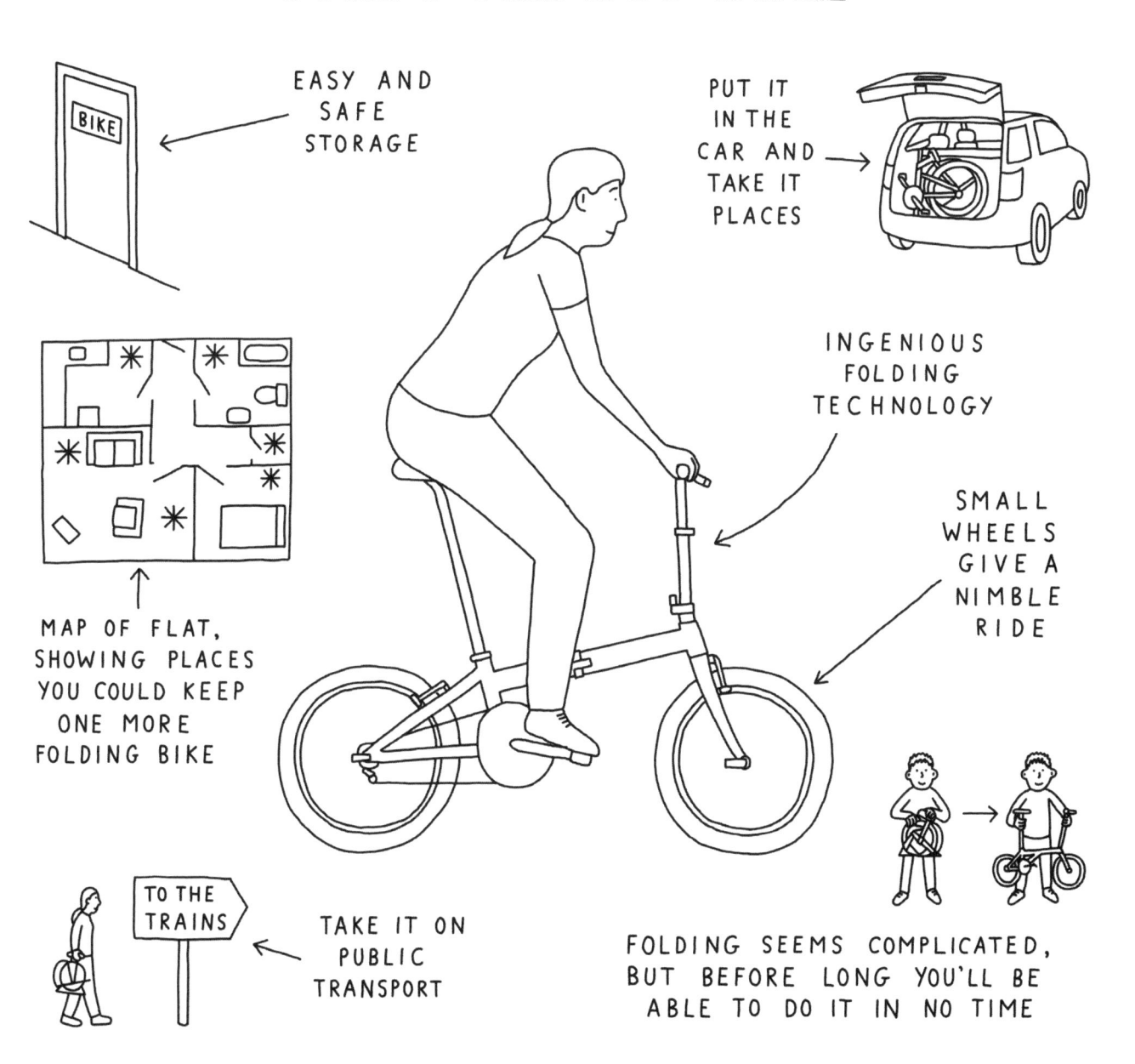

EASY AND SAFE STORAGE

PUT IT IN THE CAR AND TAKE IT PLACES

INGENIOUS FOLDING TECHNOLOGY

SMALL WHEELS GIVE A NIMBLE RIDE

MAP OF FLAT, SHOWING PLACES YOU COULD KEEP ONE MORE FOLDING BIKE

TO THE TRAINS

TAKE IT ON PUBLIC TRANSPORT

FOLDING SEEMS COMPLICATED, BUT BEFORE LONG YOU'LL BE ABLE TO DO IT IN NO TIME

BIKES THAT FOLD

POSSIBILITIES

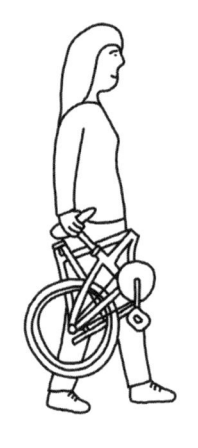

TAKE THEM ON THE TRAIN

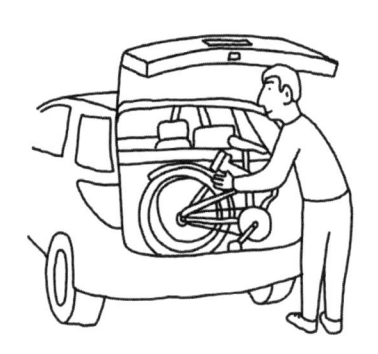

PUT THEM IN THE BOOT OF YOUR CAR

HOME
WORK

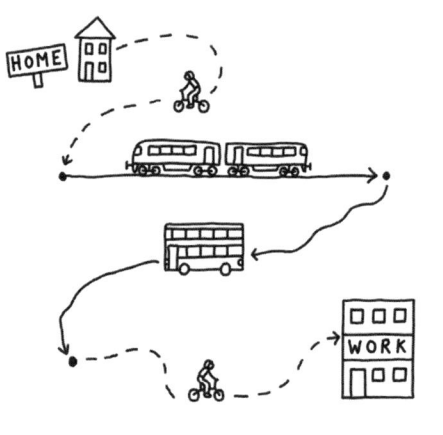

COMBINE THEM WITH OTHER FORMS OF TRANSPORT

FOLDING DEMO. NEXT SHOWING: 2 PM

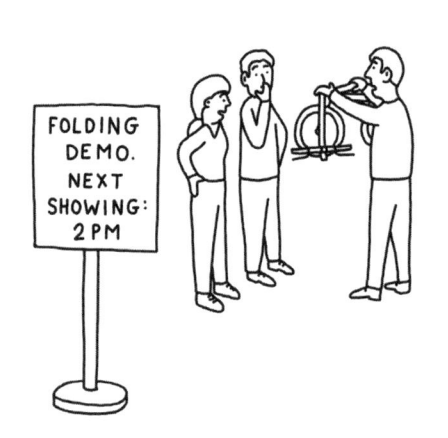

IMPRESS FRIENDS

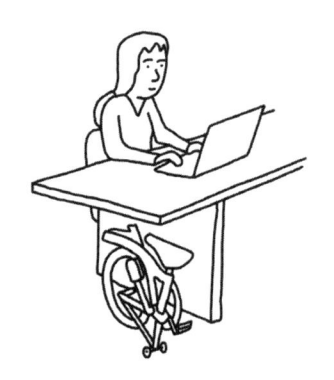

KEEP THEM SAFE FROM THIEVES

ANOTHER BIKE? I DON'T KNOW WHAT GIVES YOU THAT IDEA...

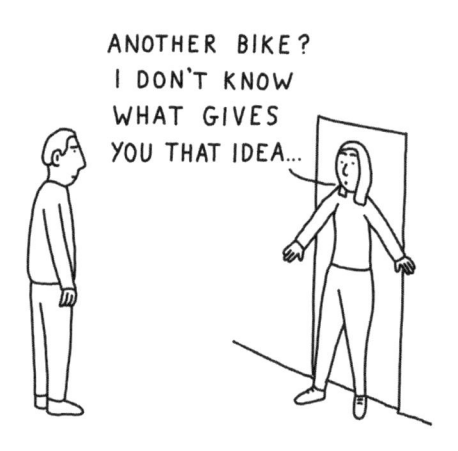

HIDE THEM IN A CUPBOARD

FOLDING TECHNOLOGIES

FOLDING-BIKE FANS SHARE THEIR ENTHUSIASM

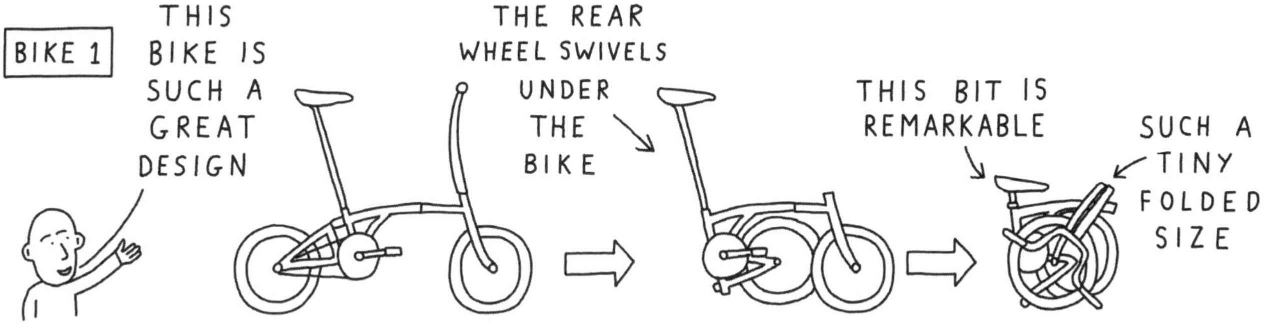
BIKE 1
THIS BIKE IS SUCH A GREAT DESIGN
THE REAR WHEEL SWIVELS UNDER THE BIKE
THIS BIT IS REMARKABLE
SUCH A TINY FOLDED SIZE

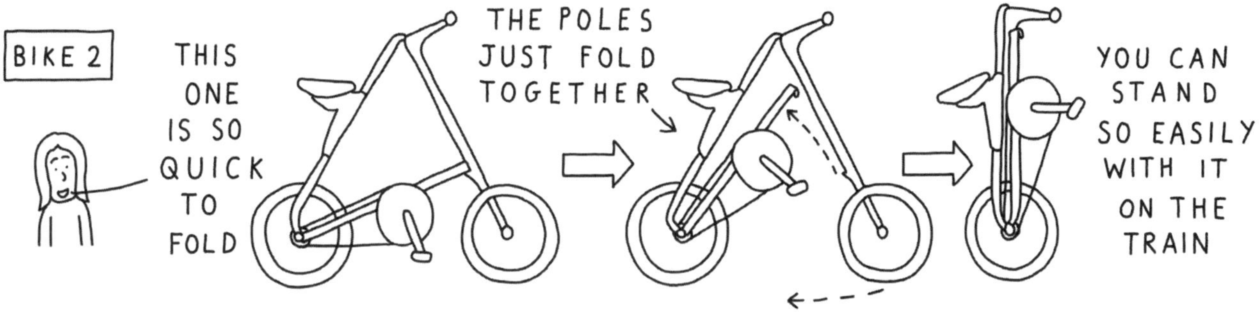
BIKE 2
THIS ONE IS SO QUICK TO FOLD
THE POLES JUST FOLD TOGETHER
YOU CAN STAND SO EASILY WITH IT ON THE TRAIN

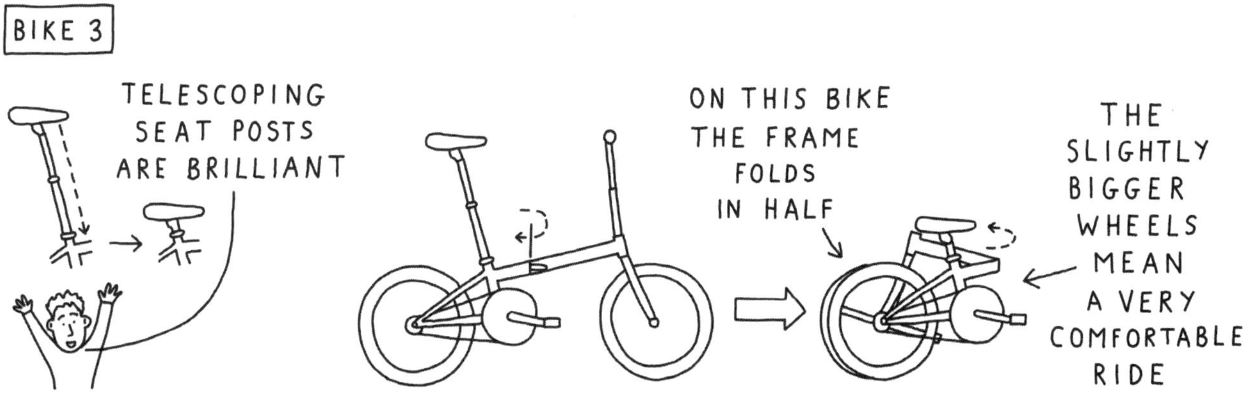
BIKE 3
TELESCOPING SEAT POSTS ARE BRILLIANT
ON THIS BIKE THE FRAME FOLDS IN HALF
THE SLIGHTLY BIGGER WHEELS MEAN A VERY COMFORTABLE RIDE

THE CARGO BIKE

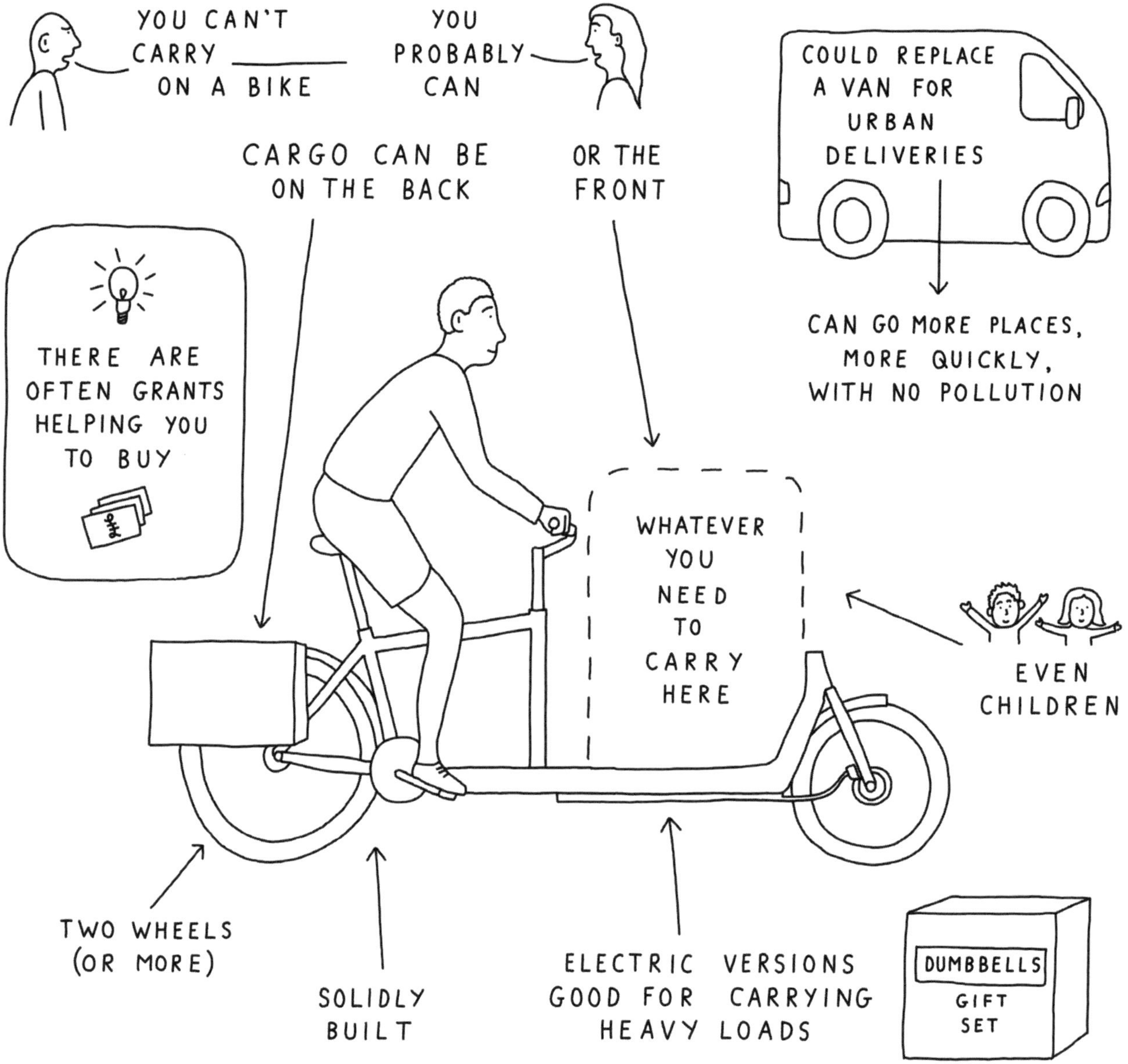
YOU CAN'T CARRY ________ ON A BIKE
YOU PROBABLY CAN
COULD REPLACE A VAN FOR URBAN DELIVERIES
CAN GO MORE PLACES, MORE QUICKLY, WITH NO POLLUTION
CARGO CAN BE ON THE BACK
OR THE FRONT
THERE ARE OFTEN GRANTS HELPING YOU TO BUY
WHATEVER YOU NEED TO CARRY HERE
EVEN CHILDREN
TWO WHEELS (OR MORE)
SOLIDLY BUILT
ELECTRIC VERSIONS GOOD FOR CARRYING HEAVY LOADS
DUMBBELLS
GIFT SET

CARGO BIKES
THINGS YOU COULD CARRY

YOUR WEEKLY SHOP

PETS

THE TOOLS OF YOUR TRADE

CHILDREN

LOCAL DELIVERIES

EVERYTHING YOU NEED FOR A DAY OUT

TAKEAWAY FOOD

A FRIDGE (YES, REALLY)

THE ELECTRIC BIKE

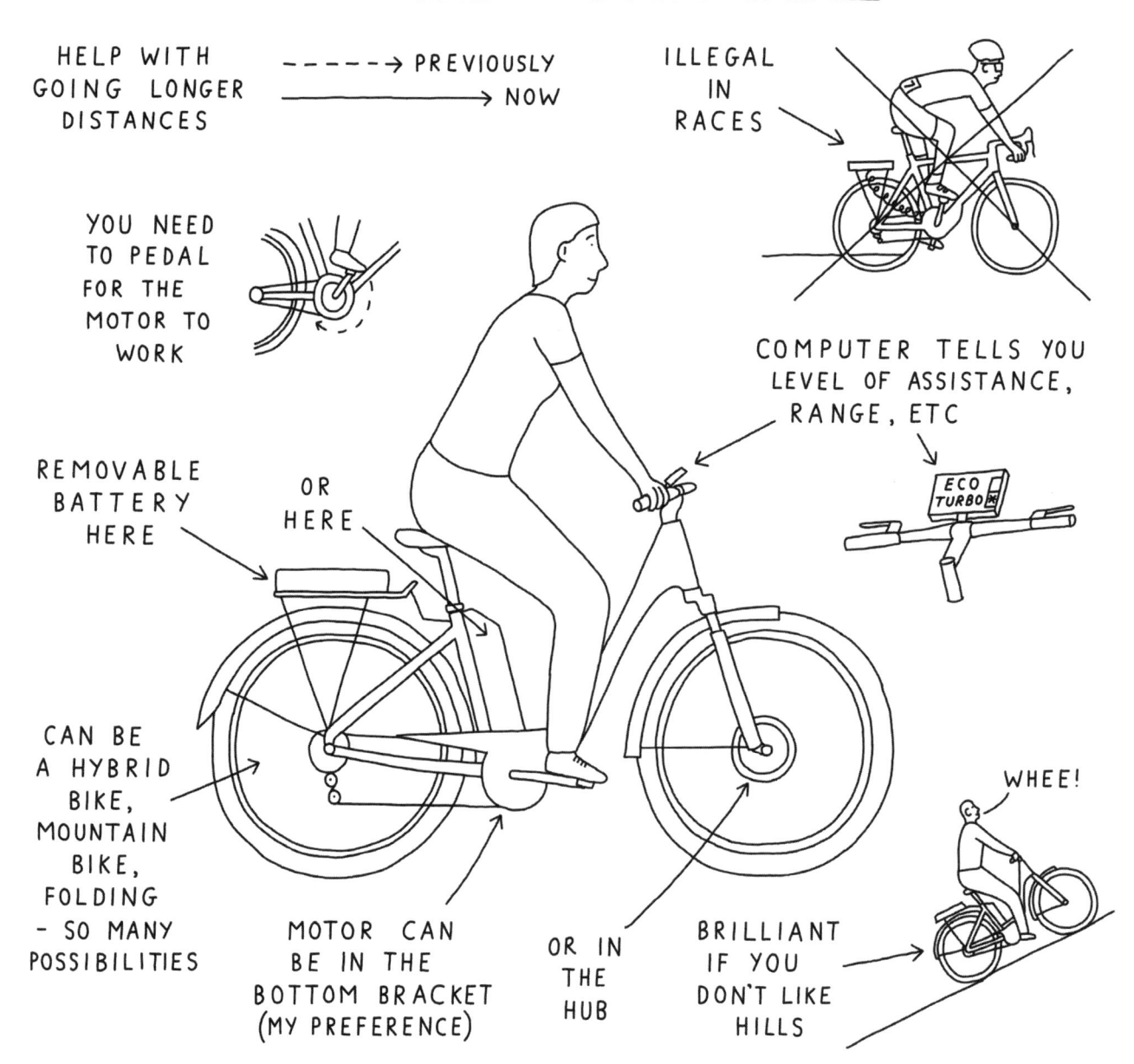

HELP WITH GOING LONGER DISTANCES

- - - - → PREVIOUSLY
———→ NOW

ILLEGAL IN RACES

YOU NEED TO PEDAL FOR THE MOTOR TO WORK

COMPUTER TELLS YOU LEVEL OF ASSISTANCE, RANGE, ETC

ECO TURBO

REMOVABLE BATTERY HERE

OR HERE

CAN BE A HYBRID BIKE, MOUNTAIN BIKE, FOLDING - SO MANY POSSIBILITIES

MOTOR CAN BE IN THE BOTTOM BRACKET (MY PREFERENCE)

OR IN THE HUB

BRILLIANT IF YOU DON'T LIKE HILLS

WHEE!

THE E-BIKE

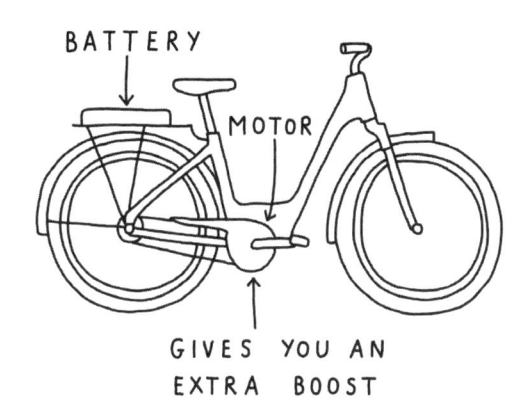

BATTERY
MOTOR
GIVES YOU AN EXTRA BOOST

OPENS RIDING A BIKE TO PEOPLE WHO COULDN'T OTHERWISE DO IT

MAKES HILLS BEARABLE

MUCH LOWER EMISSIONS AND HEALTHIER THAN OTHER POWERED ALTERNATIVES

MEANS PEOPLE OF DIFFERENT ABILITIES CAN CYCLE TOGETHER

ARE ELECTRIC BIKES 'CHEATING'? ⟶ TO BE ADDRESSED IN ANOTHER DIAGRAM [SPOILER: NO]

ELECTRIC BIKES

ARE THEY CHEATING?

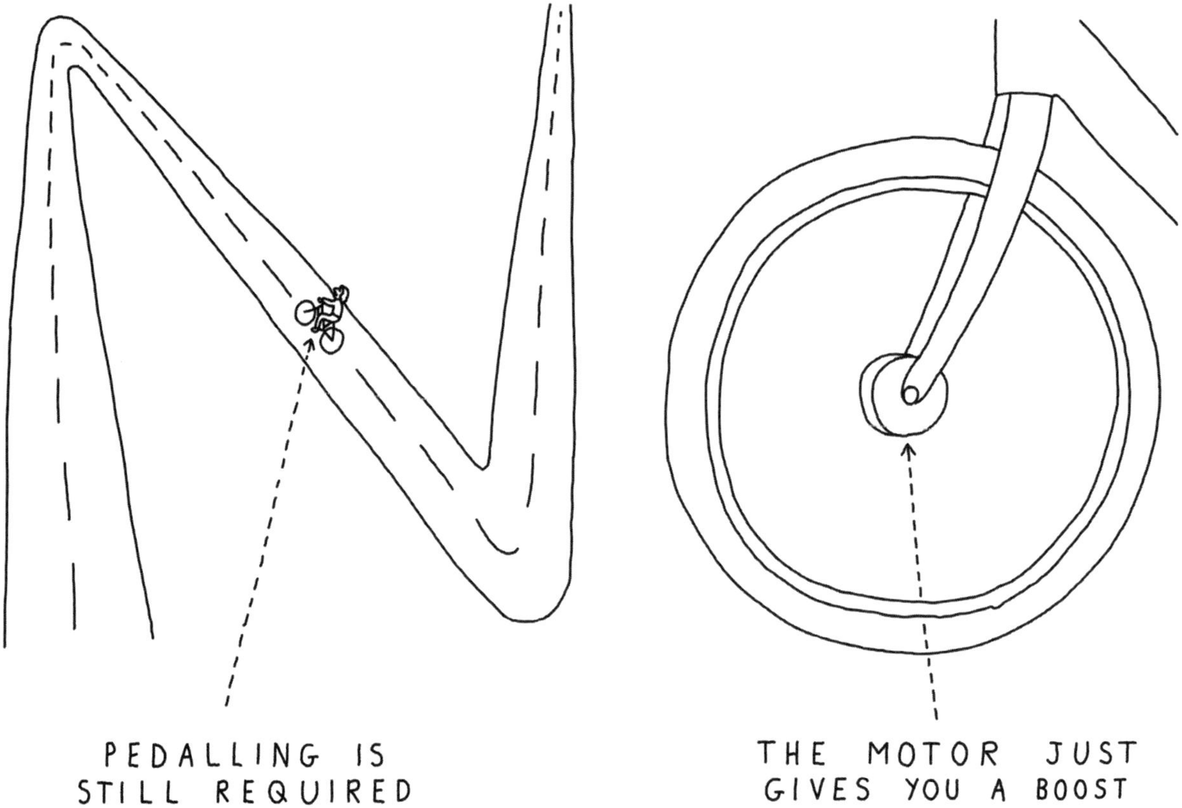
PEDALLING IS STILL REQUIRED
THE MOTOR JUST GIVES YOU A BOOST

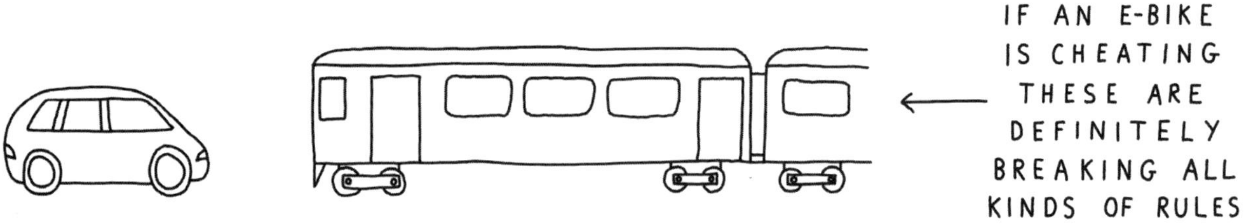
IF AN E-BIKE IS CHEATING THESE ARE DEFINITELY BREAKING ALL KINDS OF RULES

THE GRAVEL BIKE

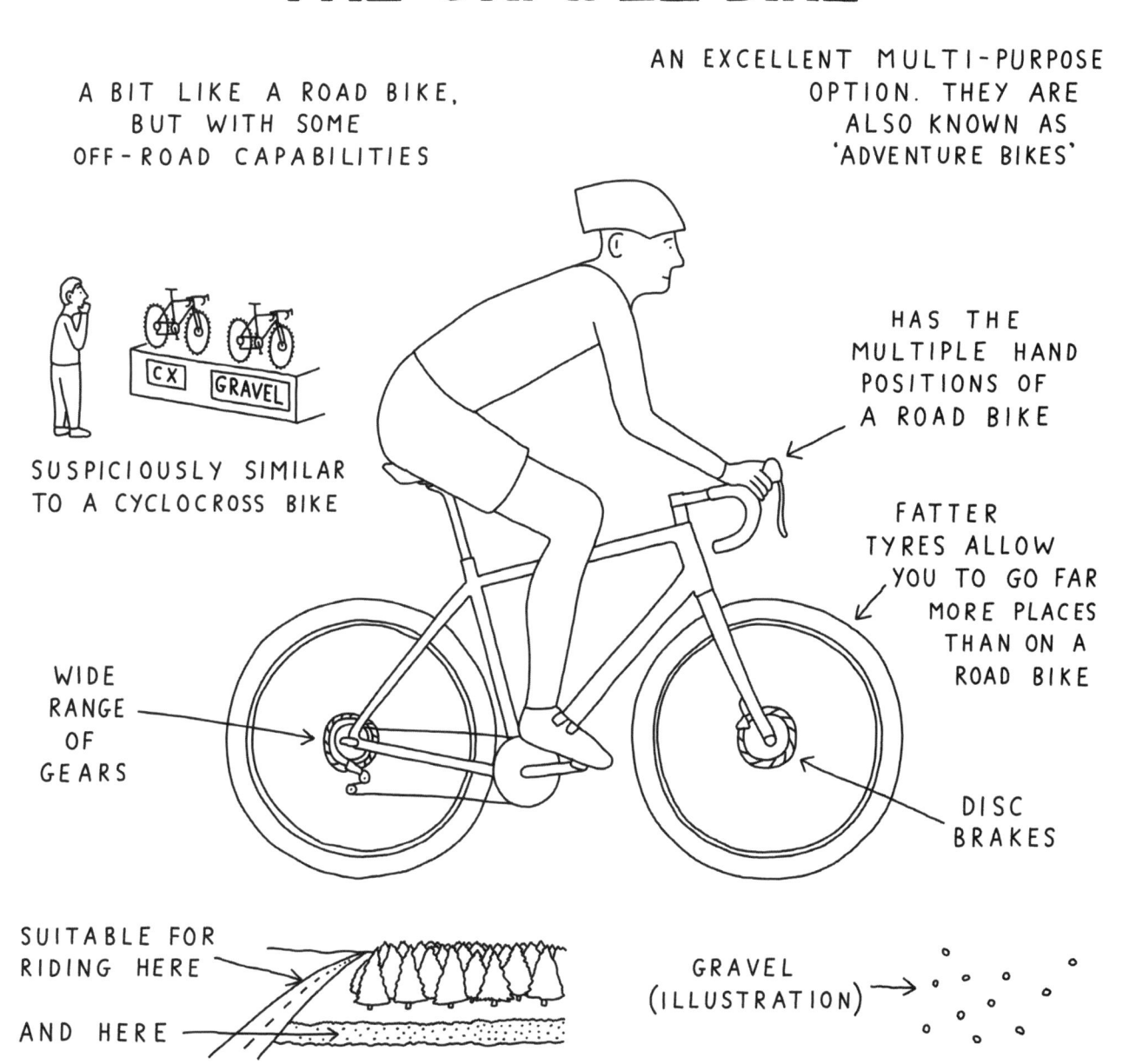

A BIT LIKE A ROAD BIKE, BUT WITH SOME OFF-ROAD CAPABILITIES

AN EXCELLENT MULTI-PURPOSE OPTION. THEY ARE ALSO KNOWN AS 'ADVENTURE BIKES'

SUSPICIOUSLY SIMILAR TO A CYCLOCROSS BIKE

HAS THE MULTIPLE HAND POSITIONS OF A ROAD BIKE

FATTER TYRES ALLOW YOU TO GO FAR MORE PLACES THAN ON A ROAD BIKE

WIDE RANGE OF GEARS

DISC BRAKES

SUITABLE FOR RIDING HERE
AND HERE

GRAVEL (ILLUSTRATION)

THE TOURING BIKE
THE ULTIMATE BIKE FOR GOING ON ADVENTURES

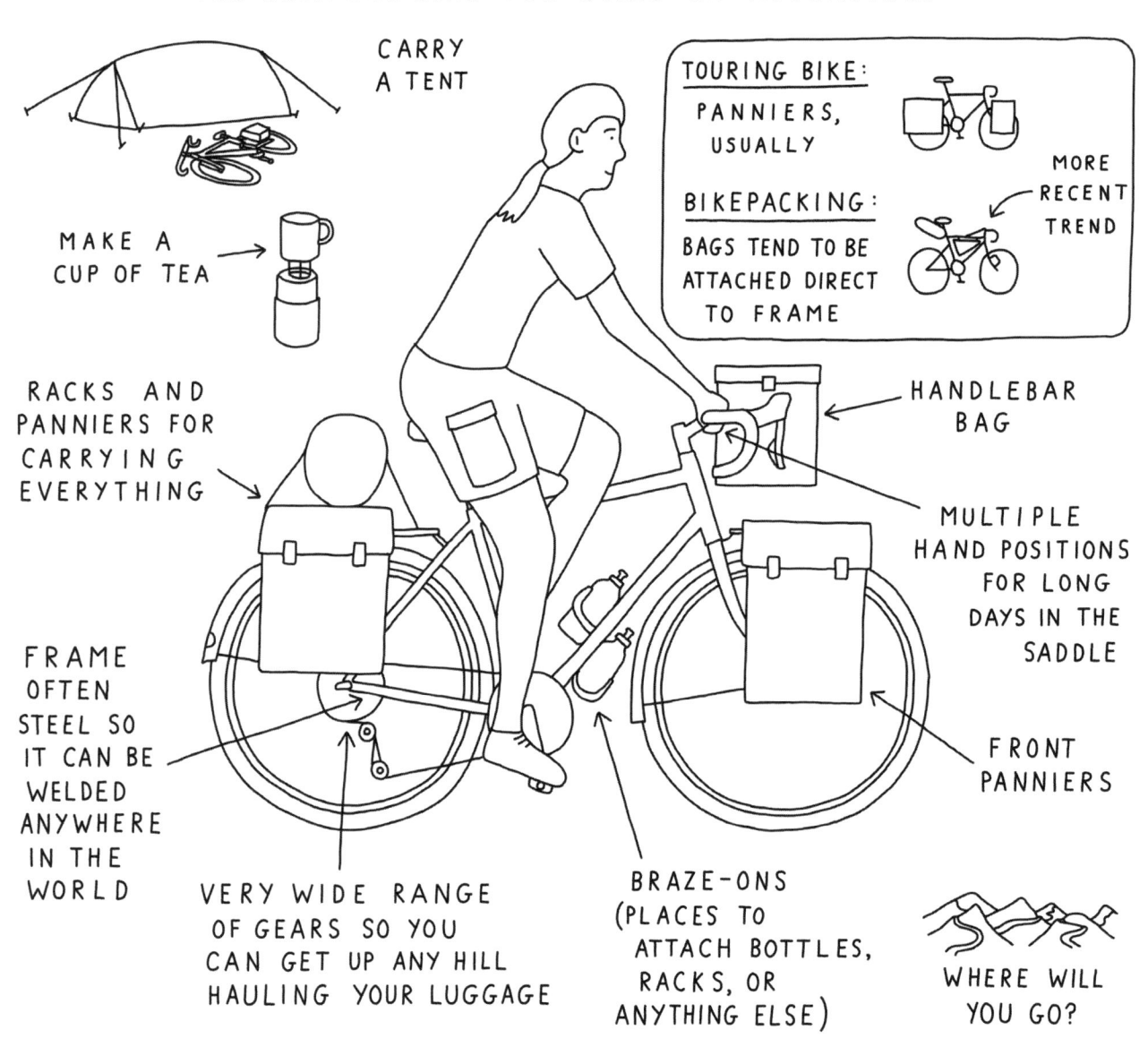

CARRY A TENT

MAKE A CUP OF TEA

TOURING BIKE: PANNIERS, USUALLY

BIKEPACKING: BAGS TEND TO BE ATTACHED DIRECT TO FRAME

MORE RECENT TREND

RACKS AND PANNIERS FOR CARRYING EVERYTHING

HANDLEBAR BAG

MULTIPLE HAND POSITIONS FOR LONG DAYS IN THE SADDLE

FRAME OFTEN STEEL SO IT CAN BE WELDED ANYWHERE IN THE WORLD

FRONT PANNIERS

VERY WIDE RANGE OF GEARS SO YOU CAN GET UP ANY HILL HAULING YOUR LUGGAGE

BRAZE-ONS (PLACES TO ATTACH BOTTLES, RACKS, OR ANYTHING ELSE)

WHERE WILL YOU GO?

THE PUB BIKE

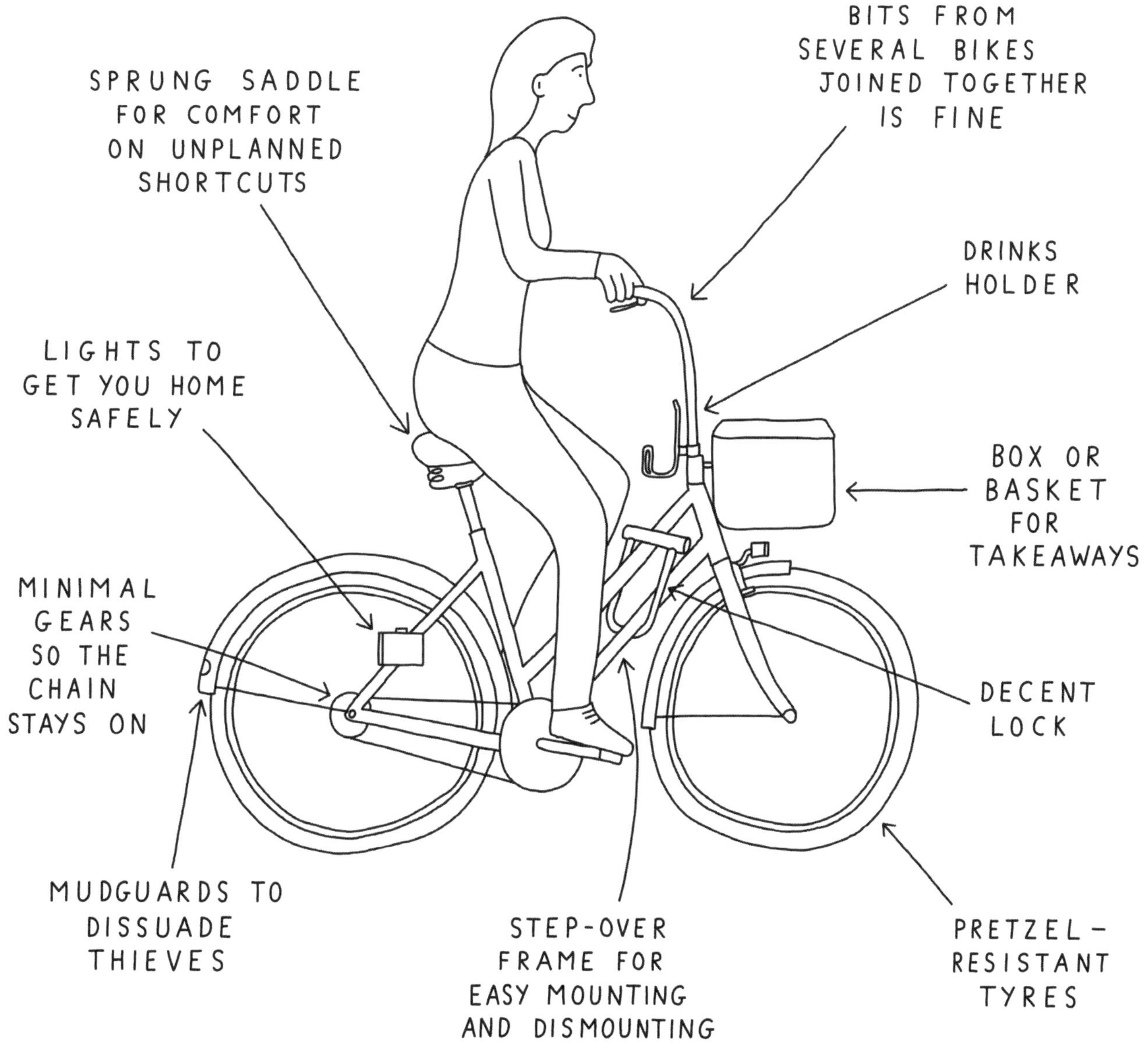
BITS FROM SEVERAL BIKES JOINED TOGETHER IS FINE
SPRUNG SADDLE FOR COMFORT ON UNPLANNED SHORTCUTS
DRINKS HOLDER
LIGHTS TO GET YOU HOME SAFELY
BOX OR BASKET FOR TAKEAWAYS
MINIMAL GEARS SO THE CHAIN STAYS ON
DECENT LOCK
MUDGUARDS TO DISSUADE THIEVES
STEP-OVER FRAME FOR EASY MOUNTING AND DISMOUNTING
PRETZEL-RESISTANT TYRES

THE TANDEM

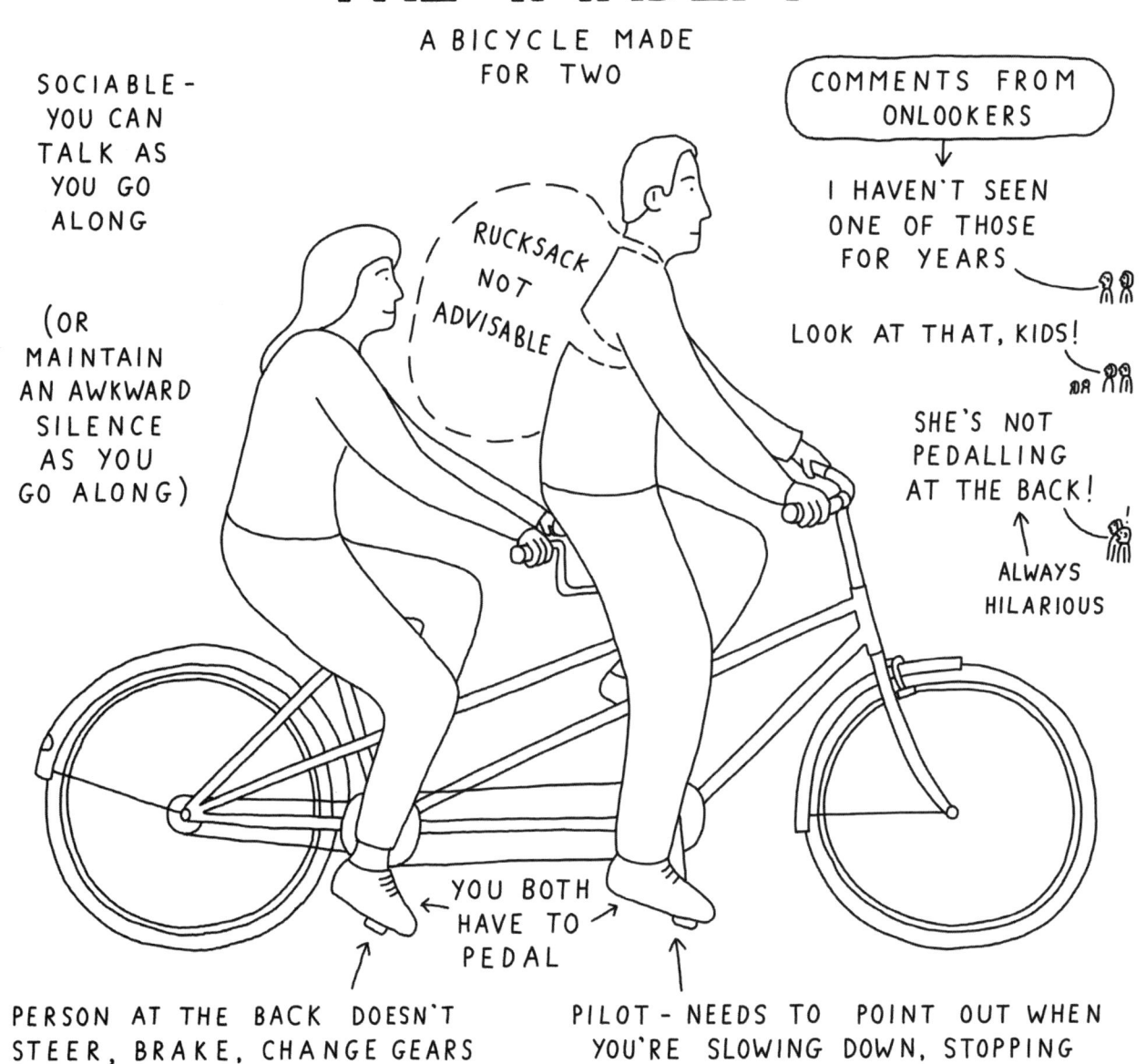

A BICYCLE MADE FOR TWO

SOCIABLE — YOU CAN TALK AS YOU GO ALONG

(OR MAINTAIN AN AWKWARD SILENCE AS YOU GO ALONG)

RUCKSACK NOT ADVISABLE

COMMENTS FROM ONLOOKERS

- I HAVEN'T SEEN ONE OF THOSE FOR YEARS
- LOOK AT THAT, KIDS!
- SHE'S NOT PEDALLING AT THE BACK! ← ALWAYS HILARIOUS

YOU BOTH HAVE TO PEDAL

PERSON AT THE BACK DOESN'T STEER, BRAKE, CHANGE GEARS OR NAVIGATE

PILOT — NEEDS TO POINT OUT WHEN YOU'RE SLOWING DOWN, STOPPING OR GOING OVER A BUMP

CHAPTER 4

ADVENTURES

CITY OR COUNTRY, NEAR OR FAR

PLACES

WHY NOT EXPLORE BY BIKE?

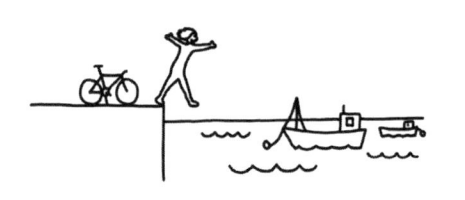

IF YOU WANT TO JUMP INTO THE SEA

LOVELY

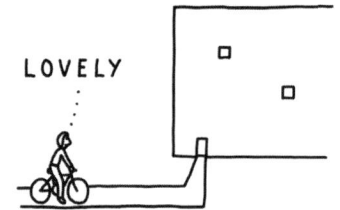

IF BRUTALIST ARCHITECTURE IS YOUR THING

AMUSEMENT PARK

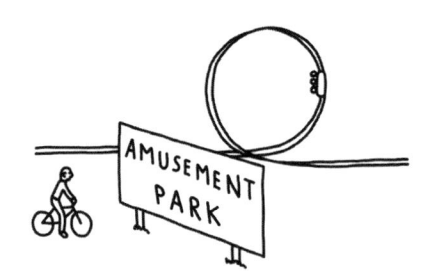

IF FEELING SLIGHTLY DIZZY IS WHAT YOU PREFER

?

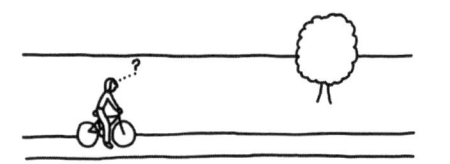

IF YOU WANT TO GET YOURSELF LOST IN WIDE OPEN SPACES

HOW DOES IT WORK?
I HAVE NO IDEA

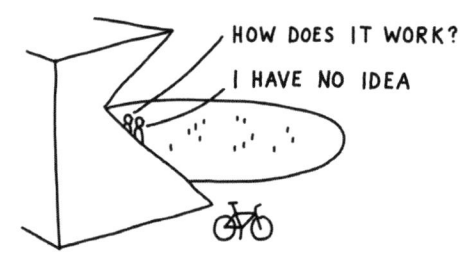

IF YOU LOVE AUSSIE-RULES FOOTBALL

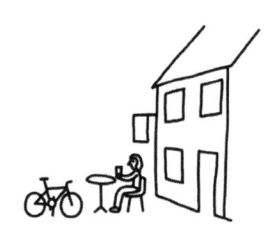

OR A LOVELY PINT OF IPA

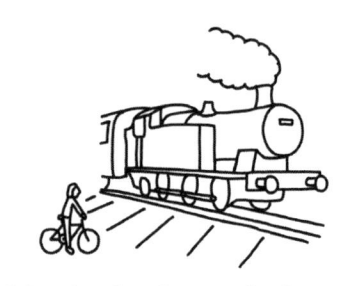

OR A GWR 0-6-2 TANK ENGINE

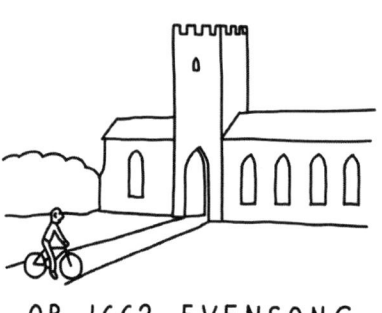

OR 1662 EVENSONG

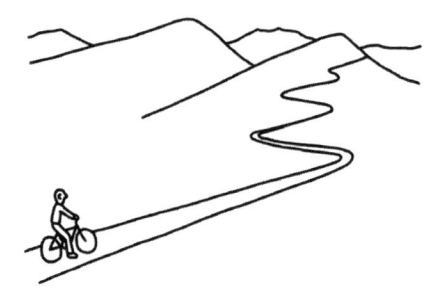

OR JUST ESCAPING FROM EVERYONE

TRAFFIC REPORT

NATIONAL ROAD NETWORK

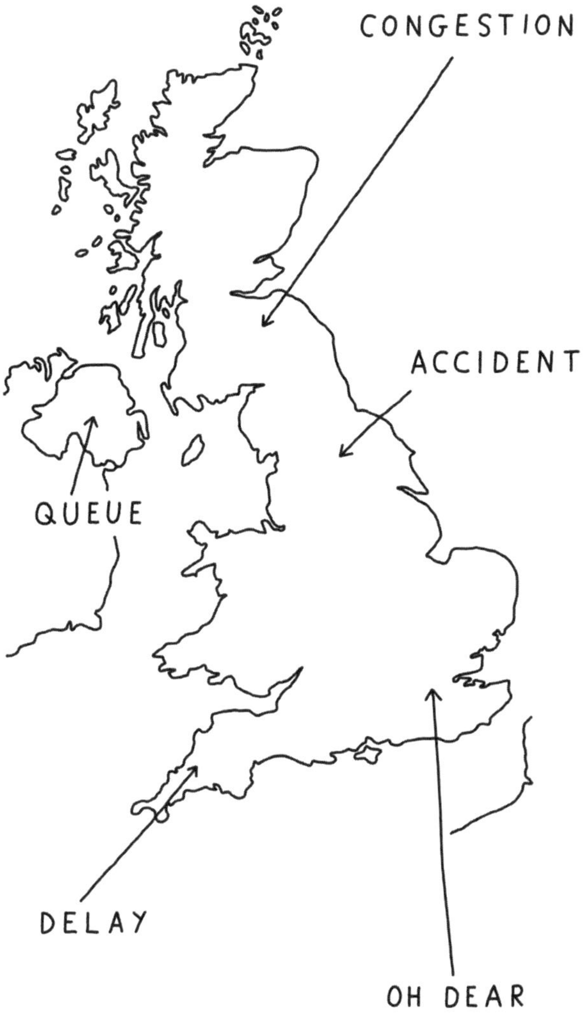
CONGESTION
ACCIDENT
QUEUE
DELAY
OH DEAR

NATIONAL CYCLE NETWORK

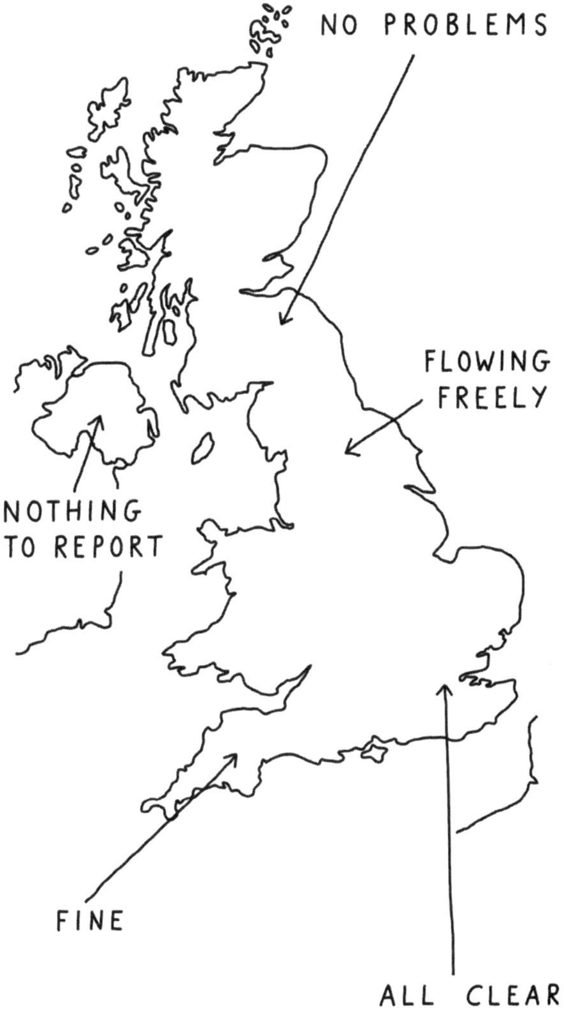
NO PROBLEMS
FLOWING FREELY
NOTHING TO REPORT
FINE
ALL CLEAR

THE HEDGE
WHAT YOU SEE OVER IT

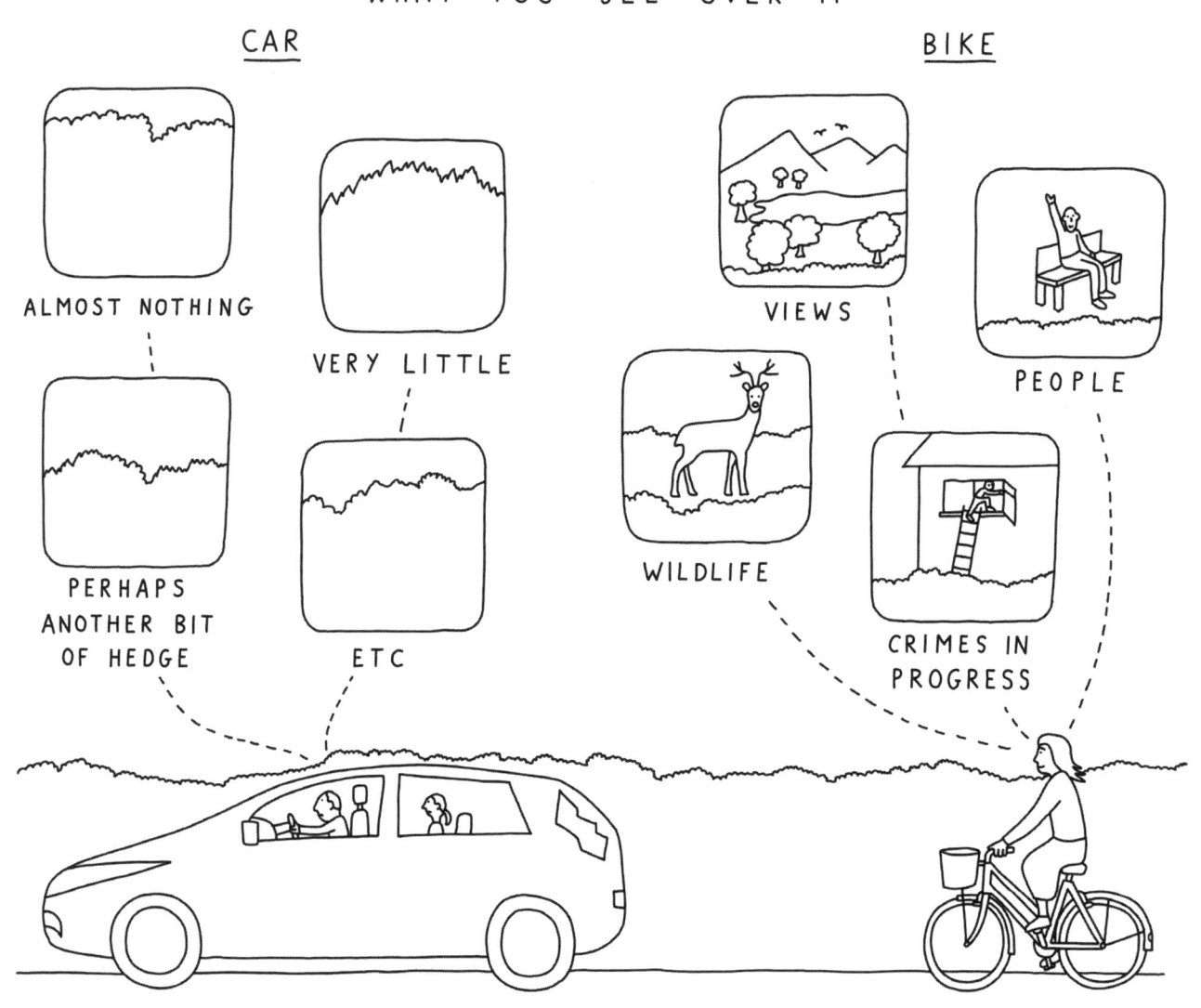

CAR

- ALMOST NOTHING
- VERY LITTLE
- PERHAPS ANOTHER BIT OF HEDGE
- ETC

BIKE

- VIEWS
- PEOPLE
- WILDLIFE
- CRIMES IN PROGRESS

[ADDITIONAL BENEFITS OF CYCLING, BEYOND THE SCOPE OF THIS DIAGRAM → +SOUNDS +SMELLS +FRESH AIR +ABILITY TO STOP AND LOOK EASILY]

LONG DISTANCE CYCLING
POPULAR ROUTES

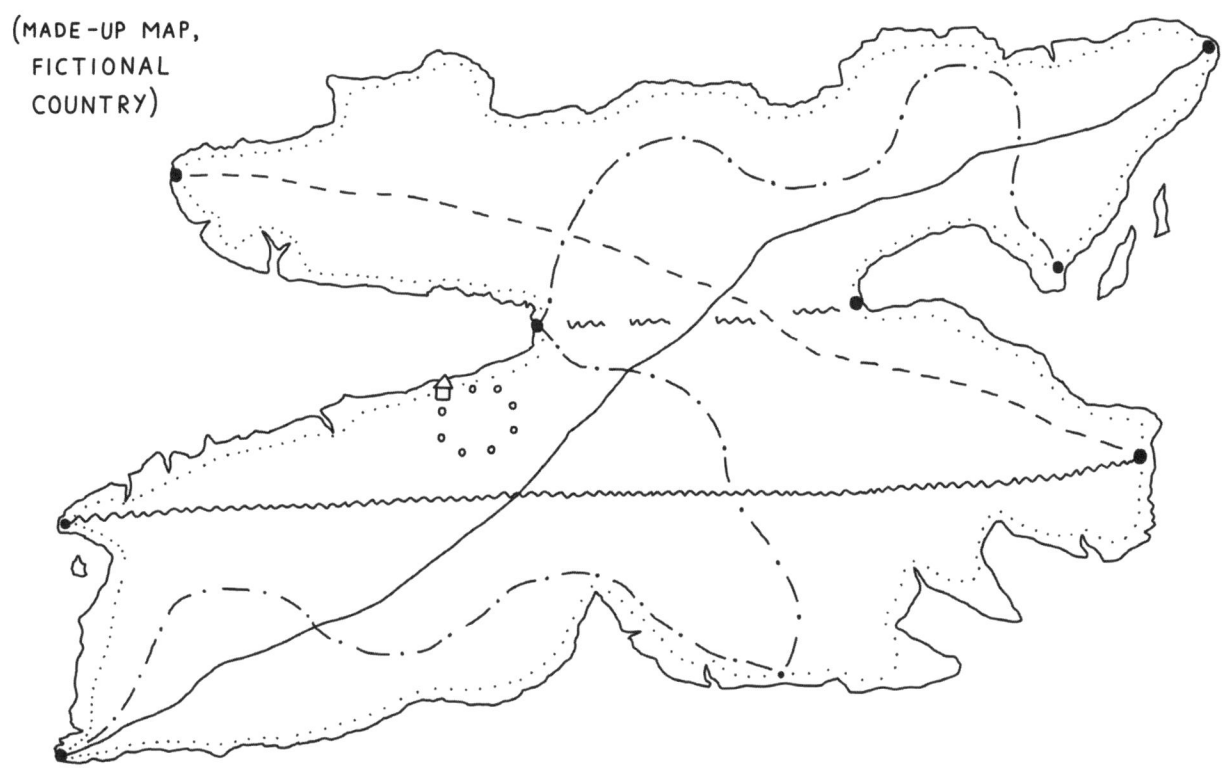

(MADE-UP MAP, FICTIONAL COUNTRY)

———————	END TO END
– – – – –	SIDE TO SIDE
· · · · · · ·	ALL THE WAY ROUND
～～～～	COAST TO COAST
～ ～ ～	COAST TO COAST (EASIER VERSION)
– · – · – ·	HERE AND THERE
⌂ · · · · ·	JUST A LITTLE BIT FURTHER FROM HOME THAN YOU WENT LAST TIME
•	BLACK DOT

BIKEPACKING

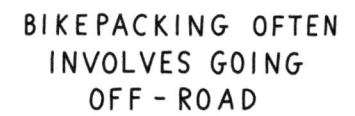

BIKEPACKING OFTEN INVOLVES GOING OFF-ROAD

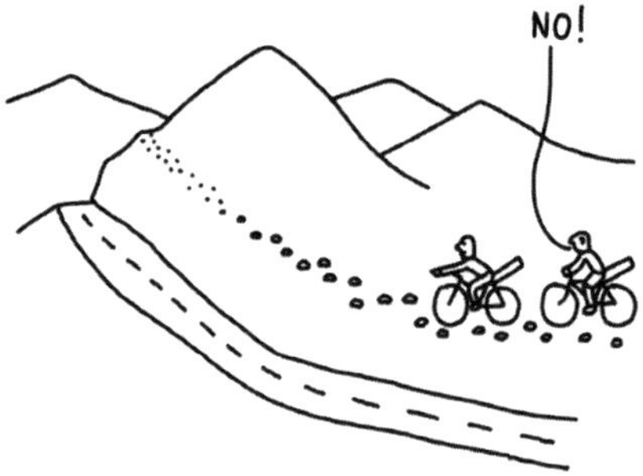
NO!

AND A FAIRLY MINIMALISTIC FORM OF CAMPING

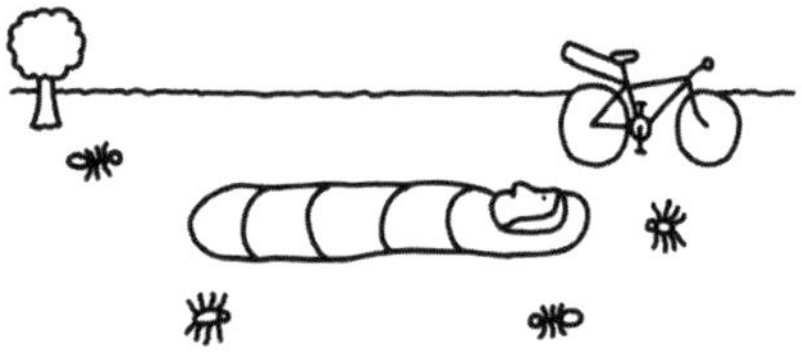

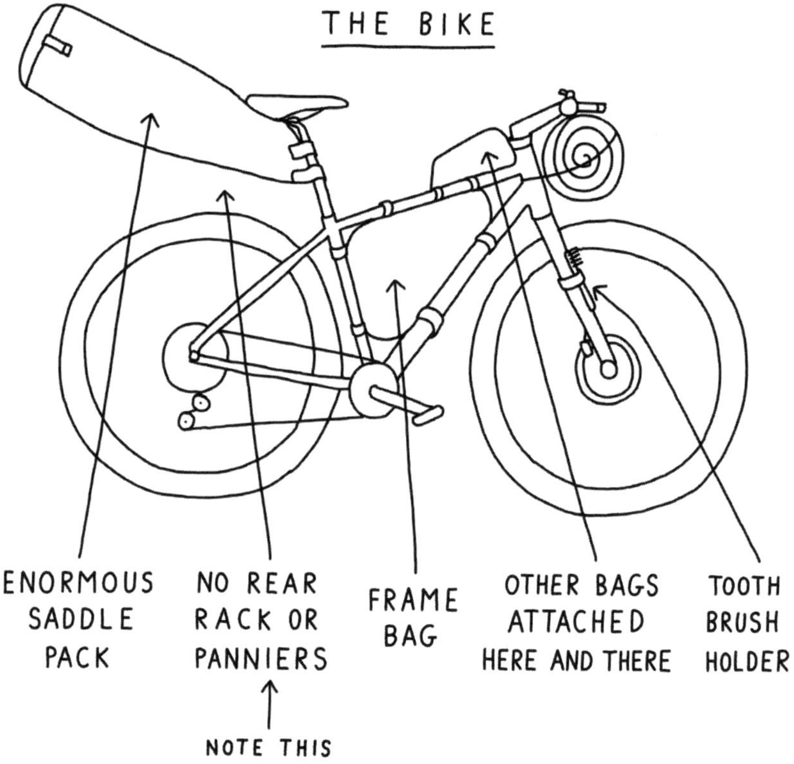
THE BIKE
ENORMOUS SADDLE PACK
NO REAR RACK OR PANNIERS
NOTE THIS
FRAME BAG
OTHER BAGS ATTACHED HERE AND THERE
TOOTH BRUSH HOLDER

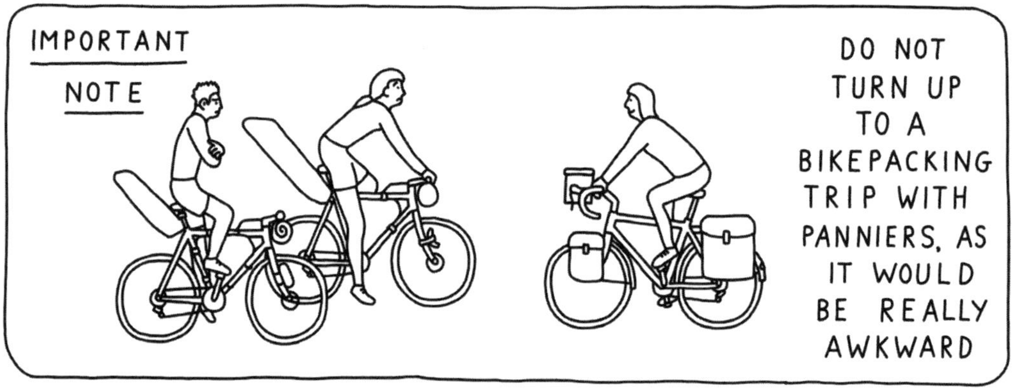
IMPORTANT NOTE
DO NOT TURN UP TO A BIKEPACKING TRIP WITH PANNIERS, AS IT WOULD BE REALLY AWKWARD

JOKE MAINLY FOR BIKEPACKERS (NONSENSICAL TO EVERYONE ELSE)

CREDIT CARD TOURING

IF YOU WANT TO TRAVEL LIGHT YOU CAN GET BY WITH JUST A CREDIT CARD

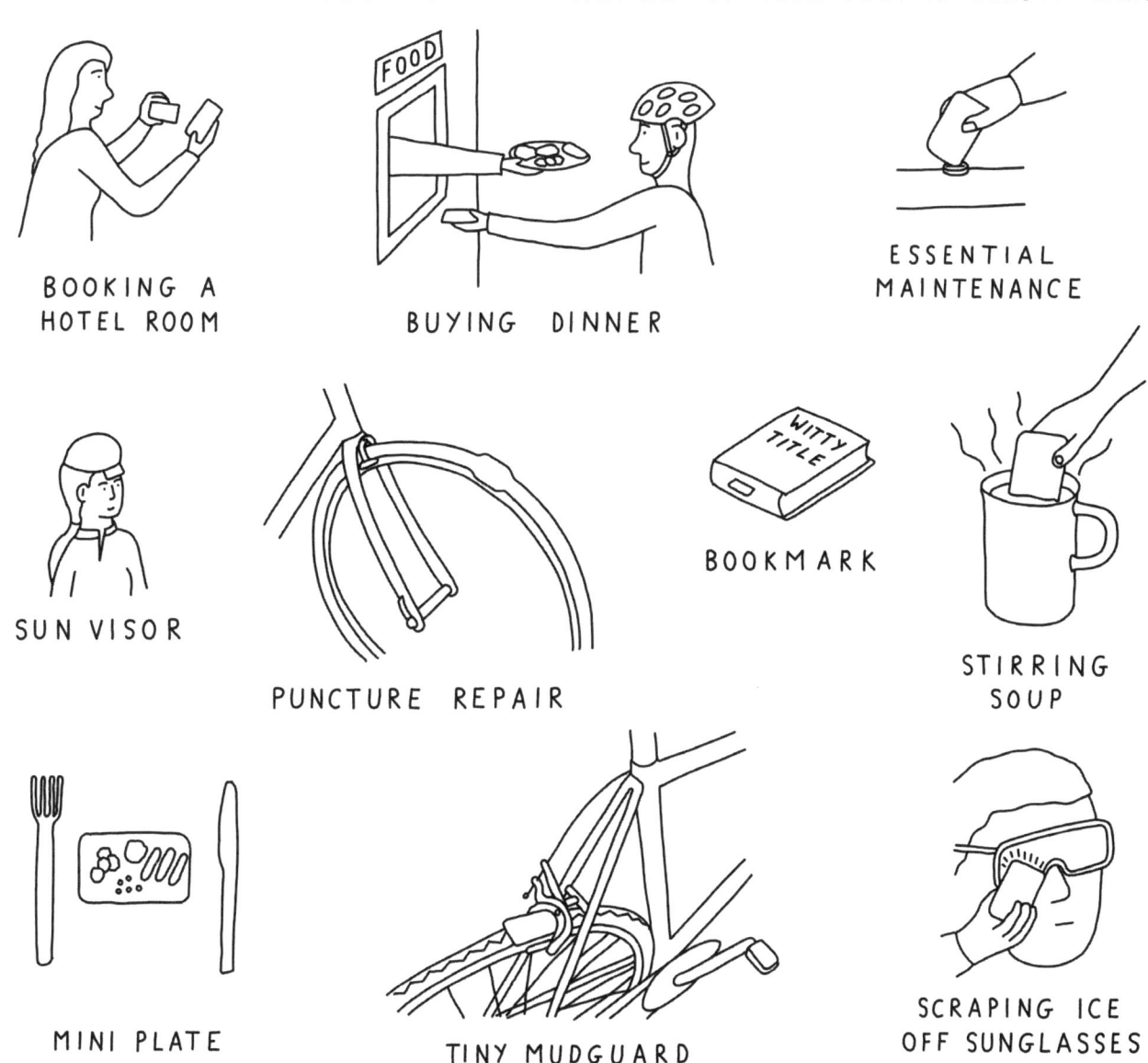

BOOKING A HOTEL ROOM

BUYING DINNER

ESSENTIAL MAINTENANCE

SUN VISOR

PUNCTURE REPAIR

BOOKMARK

STIRRING SOUP

MINI PLATE

TINY MUDGUARD

SCRAPING ICE OFF SUNGLASSES

TRAINS

HOW TO TAKE YOUR BIKE ON THEM

BOOK A SPACE (IF YOU NEED TO)

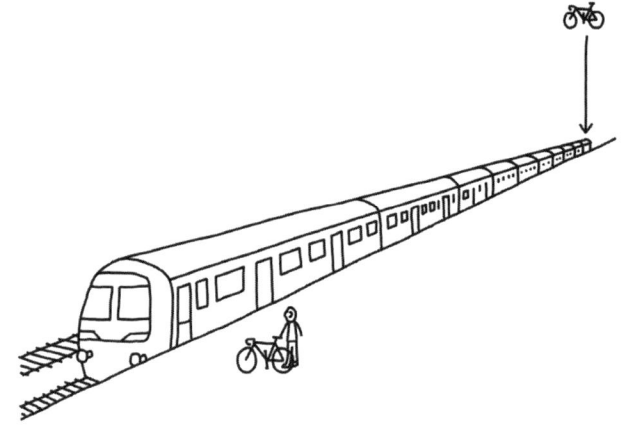

FIND THE PART OF THE TRAIN THAT HAS THE CYCLE STORAGE

DISCOVER THAT THE BIKE AREA IS FULL OF LUGGAGE, AND SPEND THE ENTIRE JOURNEY WORRYING THAT YOUR BIKE IS IN SOMEONE'S WAY

FINALLY COLLAPSE, EXHAUSTED

THE GRADIENT
IS ALWAYS UPHILL

APOLOGIES TO M.C. ESCHER

THE URBAN PELOTON

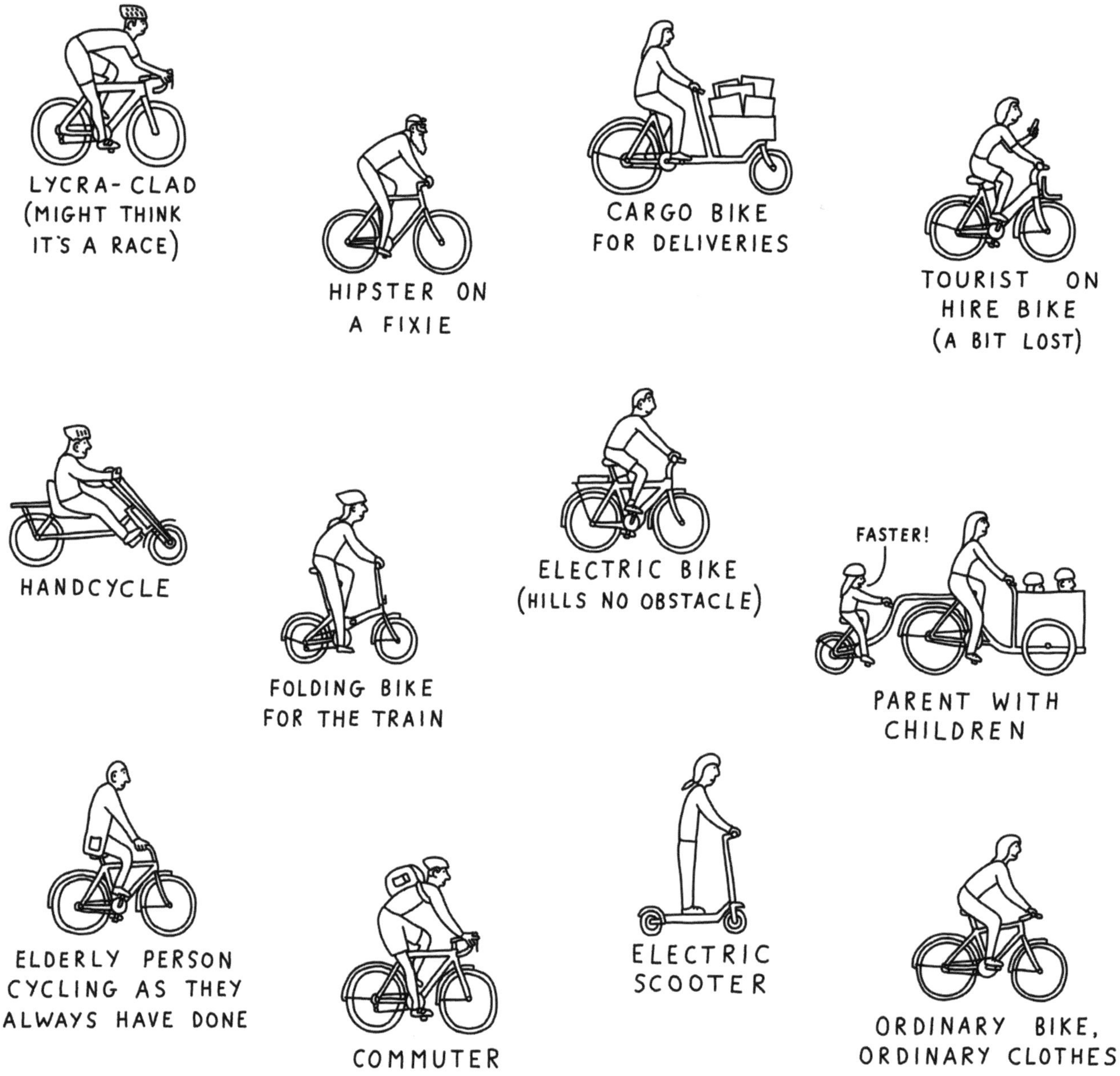
LYCRA-CLAD (MIGHT THINK IT'S A RACE)
HIPSTER ON A FIXIE
CARGO BIKE FOR DELIVERIES
TOURIST ON HIRE BIKE (A BIT LOST)
HANDCYCLE
FOLDING BIKE FOR THE TRAIN
ELECTRIC BIKE (HILLS NO OBSTACLE)
FASTER!
PARENT WITH CHILDREN
ELDERLY PERSON CYCLING AS THEY ALWAYS HAVE DONE
COMMUTER
ELECTRIC SCOOTER
ORDINARY BIKE, ORDINARY CLOTHES

CYCLING IN ALL WEATHERS
THE CONDITIONS DON'T HAVE TO DEFEAT YOU

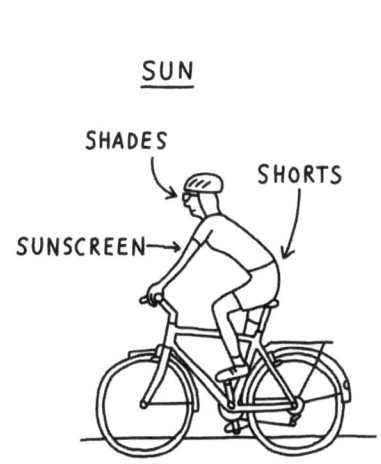

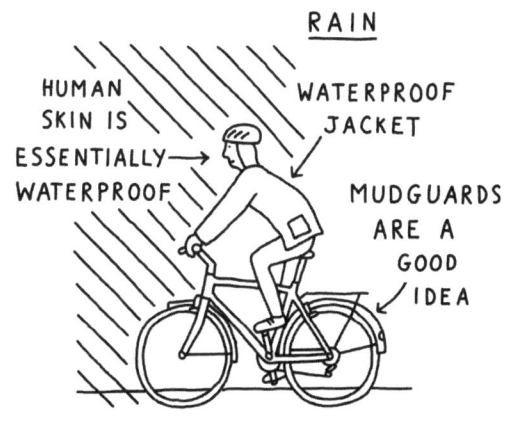

GREY AND OVERCAST

USUALLY IT IS LIKE THIS

SUN

SHADES
SHORTS
SUNSCREEN

RAIN

HUMAN SKIN IS ESSENTIALLY WATERPROOF
WATERPROOF JACKET
MUDGUARDS ARE A GOOD IDEA

COLD

ADDITIONAL COATS AND SCARVES AND GLOVES

SMALL PRINT: ICE MAY BE A REASON TO LET THE CONDITIONS DEFEAT YOU

WIND

JUST RIDE IN THE DIRECTION IT IS BLOWING

CHAPTER 5

TRAFFIC

WHY PEOPLE DON'T CYCLE

GETTING AROUND
EVERYONE NEEDS TO GET FROM A TO B

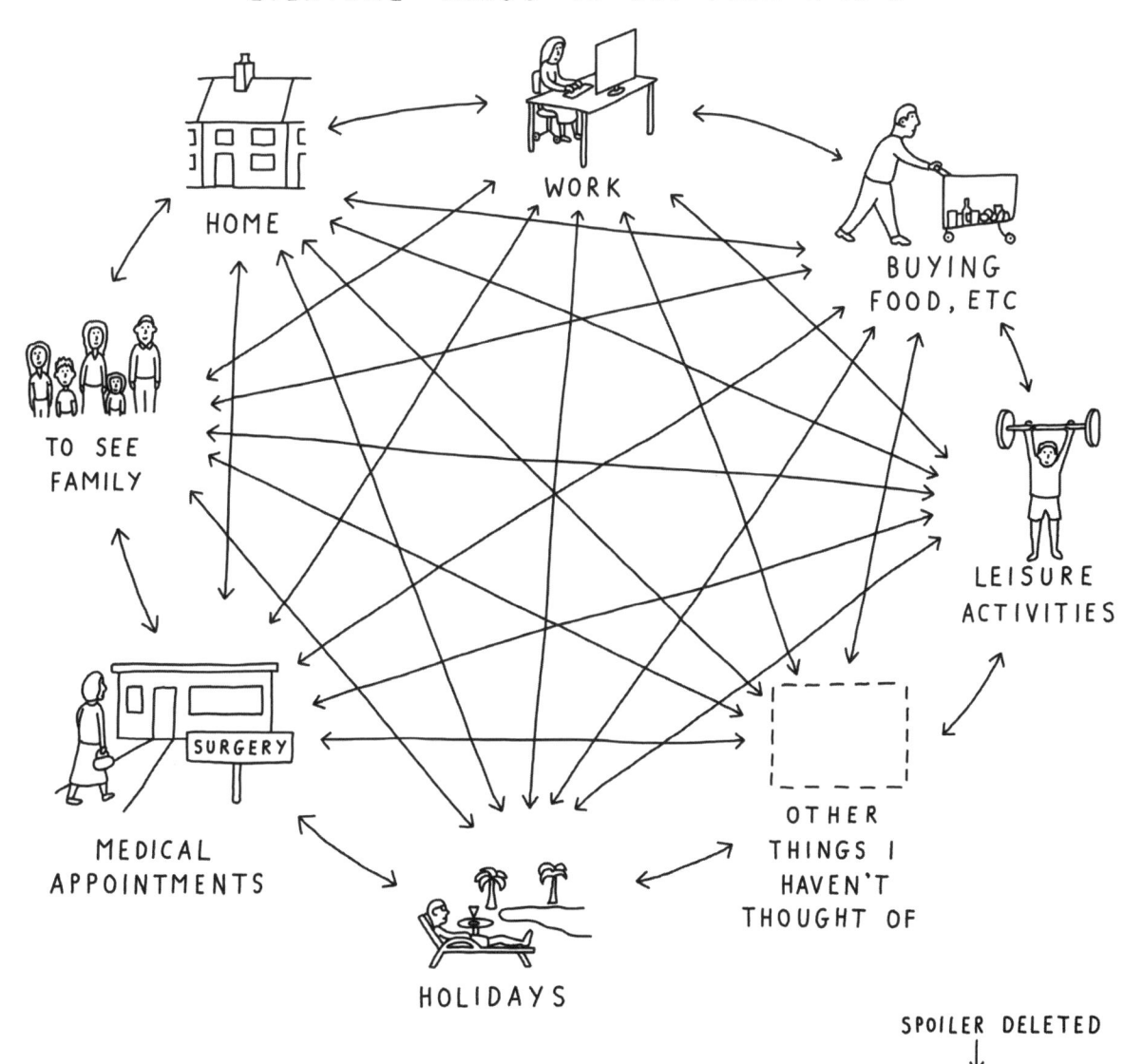

HOME

WORK

BUYING FOOD, ETC

TO SEE FAMILY

LEISURE ACTIVITIES

MEDICAL APPOINTMENTS

OTHER THINGS I HAVEN'T THOUGHT OF

HOLIDAYS

SPOILER DELETED

THIS BOOK IS ABOUT HOW WE GET THERE. THE BEST WAY IS ▓▓▓▓▓

THE STATUS QUO

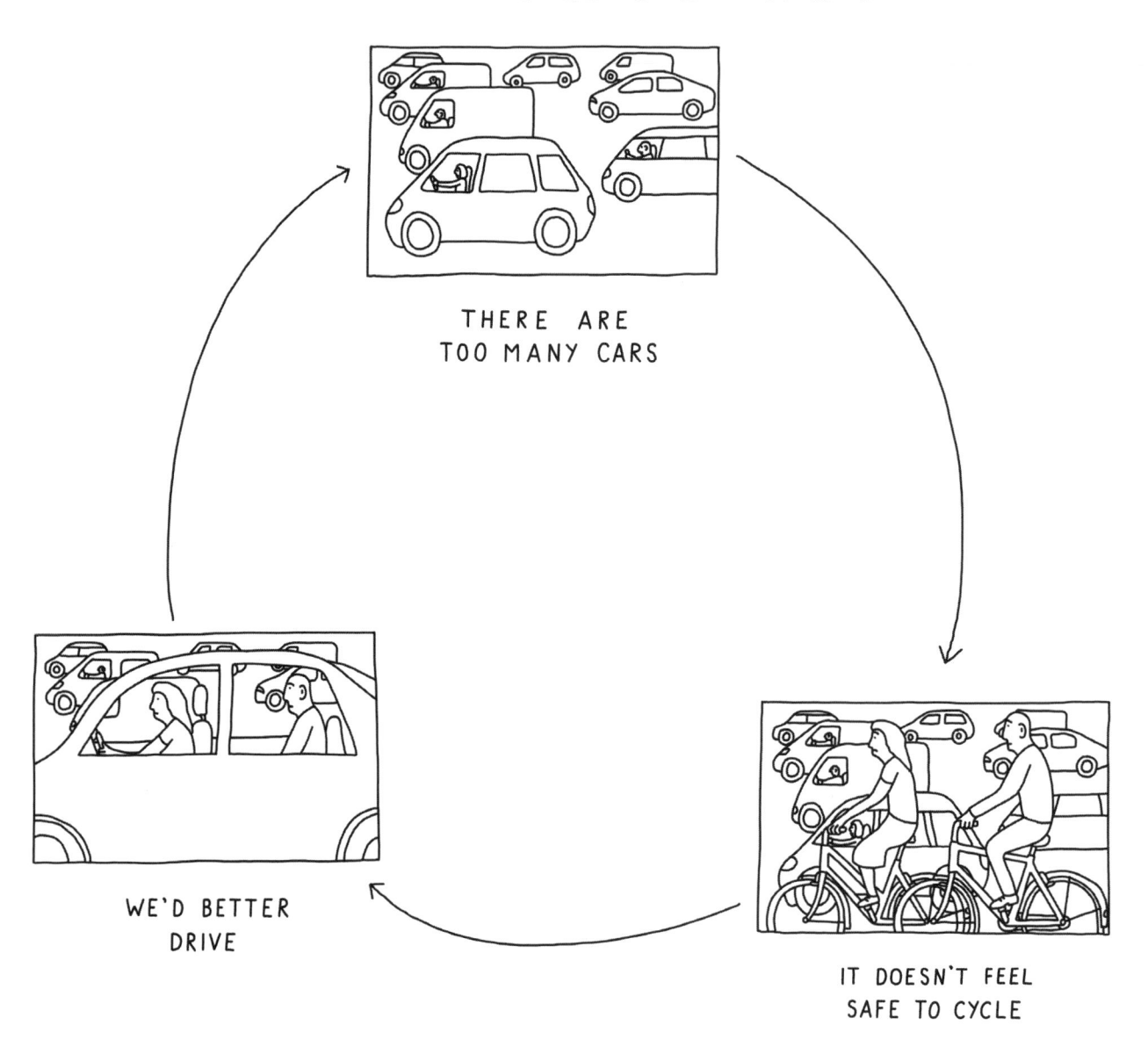

THERE ARE TOO MANY CARS

IT DOESN'T FEEL SAFE TO CYCLE

WE'D BETTER DRIVE

POLLUTION

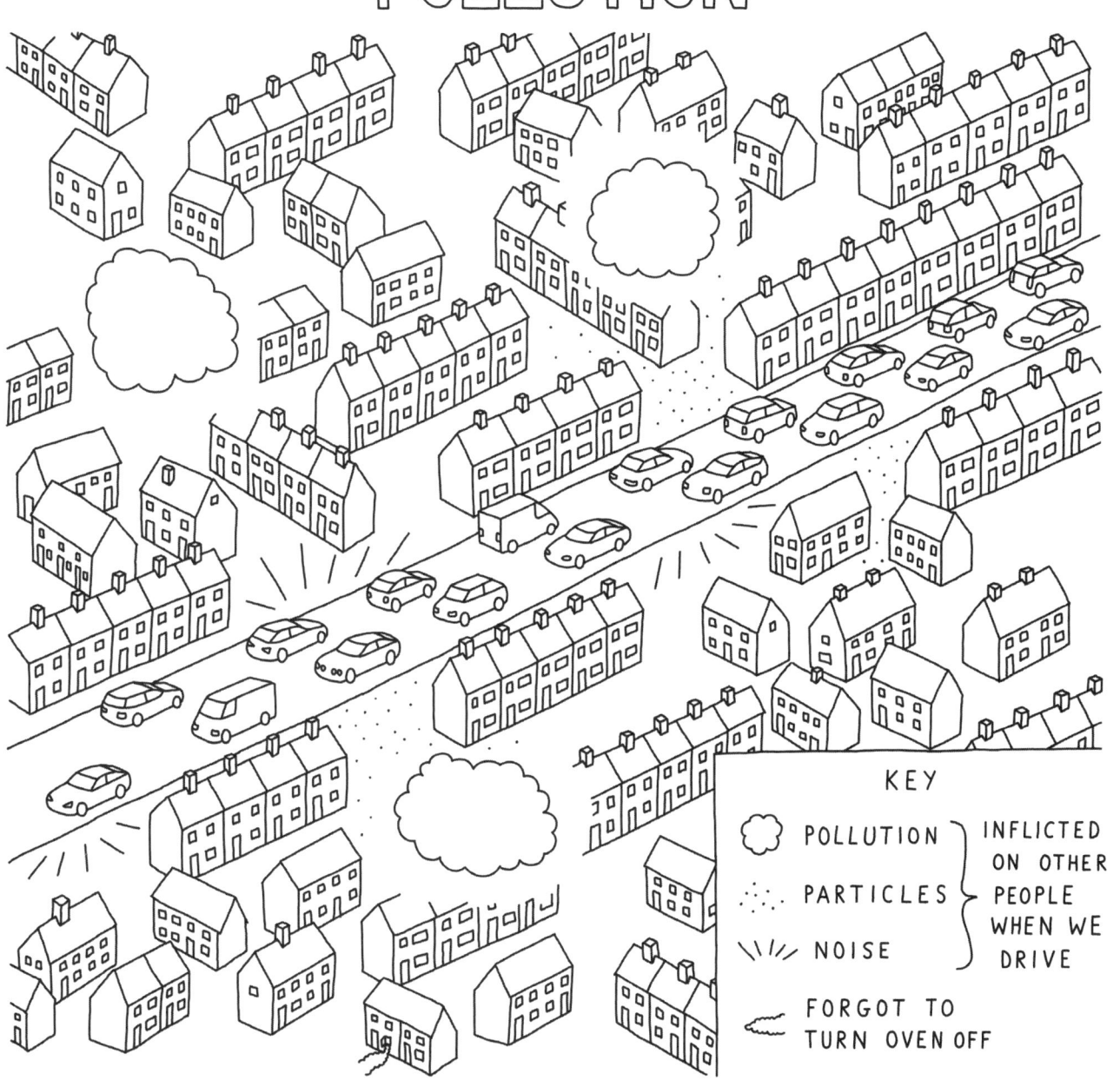

KEY

- ☁ POLLUTION ⎫
- ⋯ PARTICLES ⎬ INFLICTED ON OTHER PEOPLE WHEN WE DRIVE
- \|// NOISE ⎭
- ～ FORGOT TO TURN OVEN OFF

THE CLIMATE CRISIS

WHAT IT IS

OUR EARTH IS WARMING, DUE TO HUMAN ACTIVITY ← SCIENTIFIC FACT

THINGS IT WILL AFFECT

- THE WEATHER → EXTREMES
- FOOD SUPPLIES
- SEA LEVELS
- WILDLIFE
- PLACES YOU LOVE
- PEOPLE YOU LOVE

PROBABLY THE BIGGEST CHALLENGE FACING HUMANITY

WHAT IS CAUSING IT

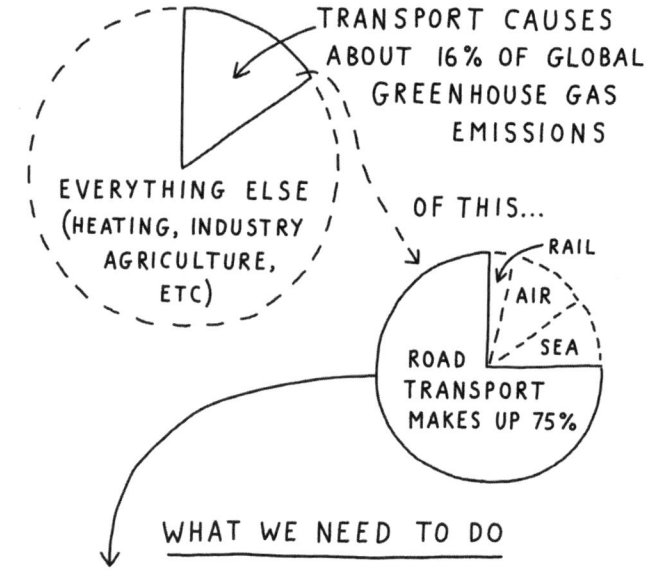

TRANSPORT CAUSES ABOUT 16% OF GLOBAL GREENHOUSE GAS EMISSIONS

EVERYTHING ELSE (HEATING, INDUSTRY, AGRICULTURE, ETC)

OF THIS... ROAD TRANSPORT MAKES UP 75% (RAIL, AIR, SEA)

WHAT WE NEED TO DO

LOTS OF THINGS, BUT REDUCING EMISSIONS FROM ROAD TRANSPORT HAS TO BE A MAJOR PART

ELECTRIC VEHICLES HAVE A ROLE TO PLAY, BUT... MANUFACTURING CAUSES HUGE GREENHOUSE GAS EMISSIONS

MANY LOCAL JOURNEYS COULD BE DONE BY BIKE

CONGESTION

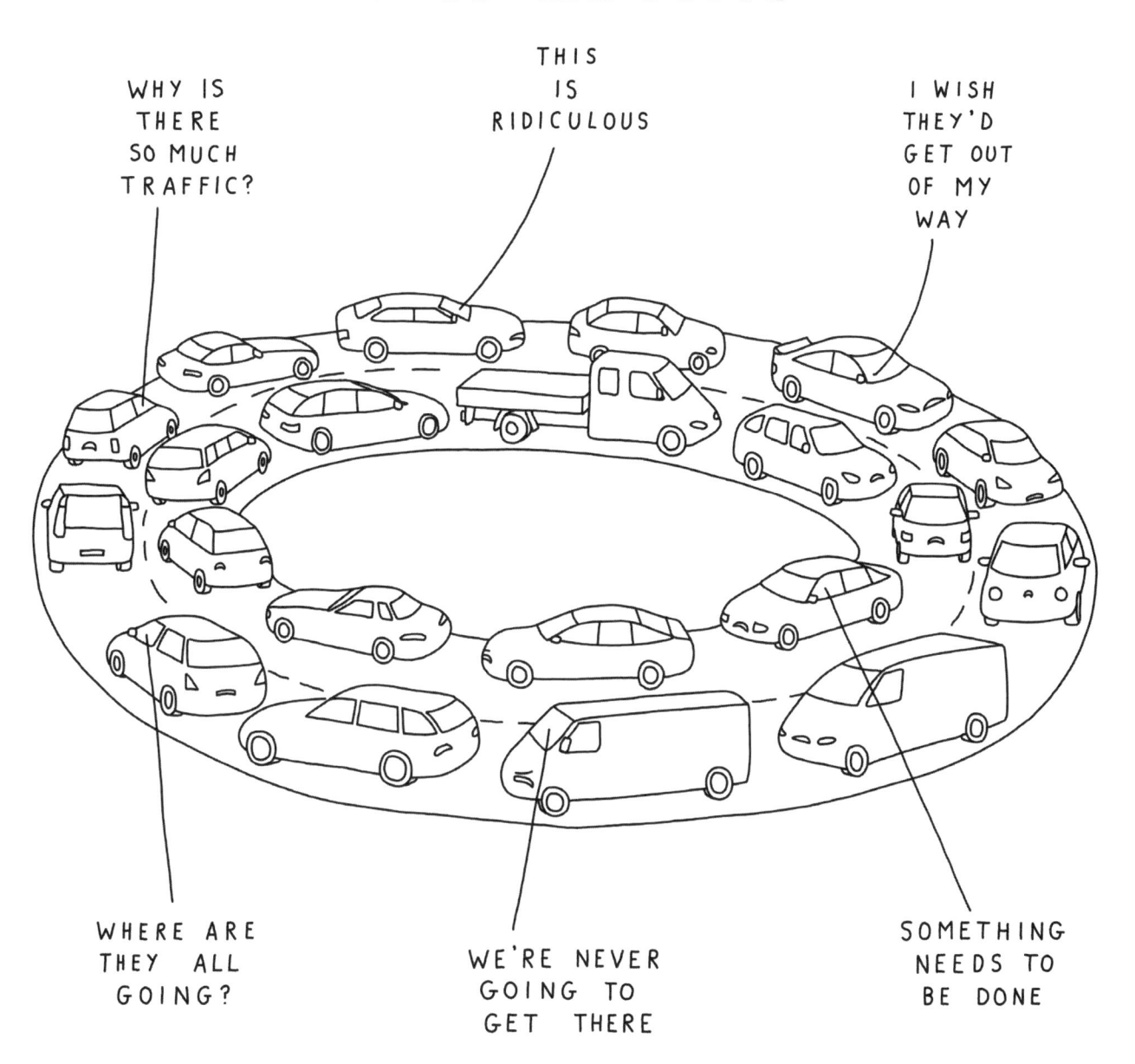

WHY IS THERE SO MUCH TRAFFIC?

THIS IS RIDICULOUS

I WISH THEY'D GET OUT OF MY WAY

WHERE ARE THEY ALL GOING?

WE'RE NEVER GOING TO GET THERE

SOMETHING NEEDS TO BE DONE

AT THE HIGHWAYS DEPARTMENT

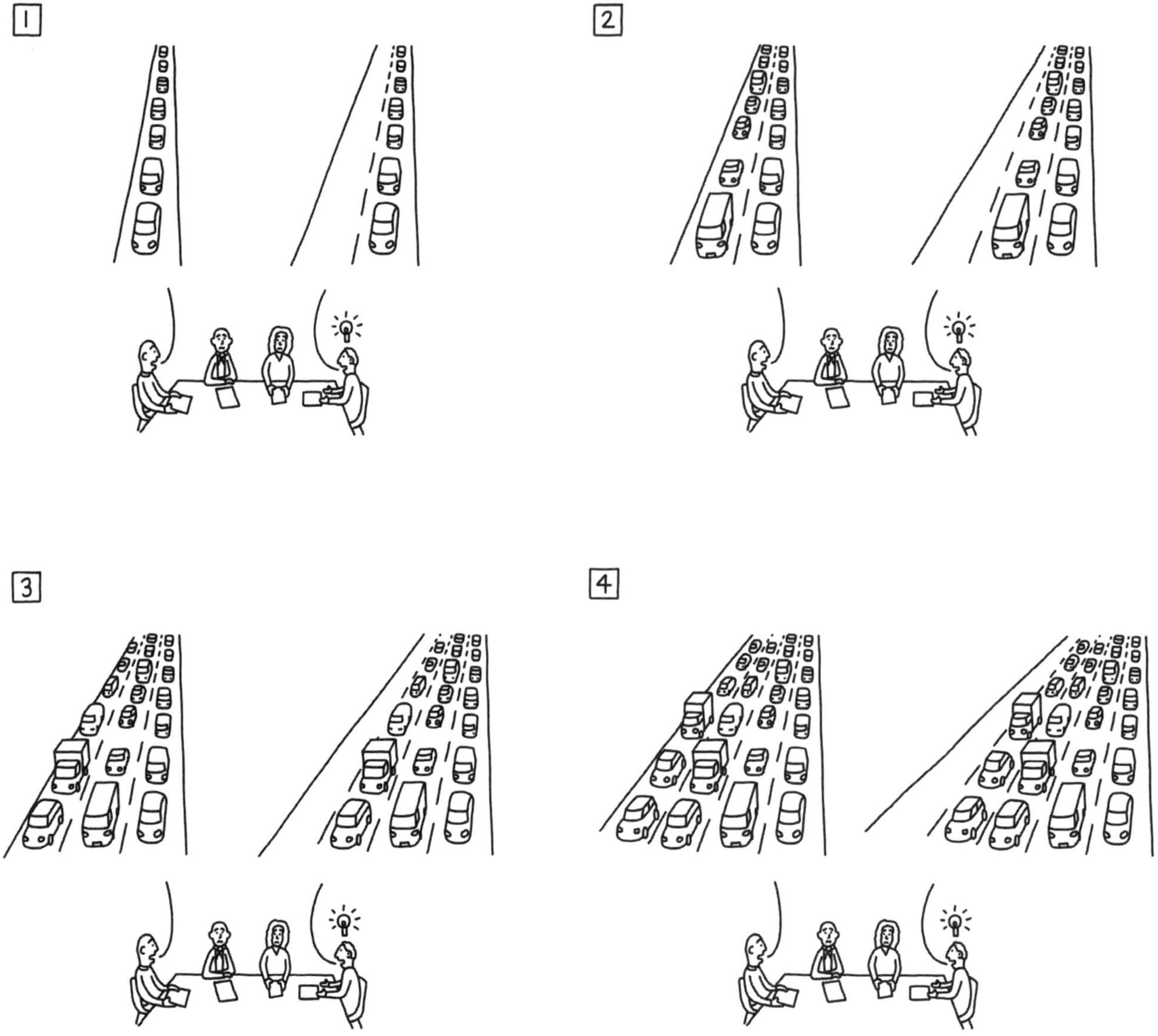
1
2
3
4

(ETC)

CARS

THEY ARE GETTING BIGGER

SOME TIME AGO ⟶ QUITE RECENTLY ⟶ NOW

WHY IS THIS?

MAYBE PEOPLE WANT BIG CARS SO THEY CAN LOOK DOWN ON PEOPLE IN SMALL CARS

BIG CARS ARE USEFUL FOR TOWING

REALLY?

BIG CARS MAKE PEOPLE FEEL IMPORTANT

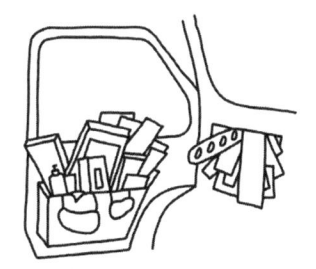

OR PERHAPS THEY HAVE A LOT OF THINGS TO FIT INTO THEIR GLOVE BOXES AND CAR DOOR POCKETS

STORAGE

OF PRIVATE PROPERTY IN THE STREET

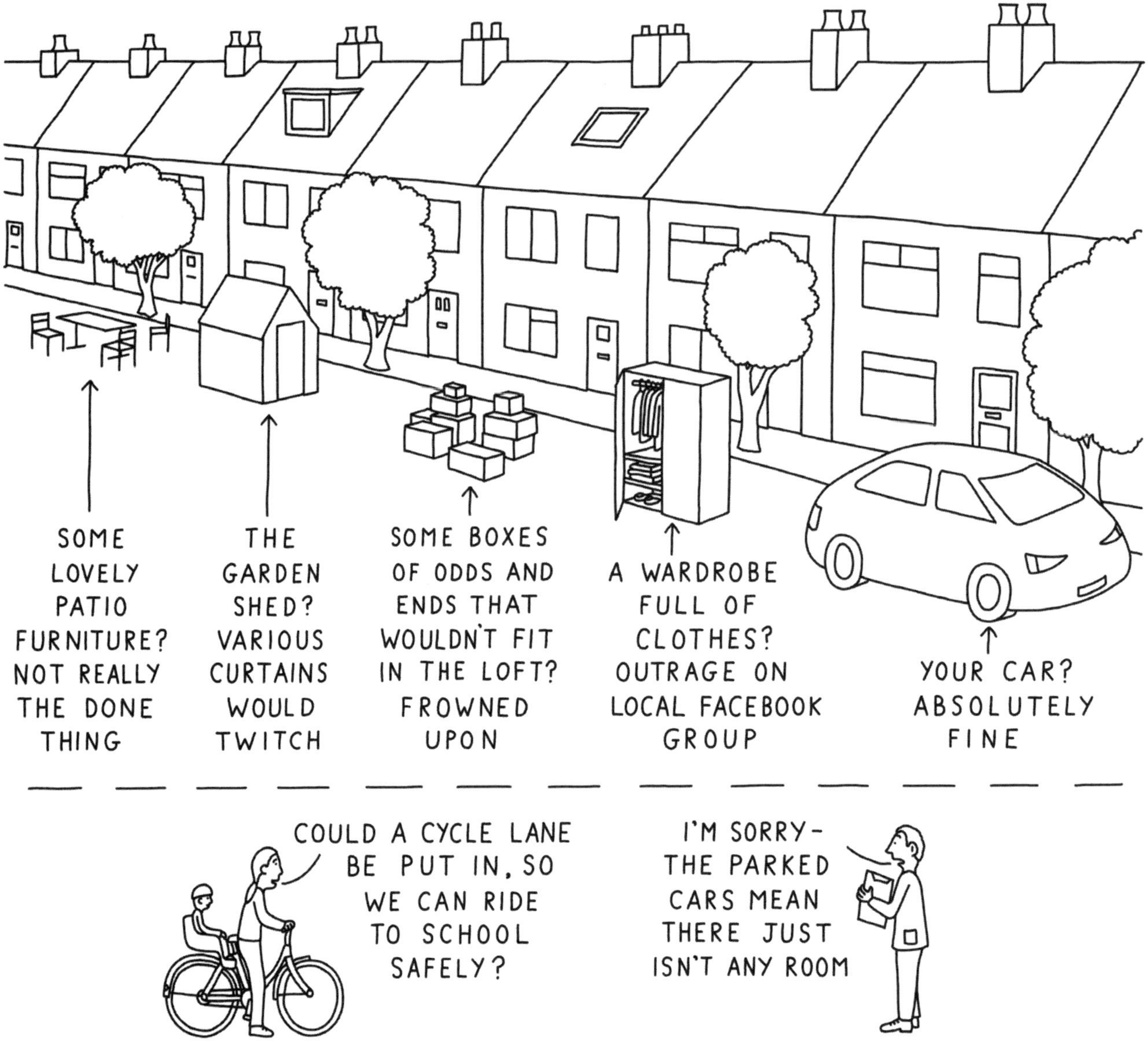
SOME LOVELY PATIO FURNITURE? NOT REALLY THE DONE THING
THE GARDEN SHED? VARIOUS CURTAINS WOULD TWITCH
SOME BOXES OF ODDS AND ENDS THAT WOULDN'T FIT IN THE LOFT? FROWNED UPON
A WARDROBE FULL OF CLOTHES? OUTRAGE ON LOCAL FACEBOOK GROUP
YOUR CAR? ABSOLUTELY FINE
COULD A CYCLE LANE BE PUT IN, SO WE CAN RIDE TO SCHOOL SAFELY?
I'M SORRY – THE PARKED CARS MEAN THERE JUST ISN'T ANY ROOM

CITY CYCLING

THE REALITY

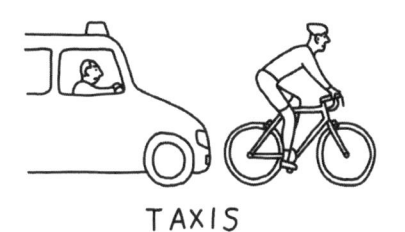

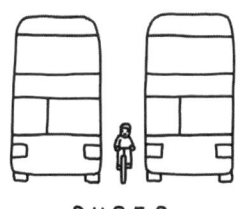

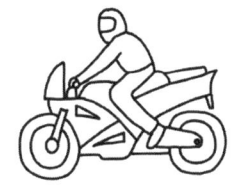

TAXIS
MOTORBIKES (SPEED LIMIT DOESN'T ALWAYS SEEM TO APPLY)
DRIVERS PASSING TOO CLOSE
BUSES
SLIPPERY
TRAM TRACKS
POTHOLES
PEDESTRIANS ON THEIR PHONES
OTHER CYCLISTS MEANDERING
CYCLE ROUTES THAT DON'T JOIN UP
A PAINTED WHITE LINE WITH NO SEGREGATION FROM TRAFFIC = WORSE THAN NO LINE
RAISED DRAIN COVERS
SUNKEN DRAIN COVERS
DRAIN COVERS THAT AREN'T QUITE SURE
UTTERLY USELESS CYCLE LANES

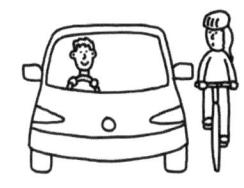

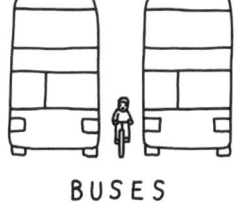

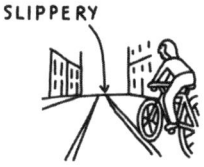

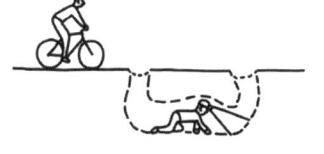

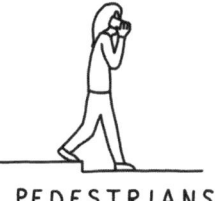

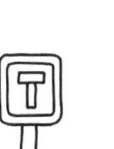

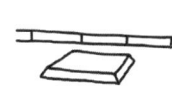

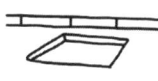

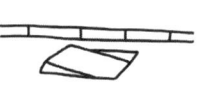

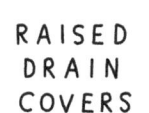

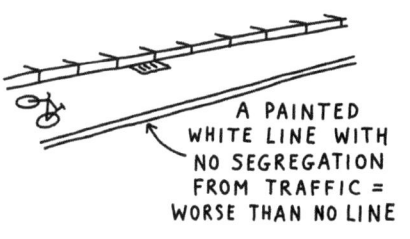

IS IT A RACE?

THINGS THAT AREN'T A RACE

YOUR DRIVE HOME FROM WORK

ARRIVING FIRST AT THE NEXT SET OF RED LIGHTS

THAT REGULAR LONG JOURNEY YOU DO

- I CAN DO IT IN UNDER THREE HOURS
- [TRIES TO APPEAR VISIBLY IMPRESSED]
- NOT LEGALLY YOU CAN'T

GETTING AHEAD OF ANYONE IN FRONT OF YOU

THINGS THAT ARE A RACE

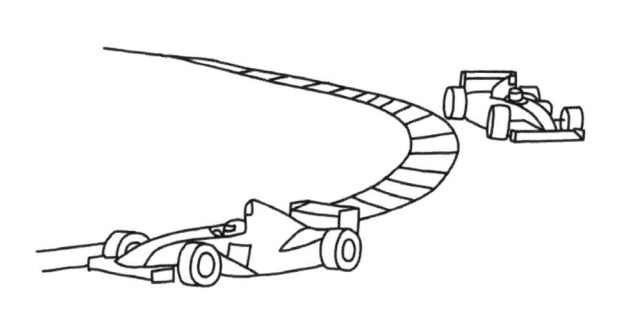

AN ACTUAL RACE

LANGUAGE

THAT AFFECTS HOW WE THINK ABOUT TRAVEL ON THE ROADS

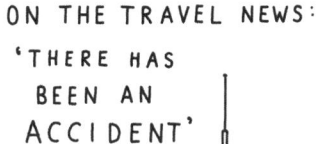

ON THE TRAVEL NEWS:

'THERE HAS BEEN AN ACCIDENT'

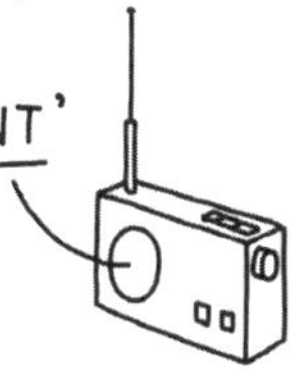

IMPLIES IT IS JUST ONE OF THOSE THINGS THAT HAPPEN. NO ONE'S FAULT, AND SOMETHING WE MUST JUST ACCEPT → 'CRASH' IS BETTER

'CYCLISTS'

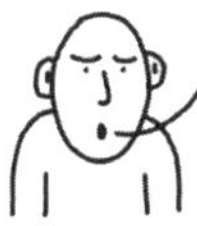

SOMETIMES USED TO MAKE PEOPLE ON BIKES SOUND AS IF THEY ARE A DIFFERENT SPECIES, RATHER THAN ORDINARY PEOPLE – FRIENDS, FAMILY, COLLEAGUES, ETC

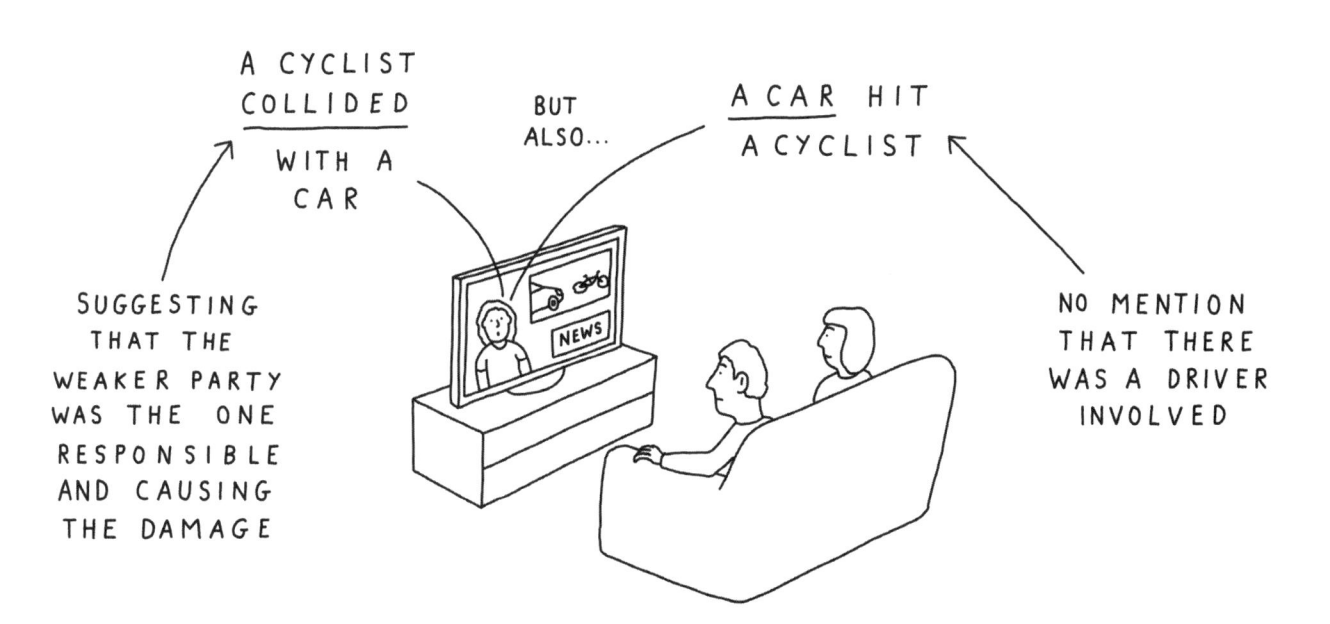

A CYCLIST COLLIDED WITH A CAR

BUT ALSO...

A CAR HIT A CYCLIST

NEWS

SUGGESTING THAT THE WEAKER PARTY WAS THE ONE RESPONSIBLE AND CAUSING THE DAMAGE

NO MENTION THAT THERE WAS A DRIVER INVOLVED

INNOVATIONS
TO HELP PHASE OUT CARS IN URBAN AREAS

JUST WON'T EVER WORK (SORRY)

DRIVERLESS CAR → **CARLESS DRIVER**

SPECIAL ADAPTATION DESIGNED TO OPTIMISE NOT GOING ANYWHERE IN GRIDLOCKED TRAFFIC

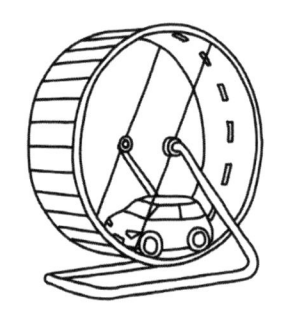

DRIVING WHEEL (FOR THOSE DETERMINED TO USE A CAR NO MATTER WHAT)

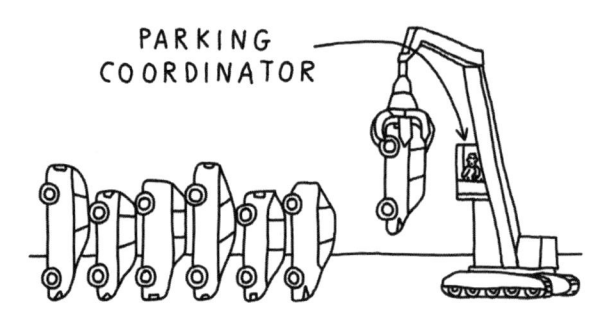

PARKING COORDINATOR

VERTICAL PARKING TO SAVE SPACE

MASSIVE INVESTMENT IN CLEAN AND SUSTAINABLE ALTERNATIVES

CAREFUL DRIVERS
WE THANK YOU

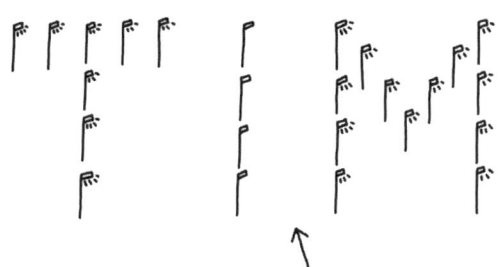

A BADGE FOR THE DRIVER WHO DIDN'T PARK ACROSS THE CYCLE PATH

A PEDESTAL FOR THE DRIVER WHO WAITED TEN SECONDS UNTIL IT WAS SAFE TO OVERTAKE

A LARGE PRESENT FOR THE DRIVER WHO WAITED UNTIL THE END OF THEIR JOURNEY TO LOOK AT THEIR PHONE

A LETTER OF COMMENDATION FOR THE DRIVER WHO TOOK CARE WHEN TURNING AT A JUNCTION

NAME IN (STREET) LIGHTS FOR THE DRIVER WHO KEPT TO THE SPEED LIMIT AT NIGHT

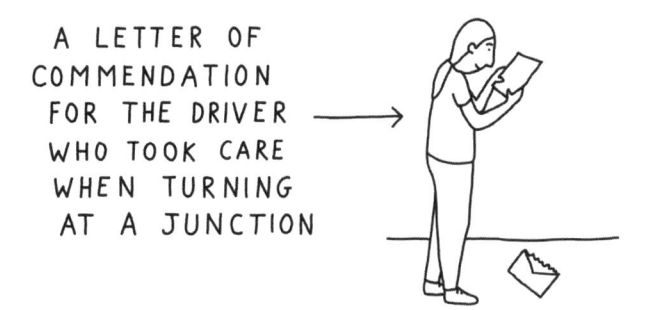

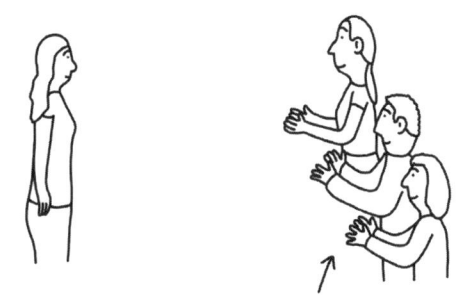

A POLITE RIPPLE OF APPLAUSE FOR THE DRIVER WHO LEFT A TWO METRE GAP WHEN OVERTAKING

THE FUTURE OF ROAD TRANSPORT

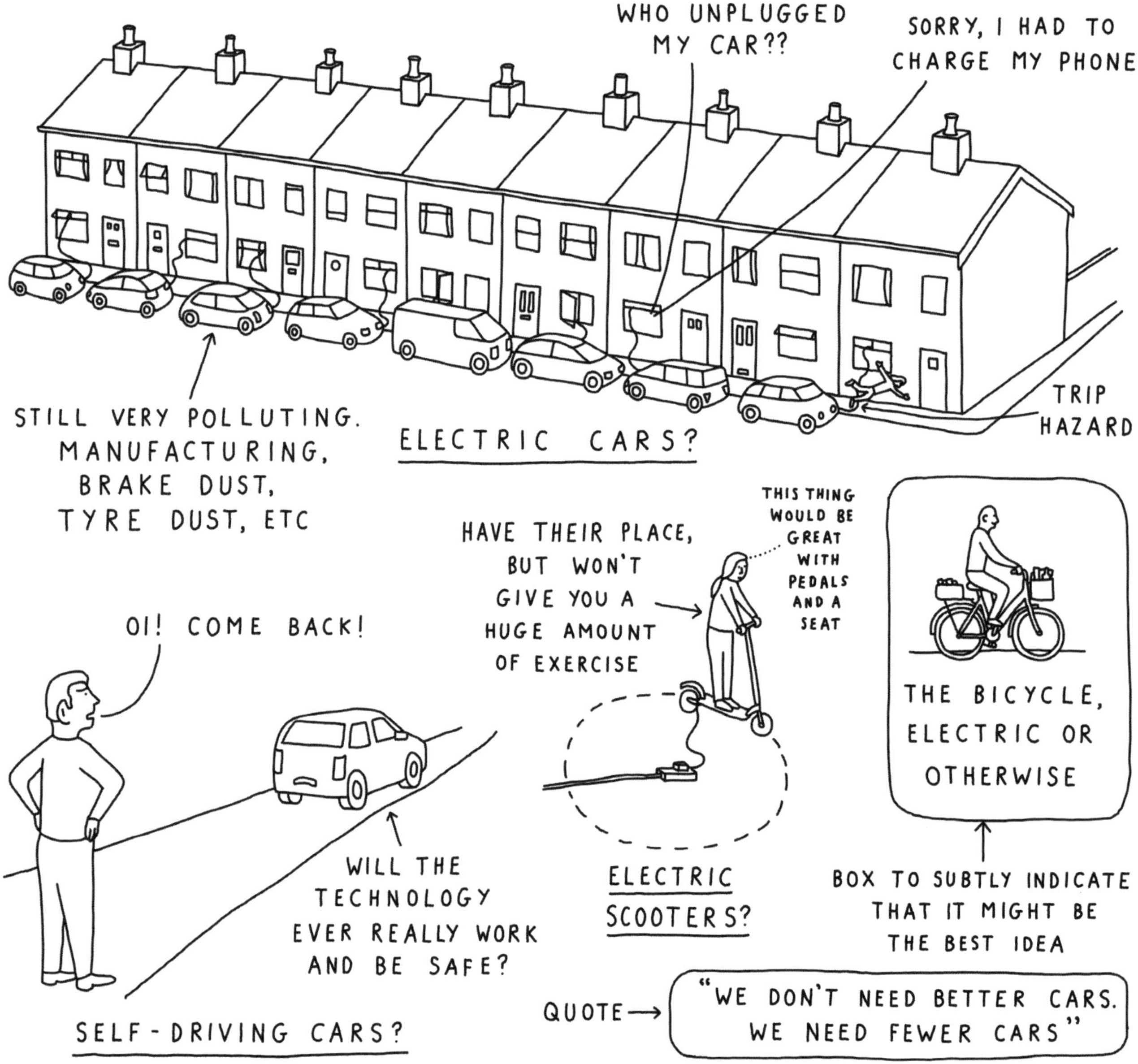
WHO UNPLUGGED MY CAR??
SORRY, I HAD TO CHARGE MY PHONE
STILL VERY POLLUTING. MANUFACTURING, BRAKE DUST, TYRE DUST, ETC
ELECTRIC CARS?
TRIP HAZARD
HAVE THEIR PLACE, BUT WON'T GIVE YOU A HUGE AMOUNT OF EXERCISE
THIS THING WOULD BE GREAT WITH PEDALS AND A SEAT
THE BICYCLE, ELECTRIC OR OTHERWISE
OI! COME BACK!
WILL THE TECHNOLOGY EVER REALLY WORK AND BE SAFE?
ELECTRIC SCOOTERS?
BOX TO SUBTLY INDICATE THAT IT MIGHT BE THE BEST IDEA
QUOTE
"WE DON'T NEED BETTER CARS. WE NEED FEWER CARS"
SELF-DRIVING CARS?

CHAPTER 6

SAFETY

WHAT WOULD MAKE CYCLING SAFER?

NATURAL ENEMIES
OF THE PERSON RIDING A BIKE

BROKEN GLASS

THE UNCERTAIN WEATHER FORECAST

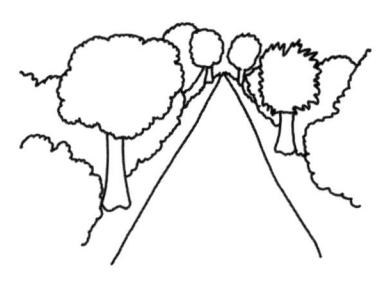

THE ISOLATED PATH

POTHOLES DISGUISED AS PUDDLES

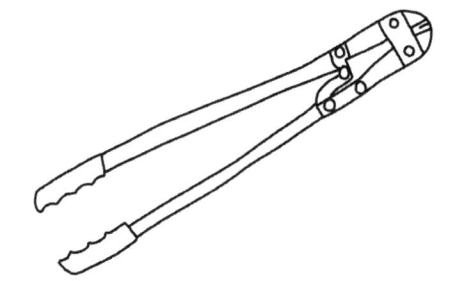

THE BOLT CUTTER

CAR DOOR

DEFICIENT LEFT INDICATOR

DEFICIENT RIGHT IDIOT

WHAT WOULD MAKE CYCLING SAFER?

ACCORDING TO PEOPLE ON THE INTERNET

HELMETS

ACCORDING TO ACTUAL STATISTICS

SEPARATING BIKES AND TRAFFIC

EDUCATING DRIVERS

ENFORCING SPEED LIMITS

DEDICATED TRAFFIC-FREE ROUTES

CLOSE PASS LAWS

DISQUALIFYING REPEAT OFFENDERS

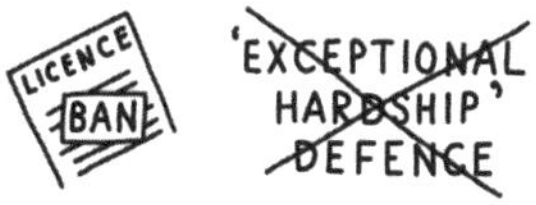

INVESTMENT IN ACTIVE TRAVEL ← NETWORK (BAD DRAWING)

CONDITIONS RELATING TO INACTIVITY ARE BY FAR THE BIGGEST KILLER →

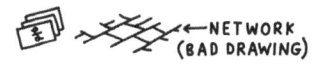

GETTING PEOPLE OFF THEIR SOFAS MAKES EVERYONE SAFER AND HEALTHIER

SAFE PASSING DISTANCES
MEASURED IN HOUSEHOLD APPLIANCES

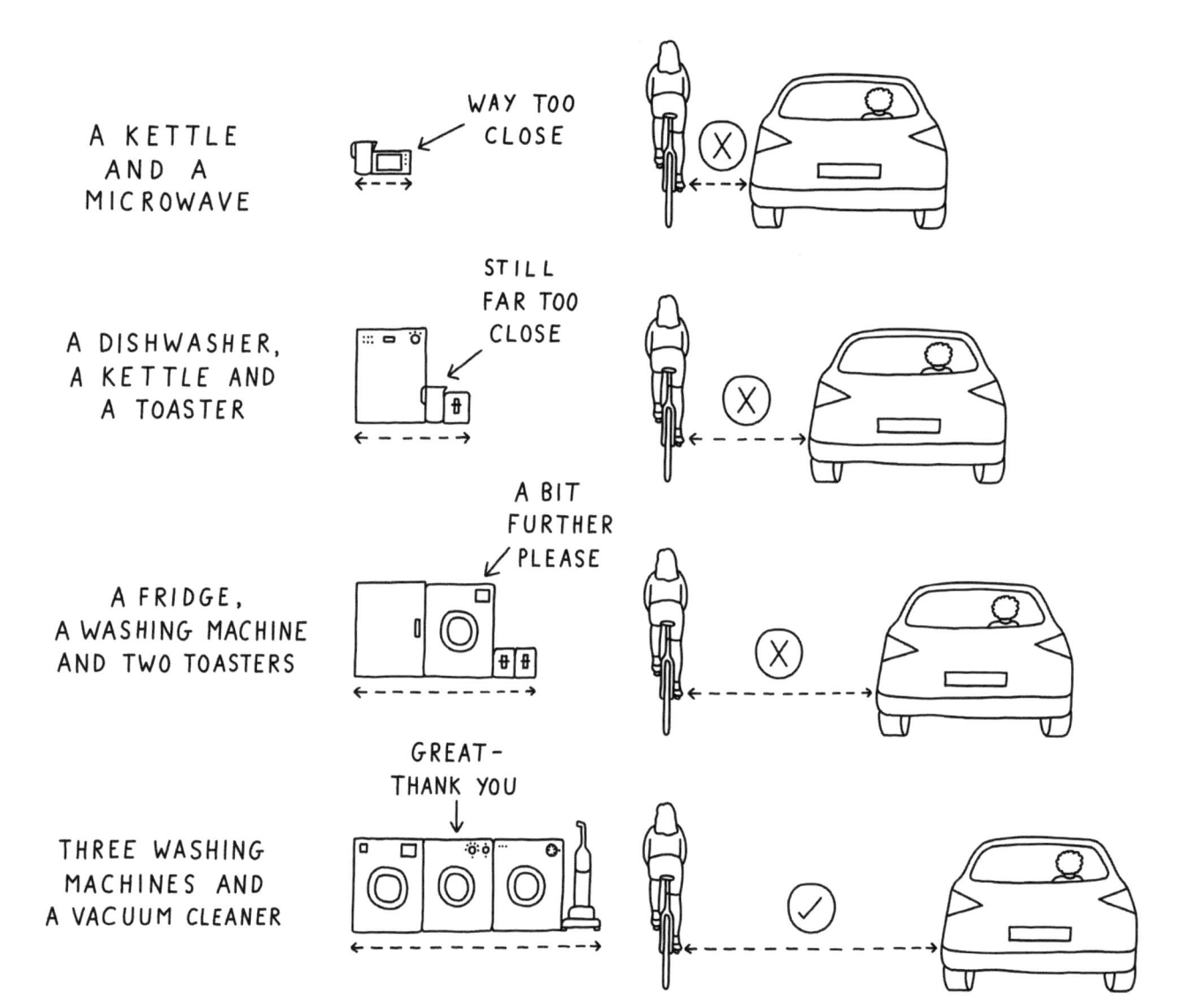

A KETTLE AND A MICROWAVE — WAY TOO CLOSE

A DISHWASHER, A KETTLE AND A TOASTER — STILL FAR TOO CLOSE

A FRIDGE, A WASHING MACHINE AND TWO TOASTERS — A BIT FURTHER PLEASE

THREE WASHING MACHINES AND A VACUUM CLEANER — GREAT - THANK YOU

THE GOLDEN RULE

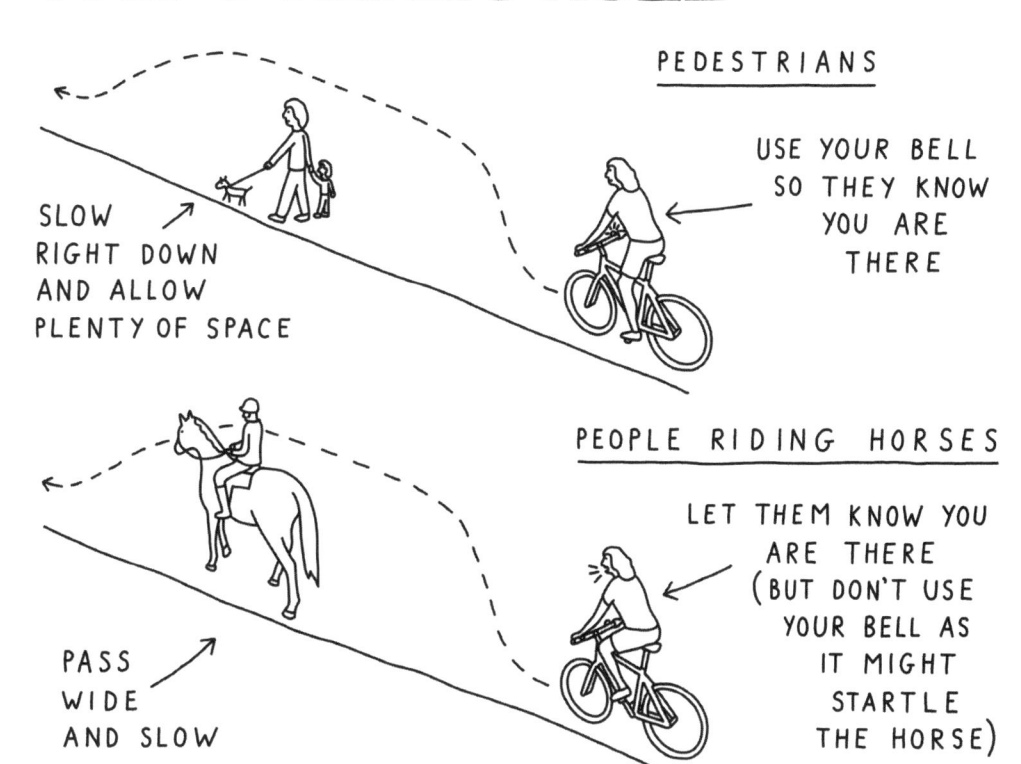

PASS OTHER PEOPLE

PEDESTRIANS — USE YOUR BELL SO THEY KNOW YOU ARE THERE

SLOW RIGHT DOWN AND ALLOW PLENTY OF SPACE

PEOPLE RIDING HORSES — LET THEM KNOW YOU ARE THERE (BUT DON'T USE YOUR BELL AS IT MIGHT STARTLE THE HORSE)

PASS WIDE AND SLOW

AS YOU WOULD LIKE TO BE PASSED

THANK THE CONSIDERATE ONES IF YOU GET A CHANCE

CAR DRIVERS — REPORT THE DANGEROUS ONES TO THE POLICE — MAYBE DRIVING JUST ISN'T FOR THEM

1.5 METRES PLUS

ROAD SAFETY

GREATER POWER SHOULD BRING GREATER RESPONSIBILITY

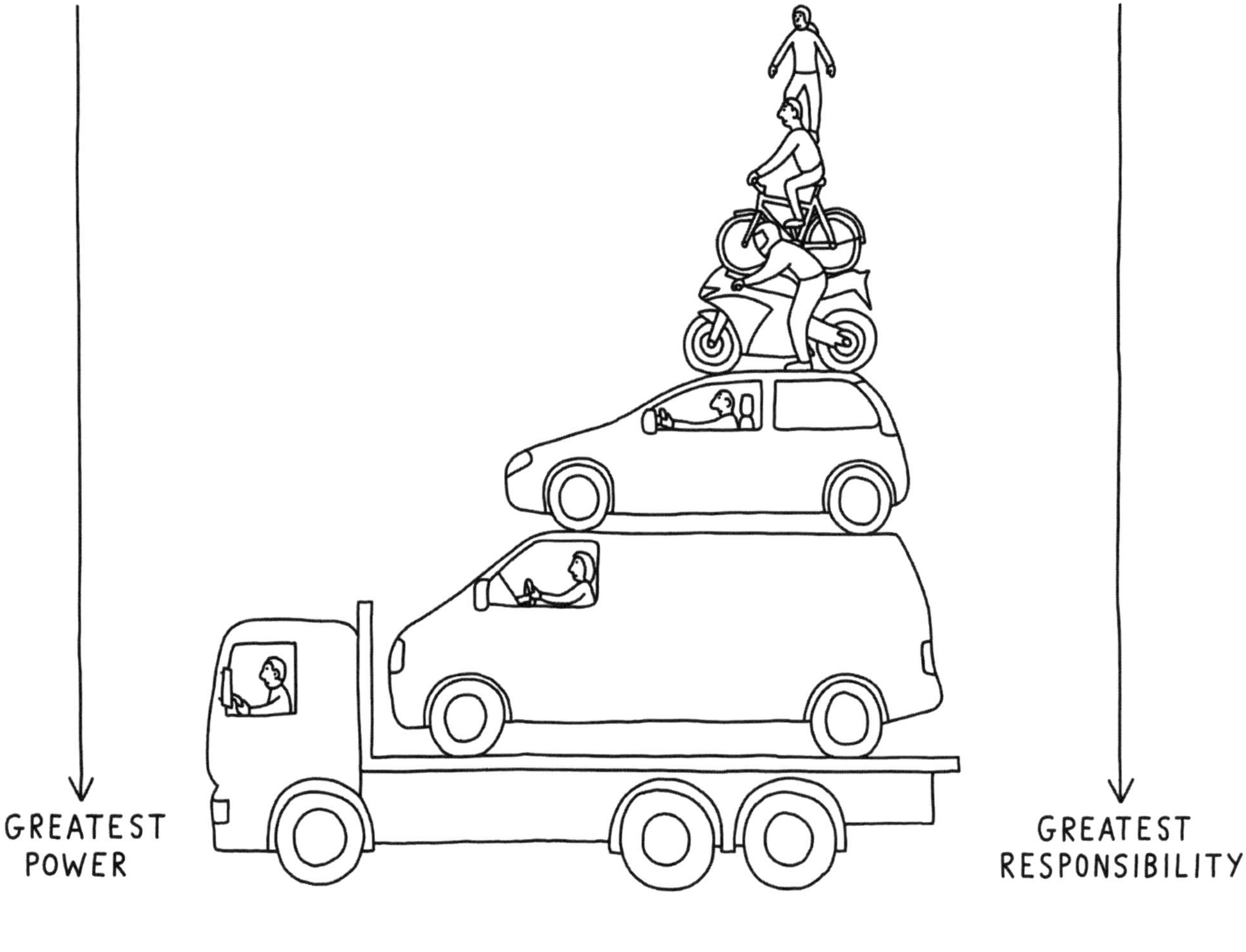
GREATEST
POWER
GREATEST
RESPONSIBILITY

A HIERARCHY OF RESPONSIBILITY SHOULD BE INCLUDED IN THE HIGHWAY CODE

HELMETS
VARIOUS COMMENTS

THE SAFEST PLACES IN THE WORLD TO CYCLE ALSO HAVE THE LOWEST RATE OF HELMET USE

NETHERLANDS DENMARK

'AH, THIS IS BECAUSE THEY HAVE GOOD INFRASTRUCTURE' I HEAR YOU SAY. MAYBE THAT'S RIGHT. IF SO IT PROVES THAT DRIVERS ARE THE PROBLEM- CYCLING IS, IN ITSELF, A SAFE ACTIVITY

A WELL-KNOWN HELMET MANUFACTURER HAS SAID THAT HELMETS ARE NOT DESIGNED TO OFFER PROTECTION IN CRASHES INVOLVING MOTOR VEHICLES

RESEARCH HAS FOUND THAT WEARING A HELMET REDUCES CHANCE OF BRAIN INJURY (AS IT DOES FOR PEDESTRIANS AND MOTORISTS TOO)

I USUALLY WEAR A HELMET WHILST RIDING A BIKE ON THE ROAD, BECAUSE MY FAITH IN DRIVERS IS VERY LOW. BUT THEN I DON'T OFTEN RIDE ON THE ROAD, BECAUSE IT SCARES ME

MY HAIR BLOWING IN THE WIND

I DON'T WEAR A HELMET TO TRUNDLE ALONG A BIKE PATH

PLACES THAT MAKE HELMETS COMPULSORY SEE BIG FALLS IN NUMBERS OF PEOPLE CYCLING, AND SO PUBLIC HEALTH SUFFERS OVERALL

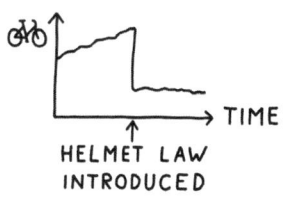

HELMET LAW INTRODUCED

ULTIMATELY IT HAS TO BE YOUR PERSONAL CHOICE. WEAR A HELMET, OR DON'T WEAR A HELMET. IT'S UP TO YOU

SAFETY

THINGS YOU SHOULD ALSO DO IF YOU INSIST OTHER PEOPLE WEAR CYCLE HELMETS

TAKE PINTS FROM PEOPLE SITTING OUTSIDE PUBS

EXTINGUISH OTHER PEOPLE'S CIGARETTES

LOCK UP ALL LADDERS

MAKE SURE NO ONE RELAXES ON THE SOFA

ALTERNATIVELY: LET PEOPLE MAKE THEIR OWN CHOICES ABOUT ALL OF THESE THINGS

SAFETY MEASURES

VARIOUS DESIGNS AVAILABLE

A GIANT INFLATABLE HELMET

I'M TURNING RIGHT!
BRAKING

INDICATORS BUILT INTO CLOTHING

A MULTITUDE OF MIRRORS

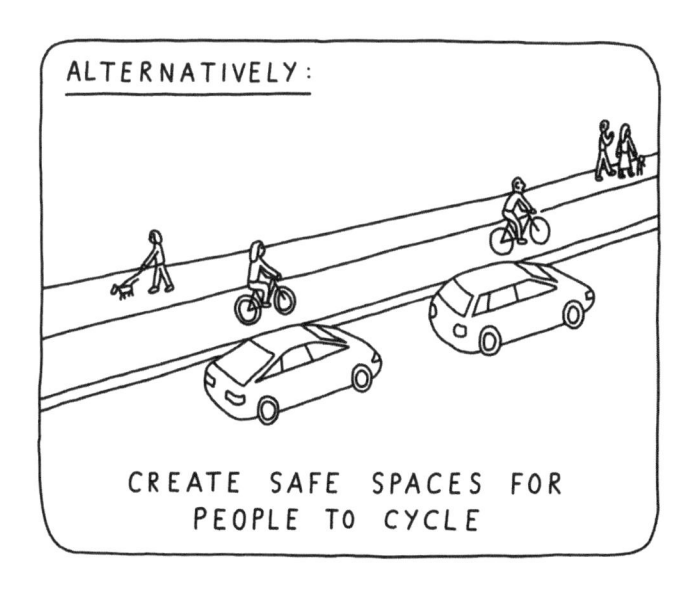

ALTERNATIVELY:

CREATE SAFE SPACES FOR PEOPLE TO CYCLE

CHAPTER 7

OBJECTIONS
COMPLAINTS ABOUT 'CYCLISTS'

CYCLE LANES

WHY DON'T CYCLISTS USE THEM?

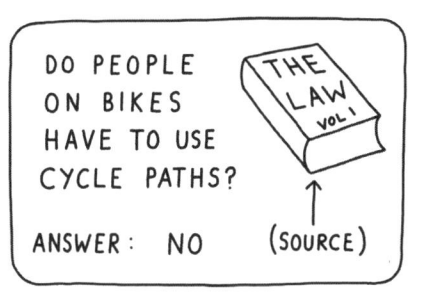

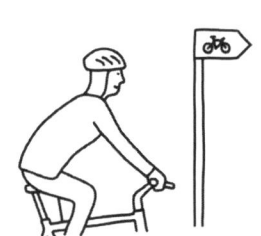

DO PEOPLE ON BIKES HAVE TO USE CYCLE PATHS?

THE LAW
VOL 1

(SOURCE)

ANSWER: NO

IF THEY ARE HIGH QUALITY, PEOPLE WILL USE THEM...

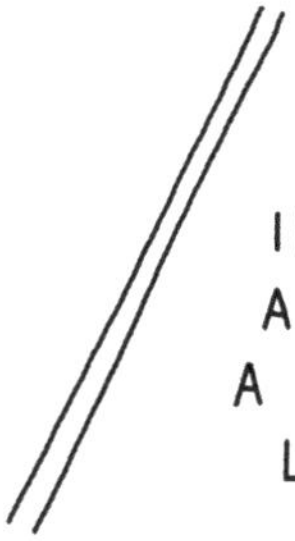

BUT IF THEY ARE JUST A PAINTED LINE...

IF YOU HAVE TO GIVE WAY AT EVERY SINGLE SIDE ROAD AND DRIVEWAY WHEN CARS DON'T...

GIVE WAY
GIVE WAY
GIVE WAY
GIVE WAY
GIVE WAY

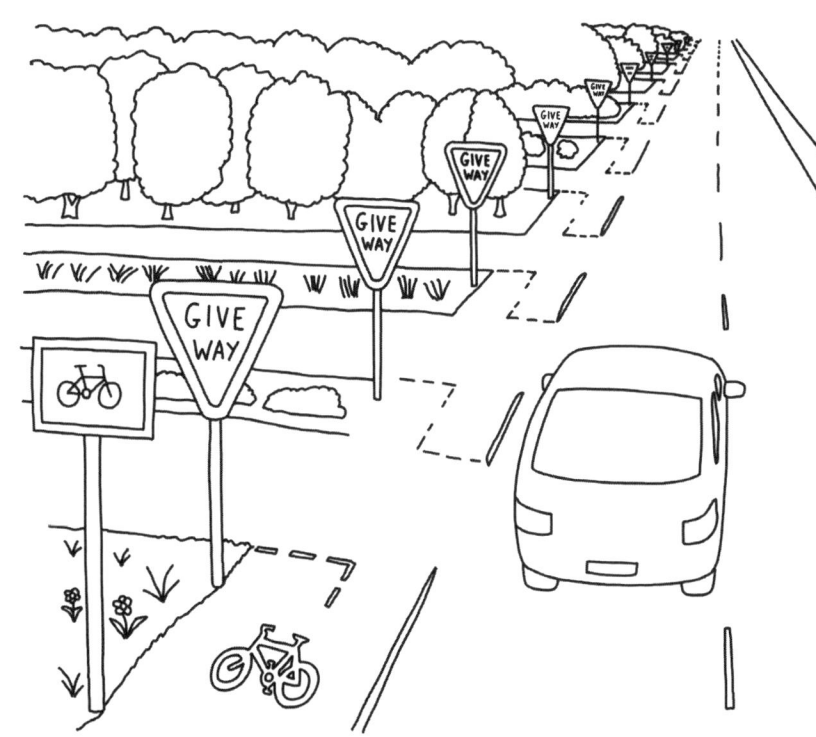

IF THE SURFACE IS TERRIBLE...

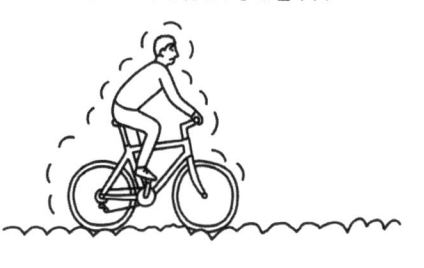

IF THEY DONT GO TO THE PLACES PEOPLE WANT TO GO...

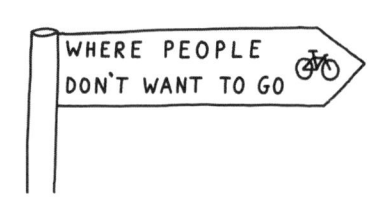

WHERE PEOPLE DON'T WANT TO GO

...THEN PEOPLE PROBABLY WON'T

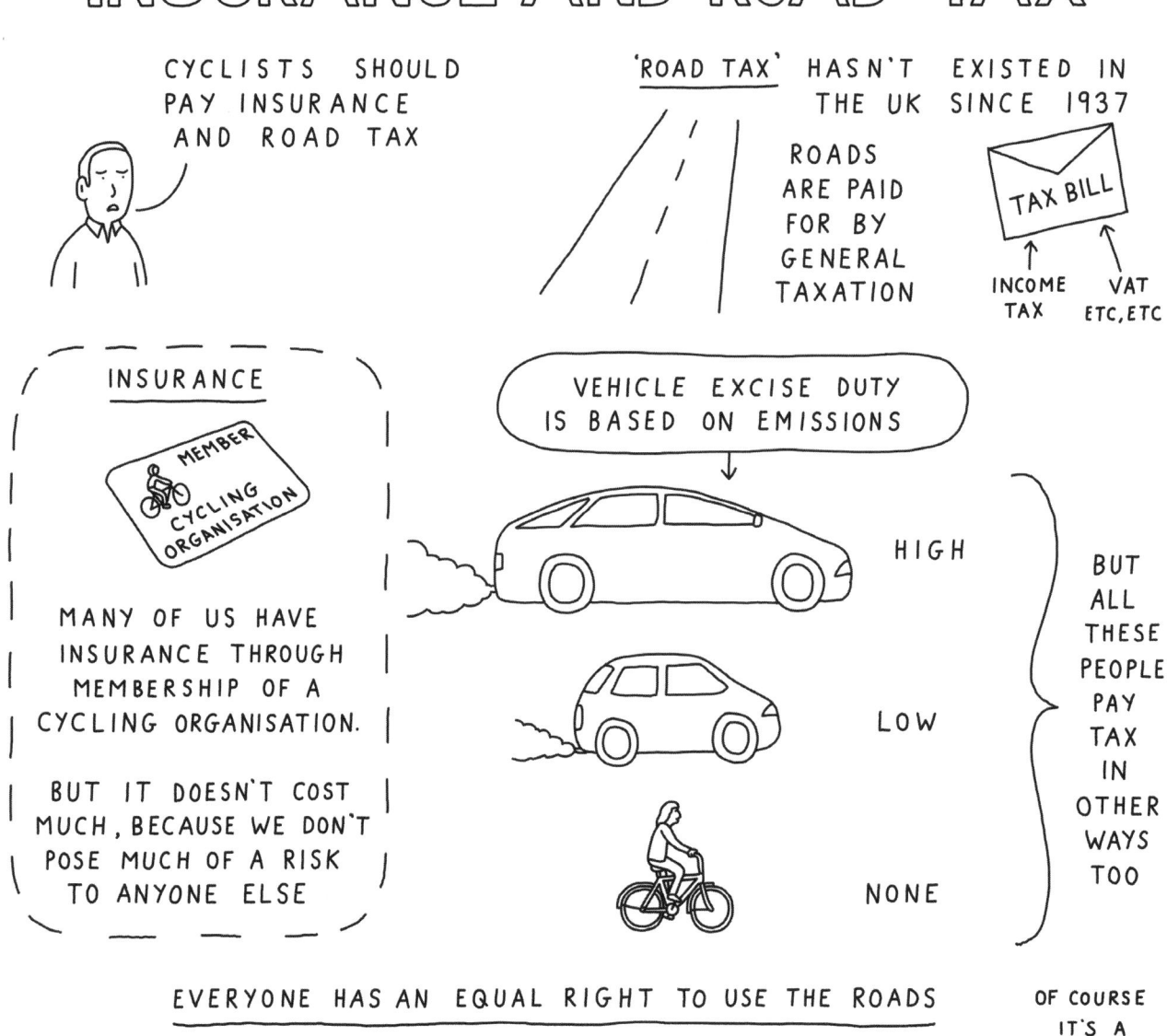

INSURANCE AND ROAD TAX

CYCLISTS SHOULD PAY INSURANCE AND ROAD TAX

'ROAD TAX' HASN'T EXISTED IN THE UK SINCE 1937

ROADS ARE PAID FOR BY GENERAL TAXATION

TAX BILL ← INCOME TAX, VAT ETC, ETC

INSURANCE

MEMBER CYCLING ORGANISATION

MANY OF US HAVE INSURANCE THROUGH MEMBERSHIP OF A CYCLING ORGANISATION.

BUT IT DOESN'T COST MUCH, BECAUSE WE DON'T POSE MUCH OF A RISK TO ANYONE ELSE

VEHICLE EXCISE DUTY IS BASED ON EMISSIONS

HIGH

LOW

NONE

BUT ALL THESE PEOPLE PAY TAX IN OTHER WAYS TOO

EVERYONE HAS AN EQUAL RIGHT TO USE THE ROADS

OF COURSE IT'S A HORSE

THE RULES OF THE ROAD
'CYCLISTS DON'T OBEY THEM'

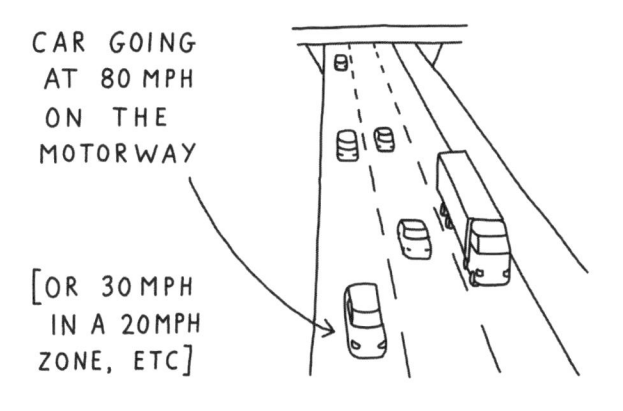

ME STOPPING AT A RED LIGHT

MOST OF US DO

CAR GOING AT 80 MPH ON THE MOTORWAY

[OR 30 MPH IN A 20MPH ZONE, ETC]

THERE WILL ALWAYS BE SOME PEOPLE WHO BREAK THE RULES

WHAT ARE THE DANGERS OF RULE-BREAKING?

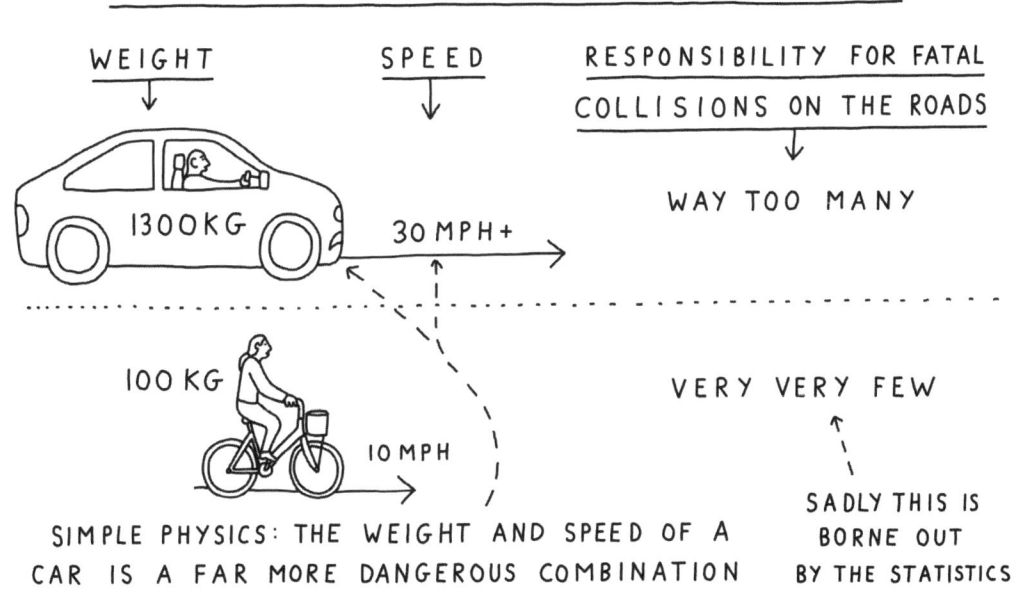

WEIGHT — SPEED

1300 KG — 30 MPH+

100 KG — 10 MPH

SIMPLE PHYSICS: THE WEIGHT AND SPEED OF A CAR IS A FAR MORE DANGEROUS COMBINATION

RESPONSIBILITY FOR FATAL COLLISIONS ON THE ROADS
↓
WAY TOO MANY

VERY VERY FEW

SADLY THIS IS BORNE OUT BY THE STATISTICS

SUMMARY
WE REALLY NEED TO FOCUS OUR ENERGY ON THE FORM OF TRANSPORT THAT DOES THE MOST DAMAGE

SINGLE FILE

'CYCLISTS SHOULD RIDE IN SINGLE FILE'

IT'S SAFER TO OVERTAKE PEOPLE ON BIKES WHEN THEY ARE RIDING TWO ABREAST

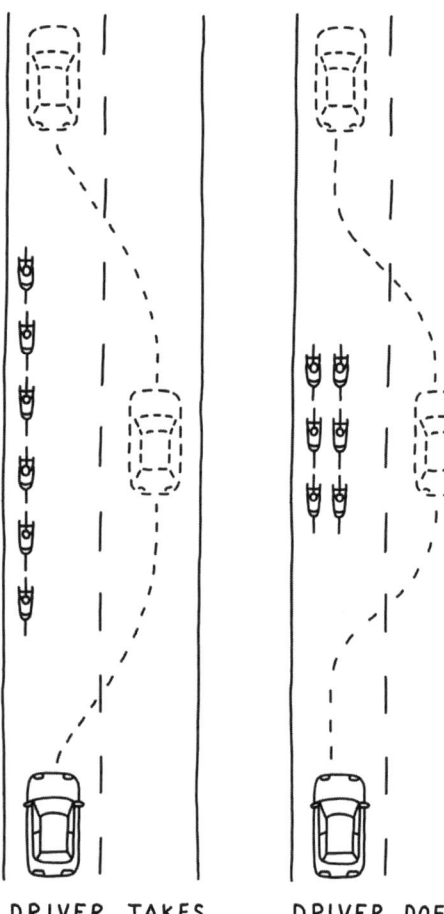

DRIVER TAKES LONGER TO OVERTAKE

DRIVER DOESN'T TAKE AS LONG TO OVERTAKE

BUT IF WE'RE GOING TO INSIST ON SINGLE FILE...

THIS SORT OF THING WOULDN'T BE ALLOWED

INTRODUCING... THE SINGLE FILE CAR

ONE SEAT WIDE

CAMERAS

'CYCLISTS SHOULDN'T BE USING CAMERAS TO CATCH UNSUSPECTING MOTORISTS'

MANY OF US WEAR CAMERAS BECAUSE WE'RE TERRIFIED OF BEING HURT ON THE ROADS AND WE KNOW OTHER PEOPLE THIS HAS HAPPENED TO

IT'S ILLEGAL TO LOOK AT YOUR PHONE WHEN DRIVING, EVEN IF THE TRAFFIC IS STOPPED. COLLISIONS HAPPEN WHEN THE TRAFFIC RESTARTS AND DRIVERS AREN'T AWARE OF THEIR SURROUNDINGS, PEDESTRIANS CROSSING, ETC ETC

MANY POLICE FORCES ACT ON CAMERA SUBMISSIONS AND THOSE THAT DON'T NEED TO START DOING SO TO KEEP PEOPLE SAFE

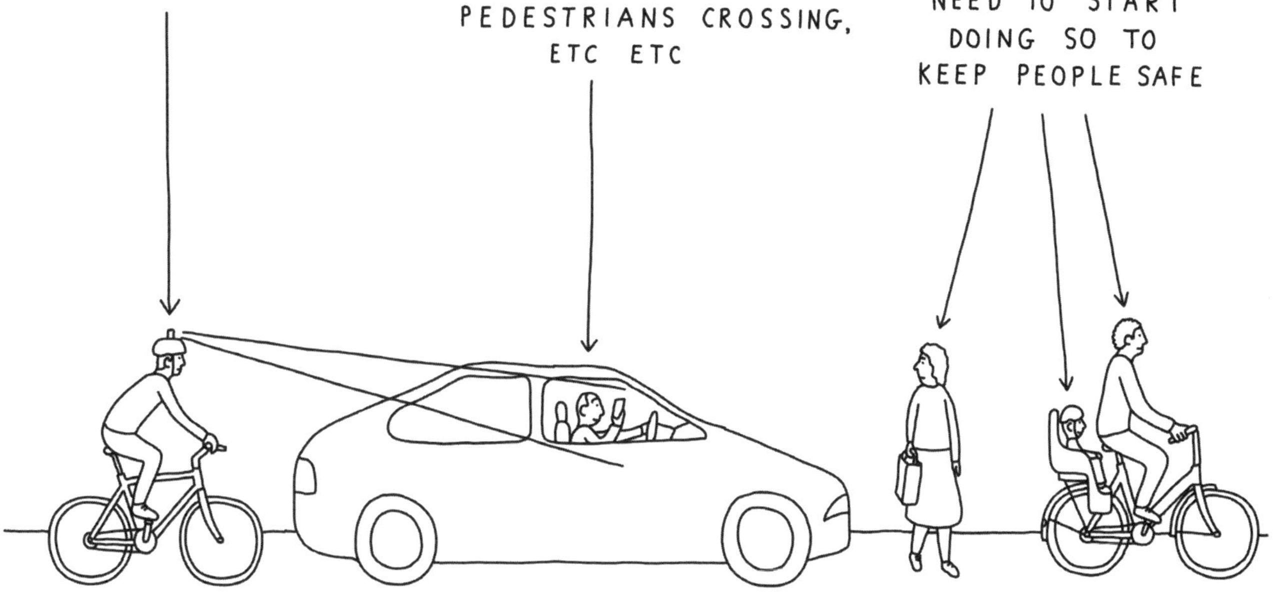

SUMMARY: IF YOU OBEY THE LAW YOU HAVE NO NEED TO WORRY

CLAMPING DOWN

'WE NEED TO CLAMP DOWN ON CYCLISTS'

CARS		BIKES	
KILL 5 PEOPLE A DAY IN UK		KILL ALMOST NO ONE	—
POLLUTION THAT AFFECTS US ALL		NO POLLUTION	—
NOISE BLIGHTING MILLIONS		SILENT	—
INCREASING BURDEN ON THE NHS	CRASHES / INACTIVITY	MAKE PEOPLE HEALTHIER	✓

IF WE'RE REALLY 'CLAMPING DOWN' ON CYCLISTS — PENALTY POINTS, INSURANCE, ETC

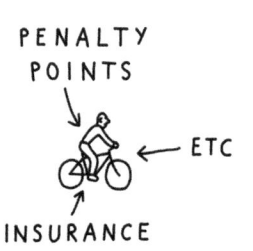

WE'LL HAVE TO CLAMP DOWN ON MOTORISTS FAR MORE SIGNIFICANTLY — INCREASE PENALTIES, SPEED LIMITERS, REDUCE SPEED LIMITS, REGULAR RETESTS

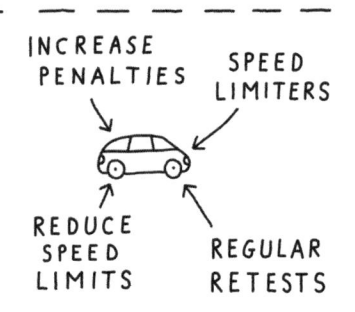

'CYCLISTS'

POSSIBLE PERCEPTIONS

DON'T PAY TAX TO USE THE ROADS?

DON'T USE THE BIKE LANES?

CAMERA-WIELDING VIGILANTE?

TAKING YOUR ROAD SPACE AWAY?

IN YOUR WAY WHEN YOU'RE DRIVING?

A LYCRA-CLAD MENACE TO SOCIETY?

IN FACT

PAY AS MUCH TAX AS YOU DO

WARY OF BIKE LANES THAT GIVE NO PROTECTION FROM UNSAFE DRIVERS

TERRIFIED BY DRIVERS WHO DON'T GIVE THEM ENOUGH SPACE

AFRAID OF GOING ON PUBLIC TRANSPORT, AND JUST WANT A SAFE WAY TO TRAVEL

AN ORDINARY PERSON GOING TO WORK

HAVE A FAMILY THAT LOVES THEM AND WANTS TO SEE THEM HOME SAFELY AT THE END OF THE DAY

CHAPTER 8

INFRASTRUCTURE

SAFE SPACES TO RIDE A BIKE

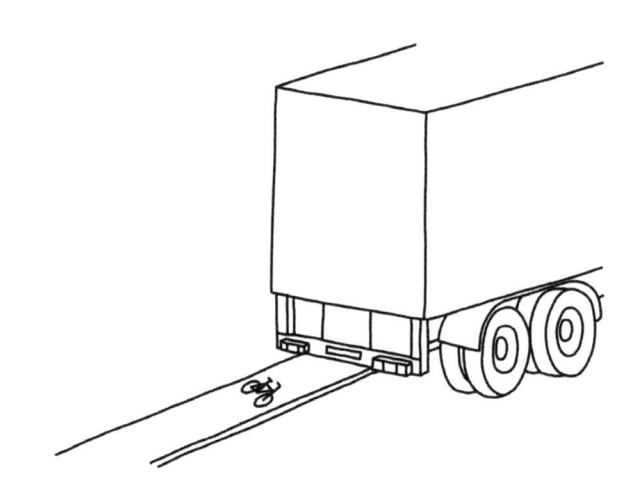

PLANNING A ROUTE

ON YOUR BIKE

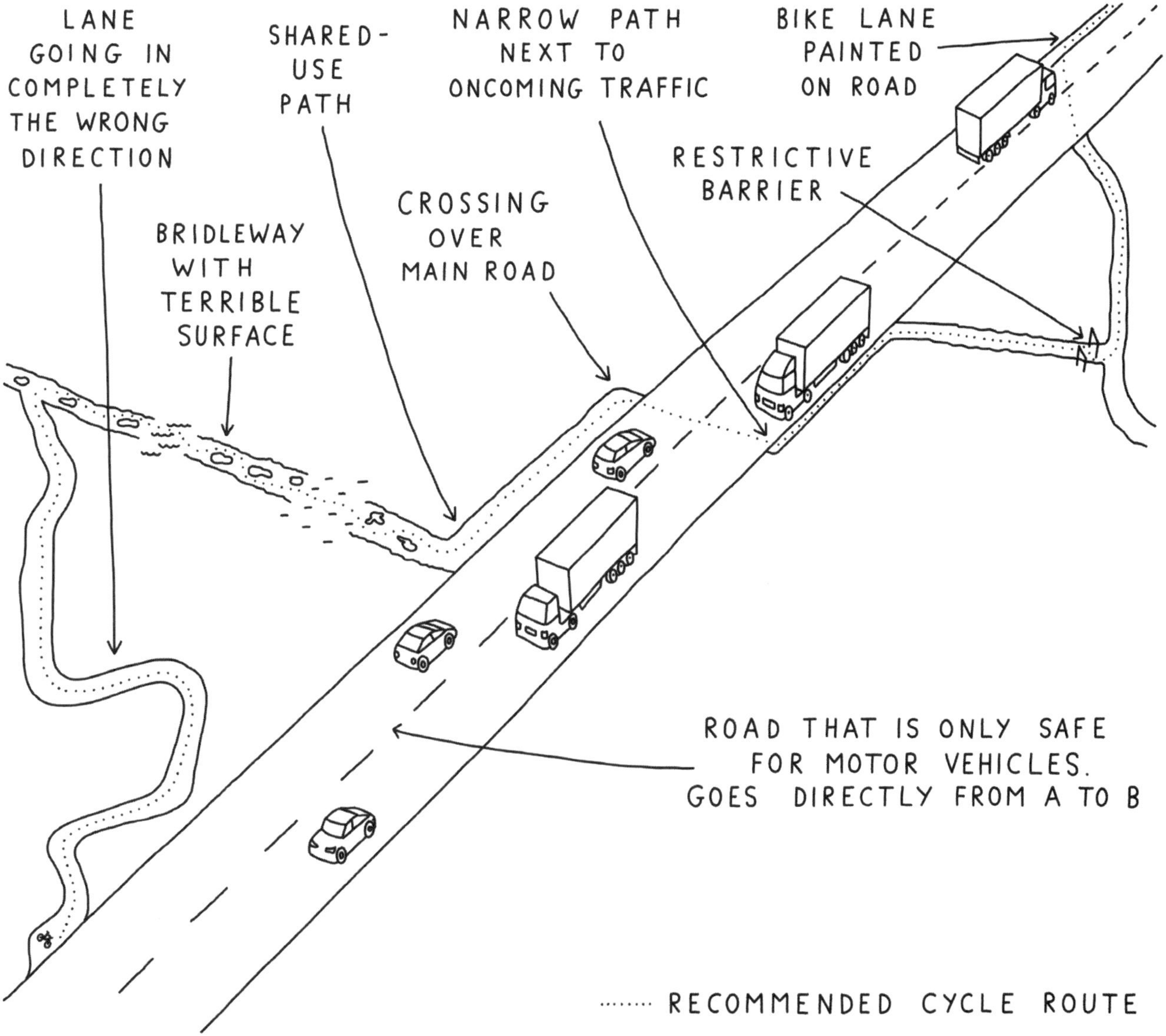
LANE GOING IN COMPLETELY THE WRONG DIRECTION
SHARED-USE PATH
NARROW PATH NEXT TO ONCOMING TRAFFIC
BIKE LANE PAINTED ON ROAD
RESTRICTIVE BARRIER
CROSSING OVER MAIN ROAD
BRIDLEWAY WITH TERRIBLE SURFACE
ROAD THAT IS ONLY SAFE FOR MOTOR VEHICLES. GOES DIRECTLY FROM A TO B
RECOMMENDED CYCLE ROUTE

THE CYCLE PATH

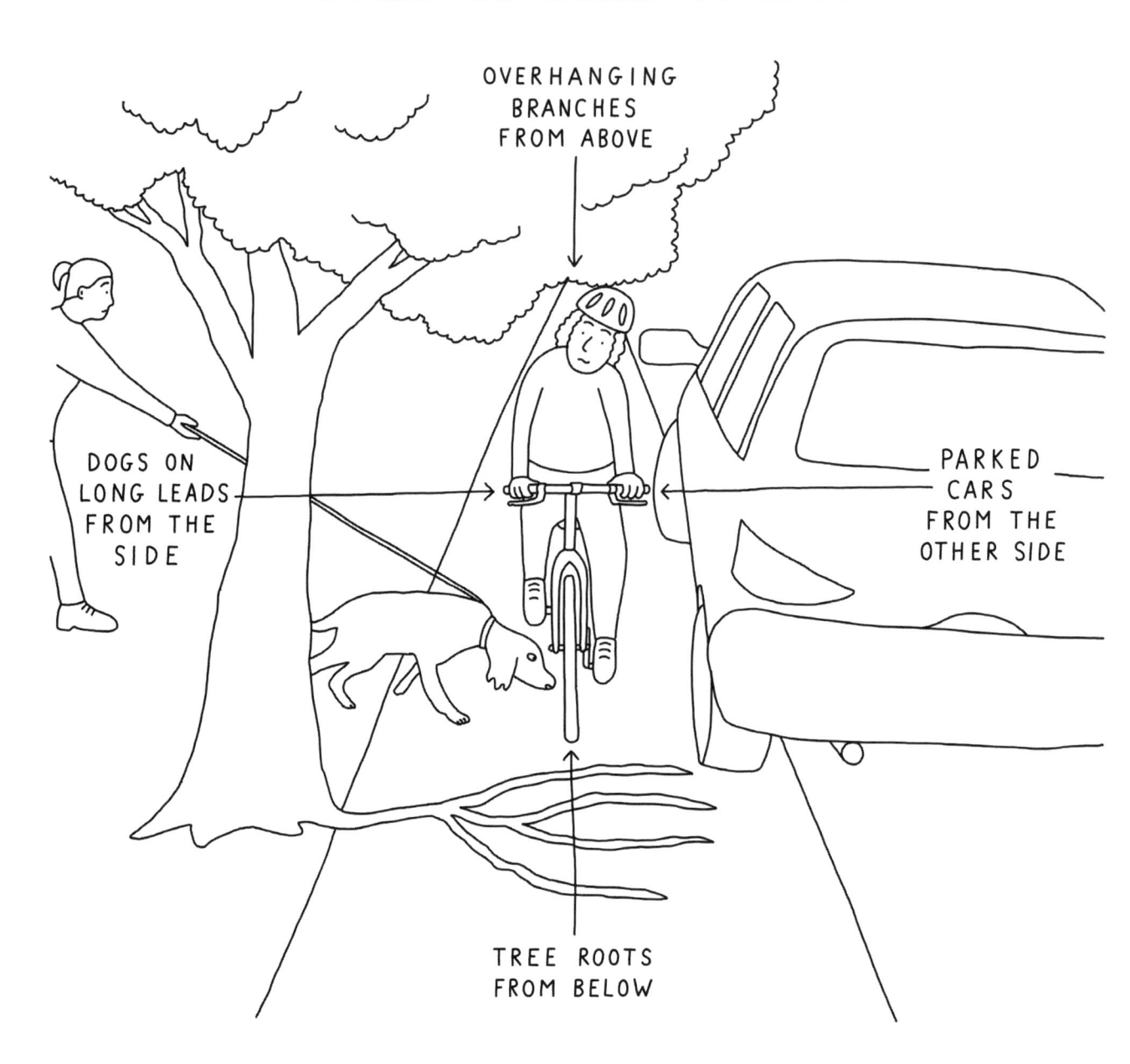

OVERHANGING BRANCHES FROM ABOVE

DOGS ON LONG LEADS FROM THE SIDE

PARKED CARS FROM THE OTHER SIDE

TREE ROOTS FROM BELOW

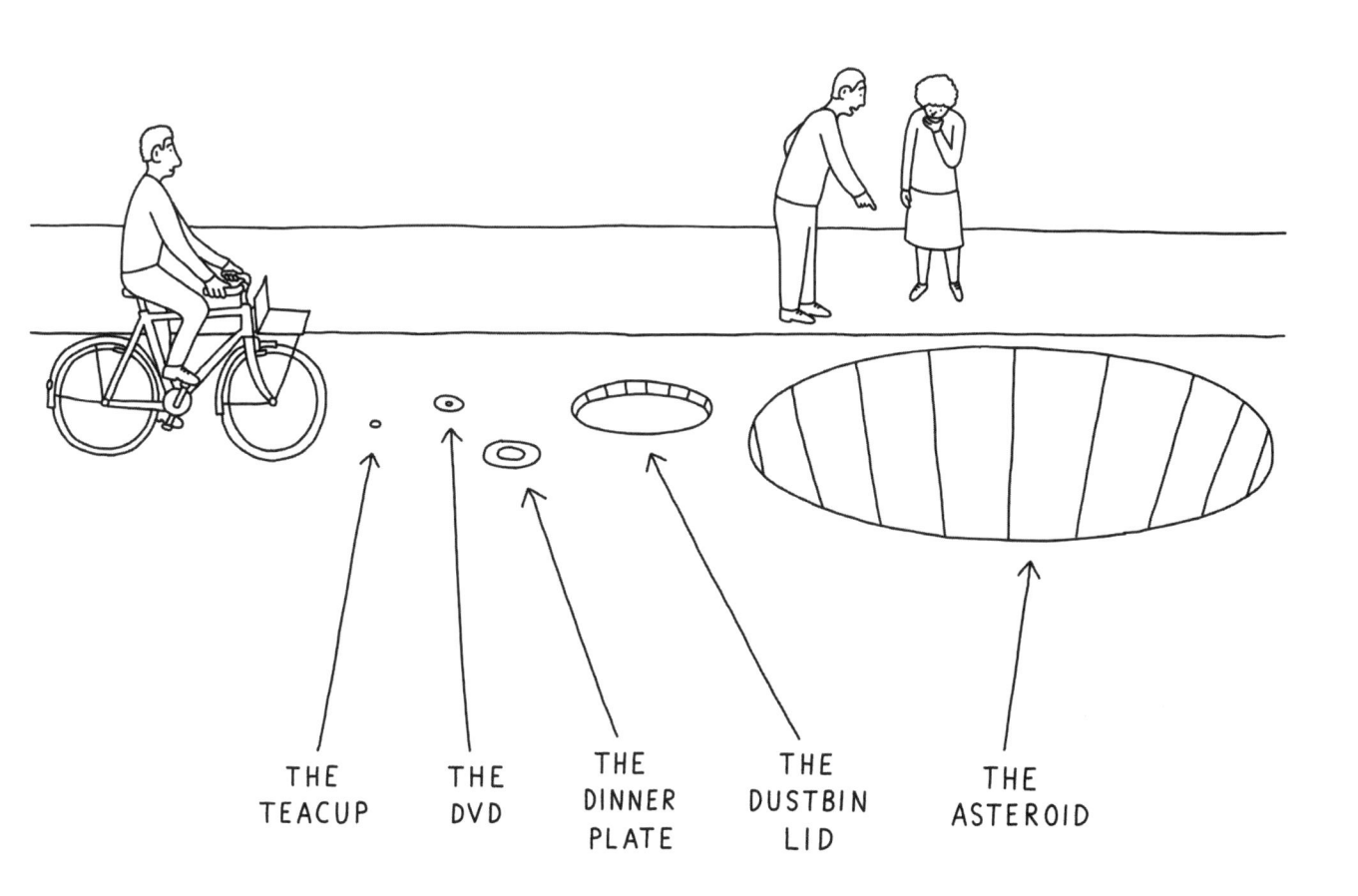

POTHOLES
A SIZE GUIDE

THE TEACUP   THE DVD   THE DINNER PLATE   THE DUSTBIN LID   THE ASTEROID

THE CYCLE NETWORK
WHAT IT SHOULD LOOK LIKE

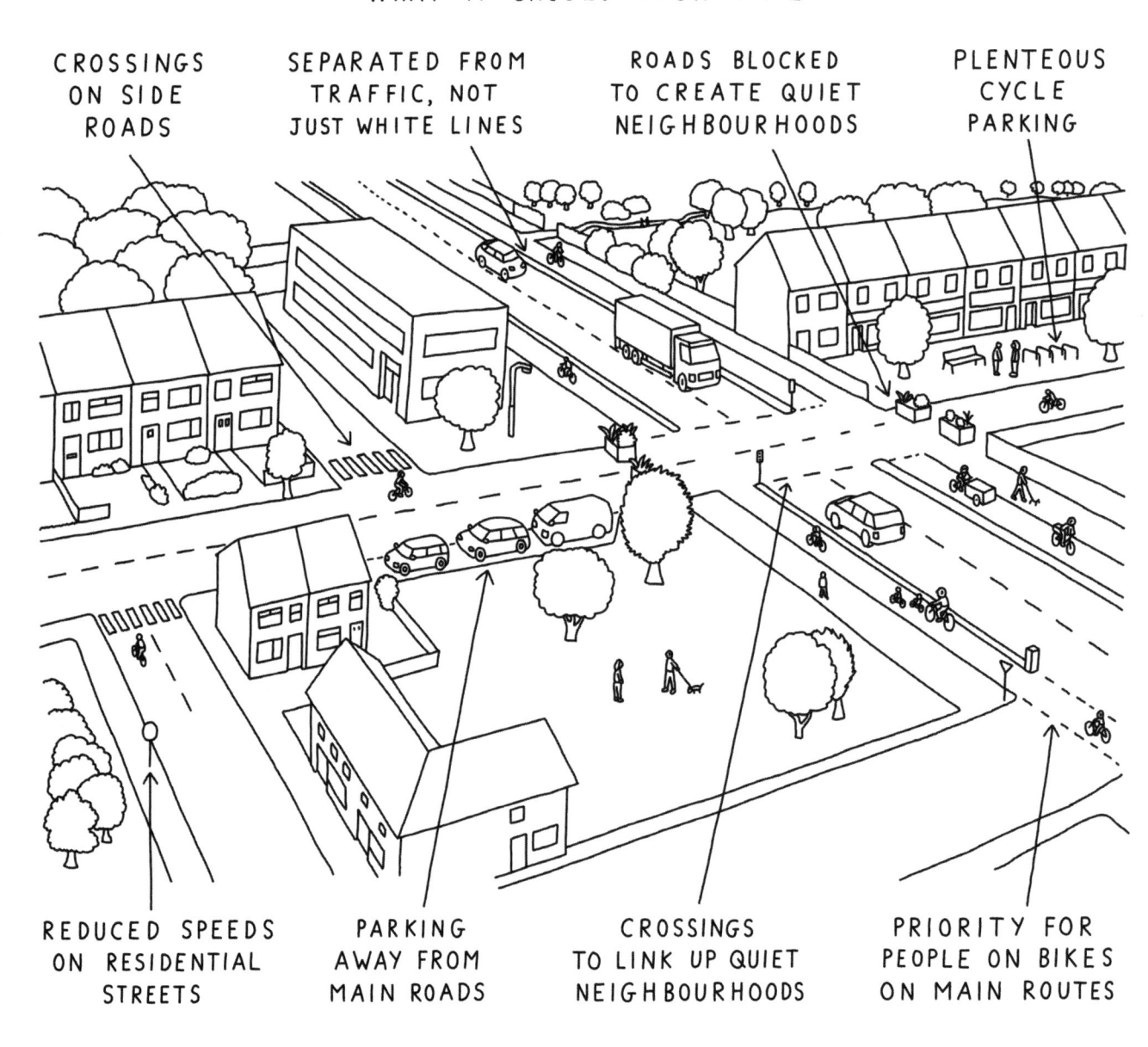

- CROSSINGS ON SIDE ROADS
- SEPARATED FROM TRAFFIC, NOT JUST WHITE LINES
- ROADS BLOCKED TO CREATE QUIET NEIGHBOURHOODS
- PLENTEOUS CYCLE PARKING
- REDUCED SPEEDS ON RESIDENTIAL STREETS
- PARKING AWAY FROM MAIN ROADS
- CROSSINGS TO LINK UP QUIET NEIGHBOURHOODS
- PRIORITY FOR PEOPLE ON BIKES ON MAIN ROUTES

CYCLE ROUTES

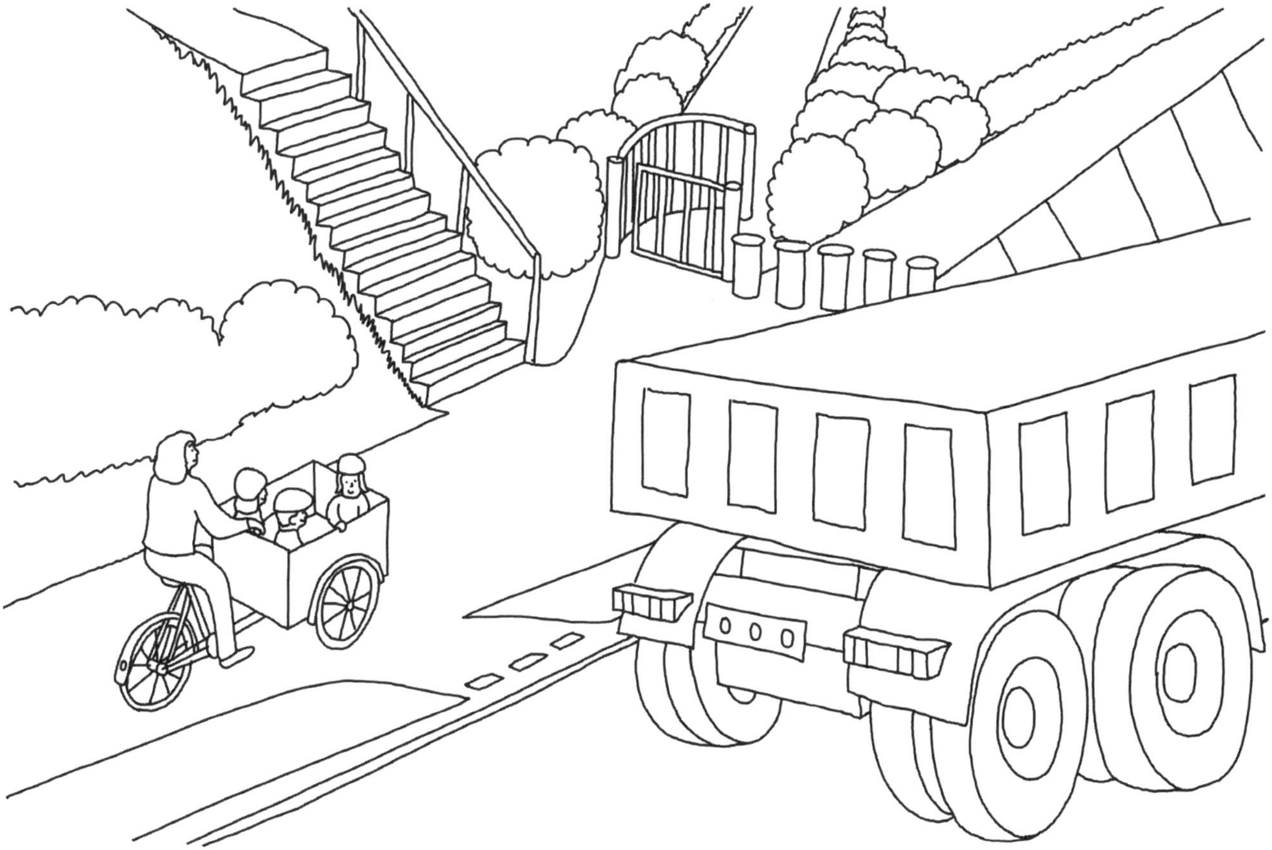

WHY THEY SHOULD BE DESIGNED BY PEOPLE WHO CYCLE

CYCLING INFRASTRUCTURE

DIFFERENT KINDS

NONE: PEOPLE MUST CYCLE ON THE ROAD

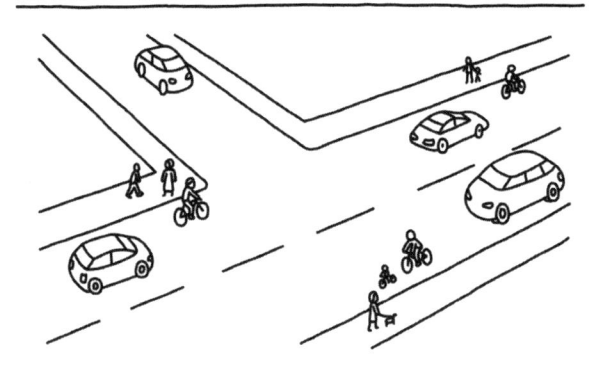

PEOPLE ON BIKES HAVE NO PROTECTION FROM UNSAFE DRIVERS

MANY PEOPLE AFRAID TO CYCLE

SHARED-USE PATH

EXCUSE ME!

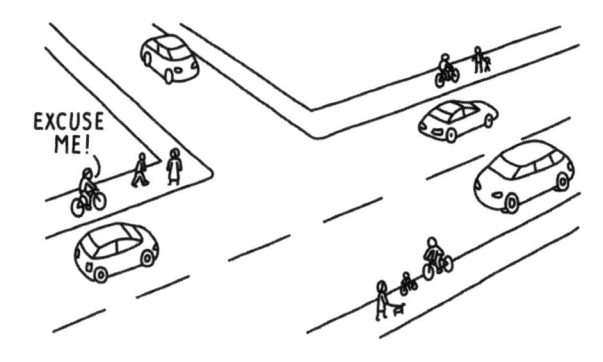

PEDESTRIANS AND PEOPLE ON BIKES GOING AT VERY DIFFERENT SPEEDS - NOT GOOD FOR EITHER

PAINTED WHITE LINE ON THE ROAD

TOO CLOSE!
OBLIVIOUS

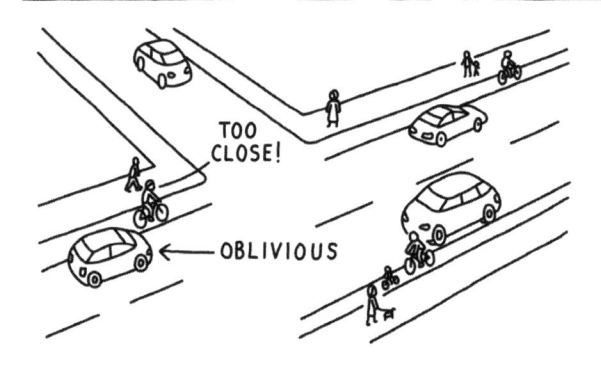

DRIVERS PASS PEOPLE ON BIKES TOO CLOSELY

WORSE THAN NO INFRASTRUCTURE AT ALL

PROTECTED CYCLEWAY

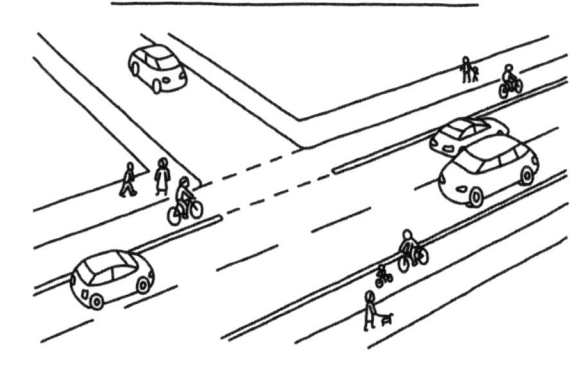

NO NEED TO STOP AT EVERY SIDE ROAD - CYCLEWAY WILL BE USED

PEOPLE FEEL SAFE RIDING A BIKE

THE SHARED-USE PATH
AS FOUND IN MANY CITIES

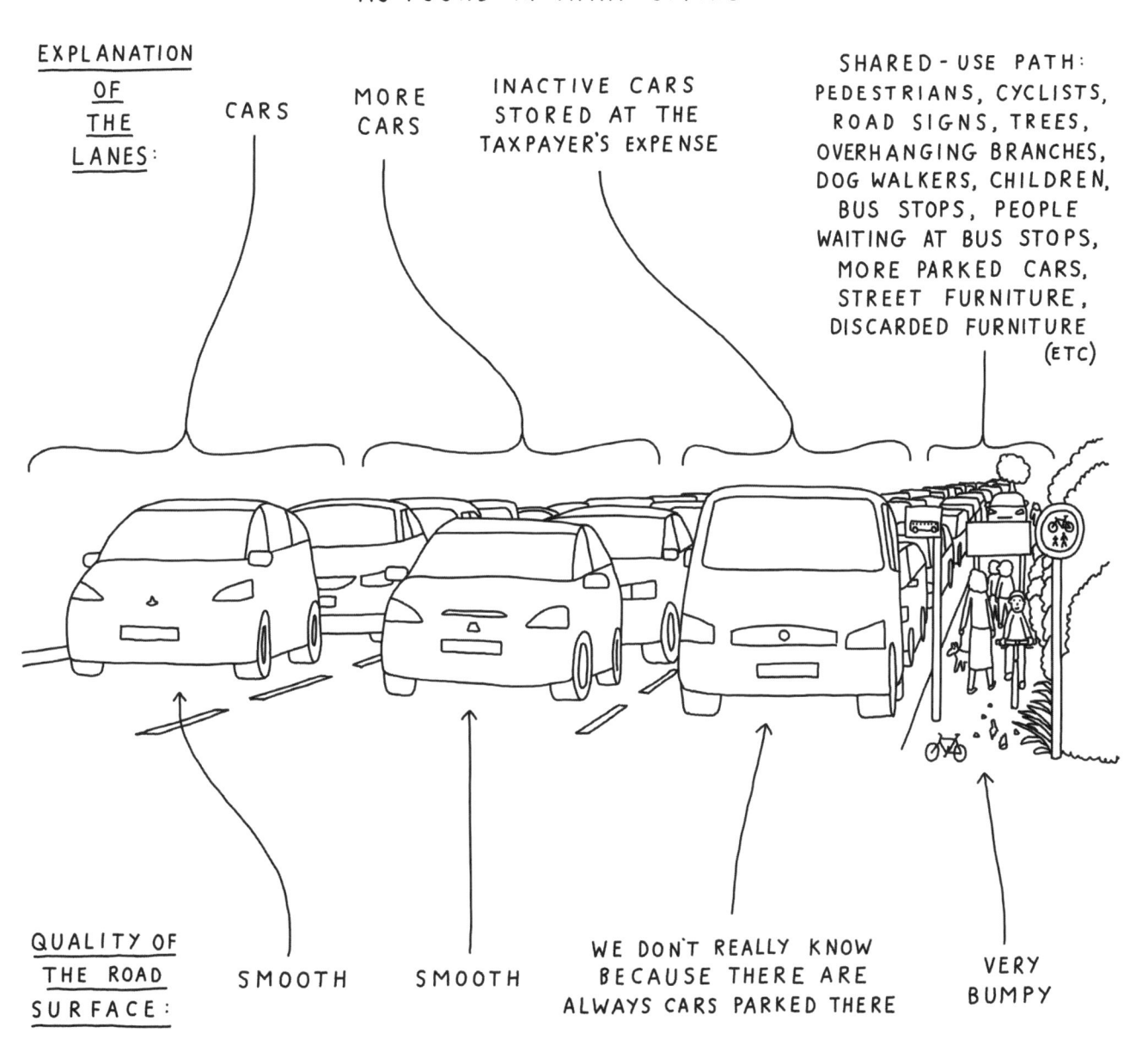

EXPLANATION OF THE LANES:

- CARS
- MORE CARS
- INACTIVE CARS STORED AT THE TAXPAYER'S EXPENSE
- SHARED-USE PATH: PEDESTRIANS, CYCLISTS, ROAD SIGNS, TREES, OVERHANGING BRANCHES, DOG WALKERS, CHILDREN, BUS STOPS, PEOPLE WAITING AT BUS STOPS, MORE PARKED CARS, STREET FURNITURE, DISCARDED FURNITURE (ETC)

QUALITY OF THE ROAD SURFACE:

- SMOOTH
- SMOOTH
- WE DON'T REALLY KNOW BECAUSE THERE ARE ALWAYS CARS PARKED THERE
- VERY BUMPY

WHITE PAINT
WAYS TO WASTE IT

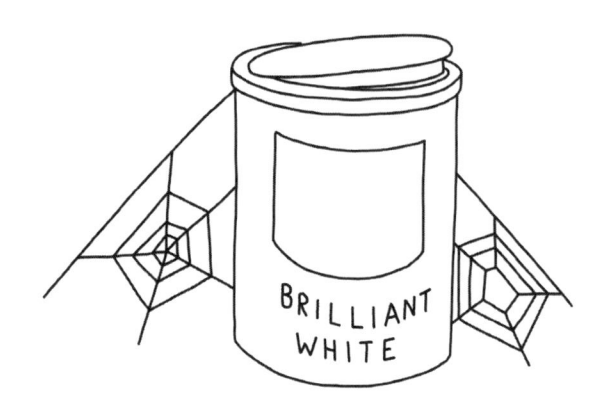

LEAVE IT IN THE GARAGE FOR 17 YEARS WITH LID NOT QUITE ON PROPERLY

REPAINT THE WALLS OF THE CHILDREN'S CRAFT ROOM

LEAVE IT UNSECURED IN THE BACK OF YOUR VAN

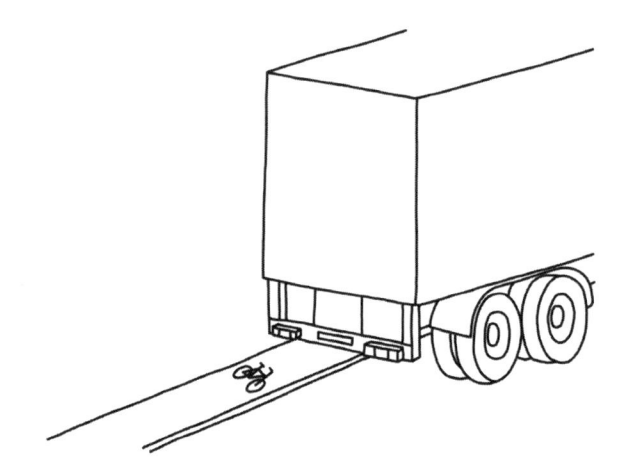

PAINT A CYCLE LANE ON THE MAIN CARRIAGEWAY OF A ROAD

LOW TRAFFIC NEIGHBOURHOODS

SOME RESIDENTIAL ROADS BLOCKED TO THROUGH TRAFFIC

WHY SOME PEOPLE LIKE LOW TRAFFIC NEIGHBOURHOODS

SAFE ROUTES TO RIDE A BIKE

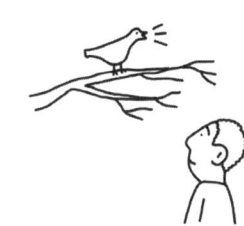

PLACES YOU CAN HEAR THE BIRDS SINGING

CHILDREN CAN PLAY OUTSIDE (LIKE WE COULD)

WHY OTHER PEOPLE DO NOT LIKE LOW TRAFFIC NEIGHBOURHOODS

LIKE TO DRIVE TWO MINUTES TO THE SHOPS

BUT IT WON'T HAVE ANY COLOUR IN OCTOBER

HORTICULTURAL CONCERNS

'BUT I'VE ALWAYS GONE THIS WAY'

SIGNS
ALTERNATIVES TO UNHELPFUL SIGNAGE

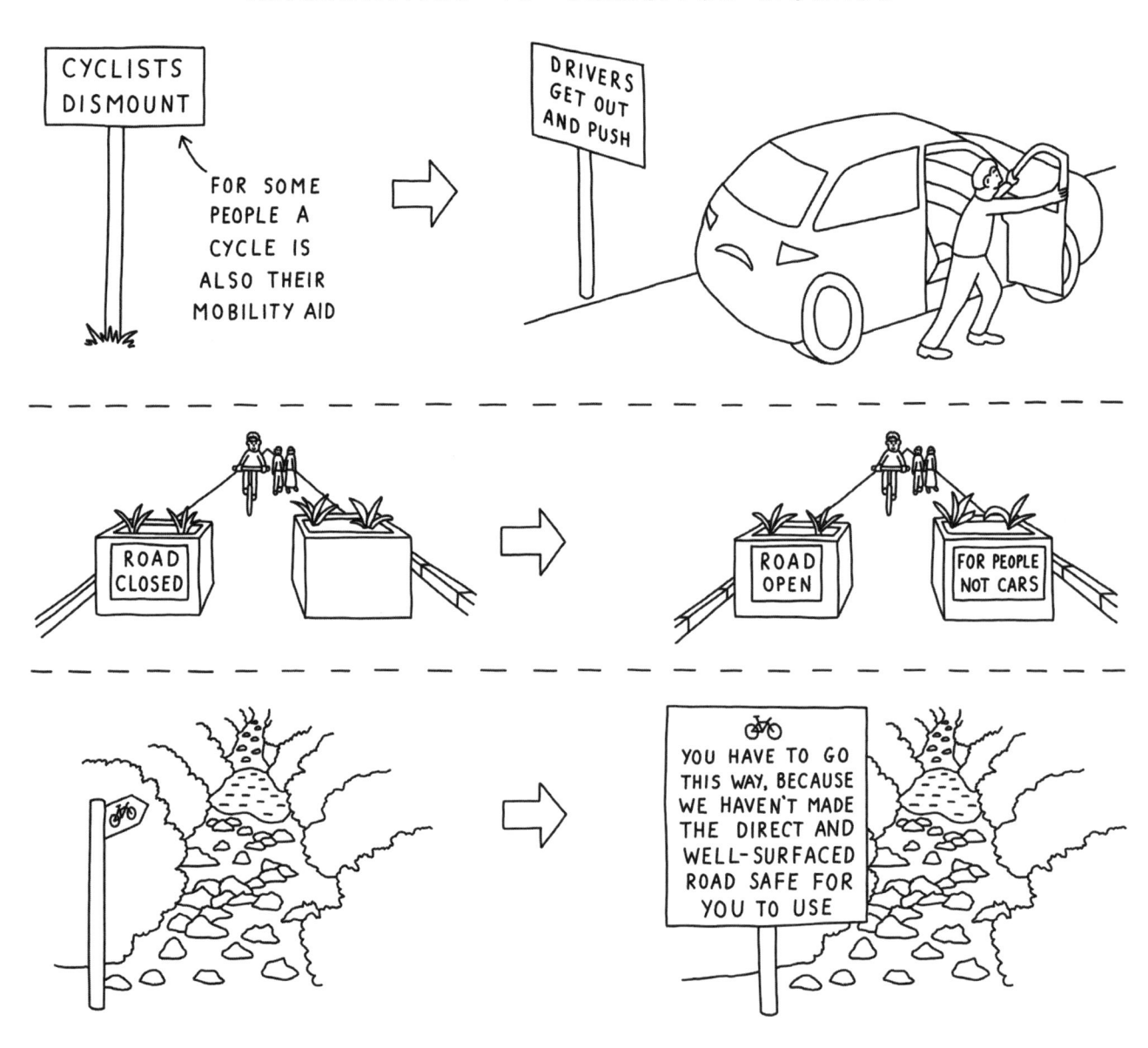

CYCLISTS DISMOUNT ← FOR SOME PEOPLE A CYCLE IS ALSO THEIR MOBILITY AID

→ DRIVERS GET OUT AND PUSH

ROAD CLOSED → ROAD OPEN / FOR PEOPLE NOT CARS

→ YOU HAVE TO GO THIS WAY, BECAUSE WE HAVEN'T MADE THE DIRECT AND WELL-SURFACED ROAD SAFE FOR YOU TO USE

PLANNING
OF NEW HOUSING DEVELOPMENTS

HOW THINGS OFTEN ARE

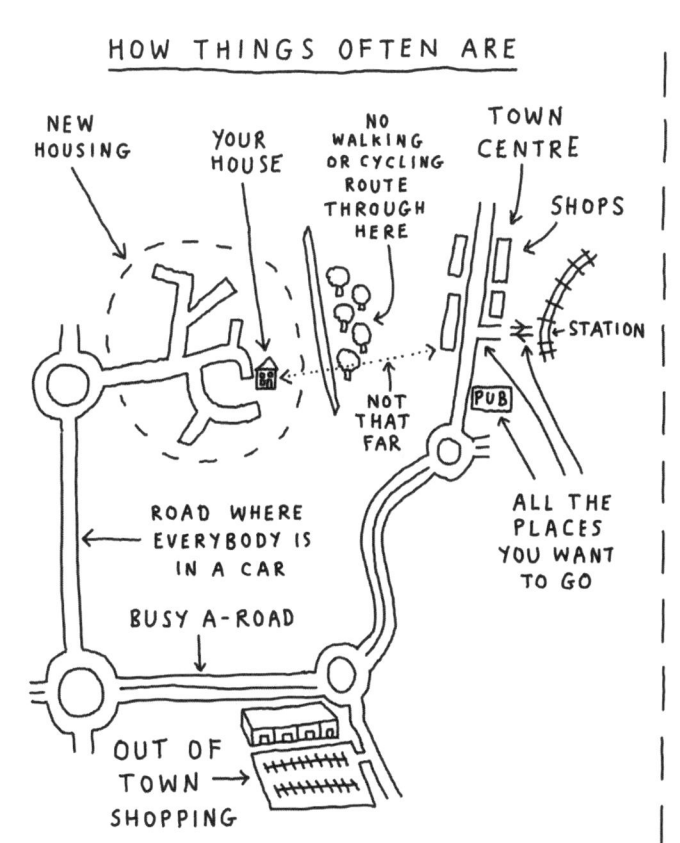

- NEW HOUSING
- YOUR HOUSE
- NO WALKING OR CYCLING ROUTE THROUGH HERE
- TOWN CENTRE
- SHOPS
- STATION
- PUB
- NOT THAT FAR
- ALL THE PLACES YOU WANT TO GO
- ROAD WHERE EVERYBODY IS IN A CAR
- BUSY A-ROAD
- OUT OF TOWN SHOPPING
- EVERYONE DRIVES (BECAUSE THERE IS NO OTHER OPTION)

RESULTS:
- CONGESTION
- POLLUTION
- QUALITY OF LIFE SUFFERS
- PEOPLE DON'T VISIT THE TOWN CENTRE

HOW TO CHANGE THINGS

- PROVIDE WALKING AND CYCLING ROUTES 
- DESIGN FOR LOW TRAFFIC SPEED AND VOLUME — A PLACE YOU'D LIKE TO SPEND TIME
- STREET HIERARCHY — MAKE IT QUICKER TO WALK AND CYCLE
- PROVIDE PUBLIC TRANSPORT OPTIONS — FREQUENT, SIMPLE TICKETING
- PARKING MANAGEMENT — SO CAR ISN'T ALWAYS FIRST CHOICE
- TRAVEL PLANNING — PERSONAL TRAVEL PLAN, INFO, MAP

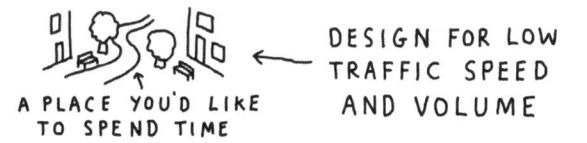

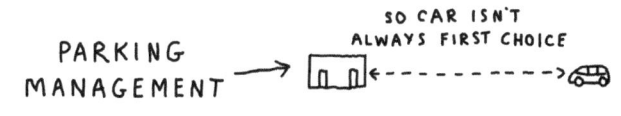

THE BIKE PATH

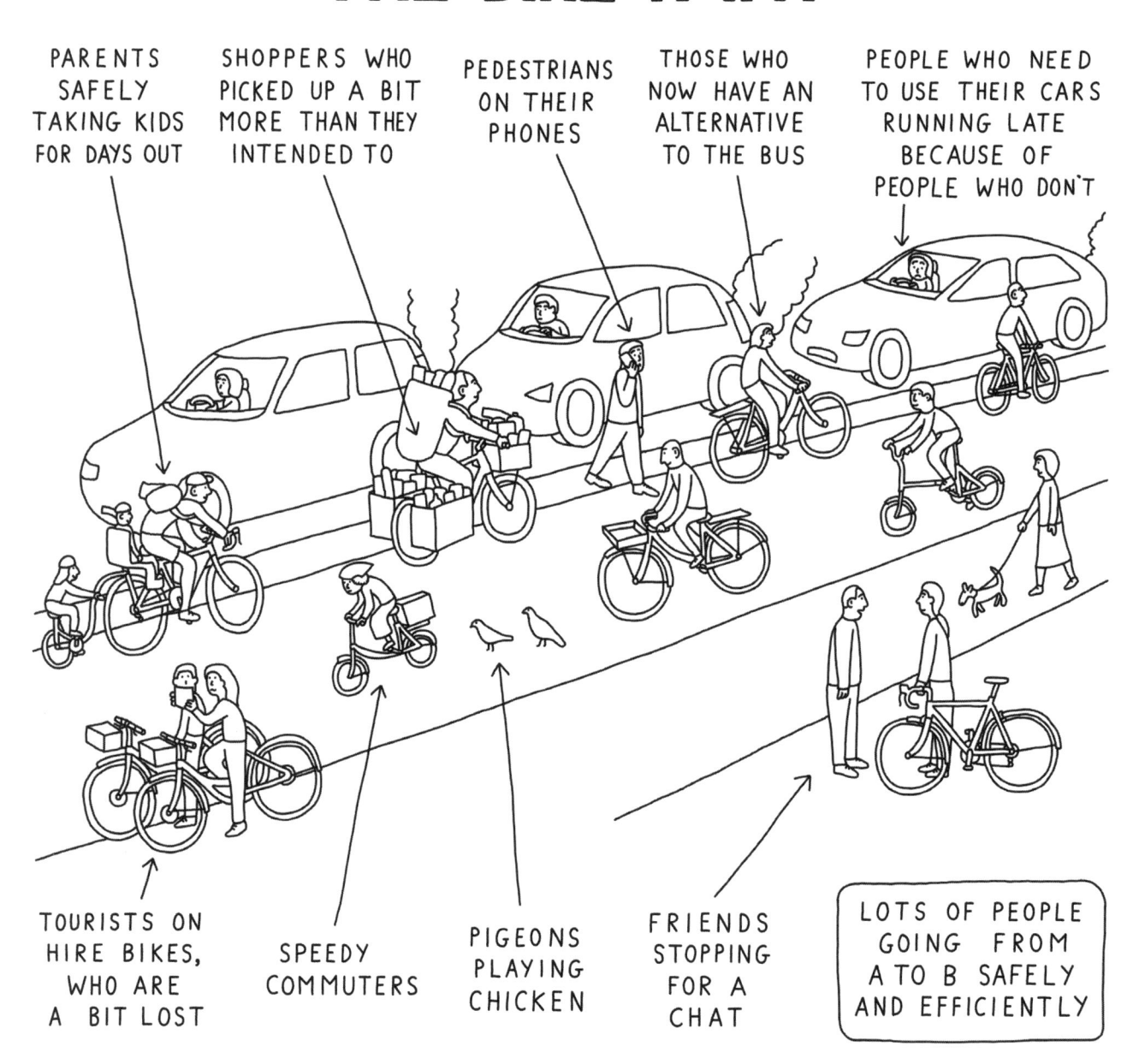

- PARENTS SAFELY TAKING KIDS FOR DAYS OUT
- SHOPPERS WHO PICKED UP A BIT MORE THAN THEY INTENDED TO
- PEDESTRIANS ON THEIR PHONES
- THOSE WHO NOW HAVE AN ALTERNATIVE TO THE BUS
- PEOPLE WHO NEED TO USE THEIR CARS RUNNING LATE BECAUSE OF PEOPLE WHO DON'T
- TOURISTS ON HIRE BIKES, WHO ARE A BIT LOST
- SPEEDY COMMUTERS
- PIGEONS PLAYING CHICKEN
- FRIENDS STOPPING FOR A CHAT
- LOTS OF PEOPLE GOING FROM A TO B SAFELY AND EFFICIENTLY

CHAPTER 9

CYCLING: A FORCE FOR GOOD

HOW TO CHANGE THE WORLD (ON A BIKE)

POSSIBILITIES

OPENED UP BY CYCLING

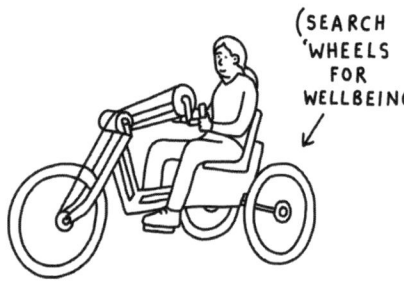

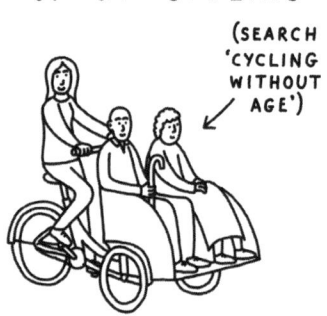

(SEARCH 'WHEELS FOR WELLBEING')

CYCLES FOR PEOPLE WITH A DISABILITY

(SEARCH 'CYCLING WITHOUT AGE')

RICKSHAW RIDES FOR THE ELDERLY

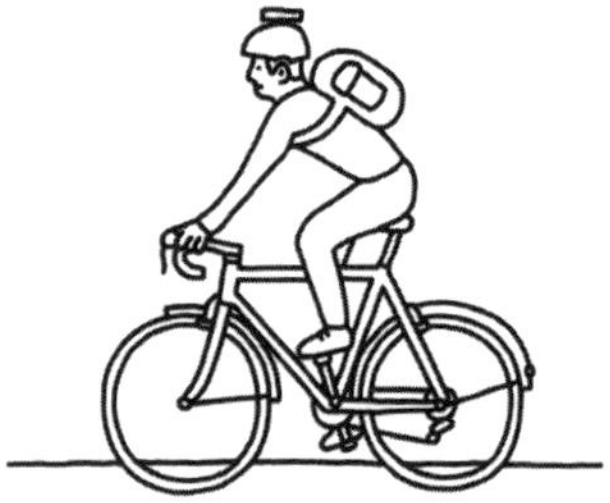

USING A COMMUTE TO GET FIT

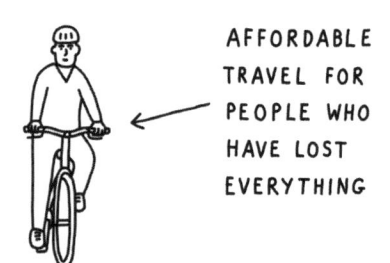

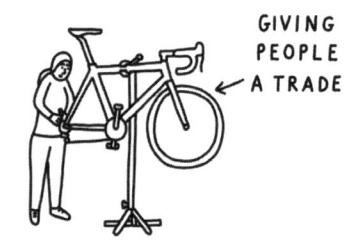

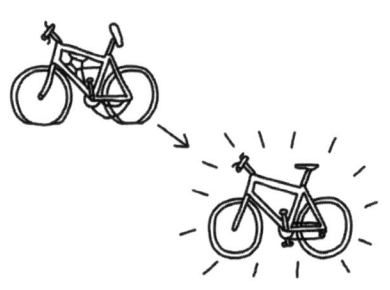

AFFORDABLE TRAVEL FOR PEOPLE WHO HAVE LOST EVERYTHING

BIKES FOR REFUGEES

GIVING PEOPLE A TRADE

COMMUNITY CYCLING WORKSHOPS

BIKE RECYCLING PROJECTS

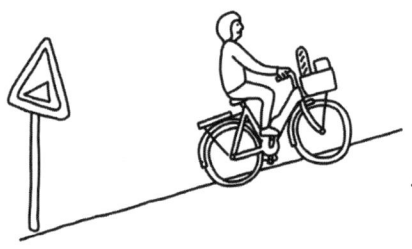

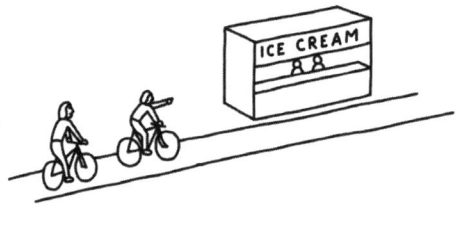

ELECTRIC BIKES, FOR A BOOST UP THE HILLS

ICE CREAM

CREATING JOBS THROUGH TOURISM

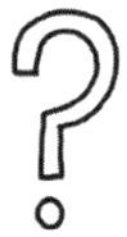

THE POSSIBILITIES ARE LIMITLESS

SPORT OR TRANSPORT?

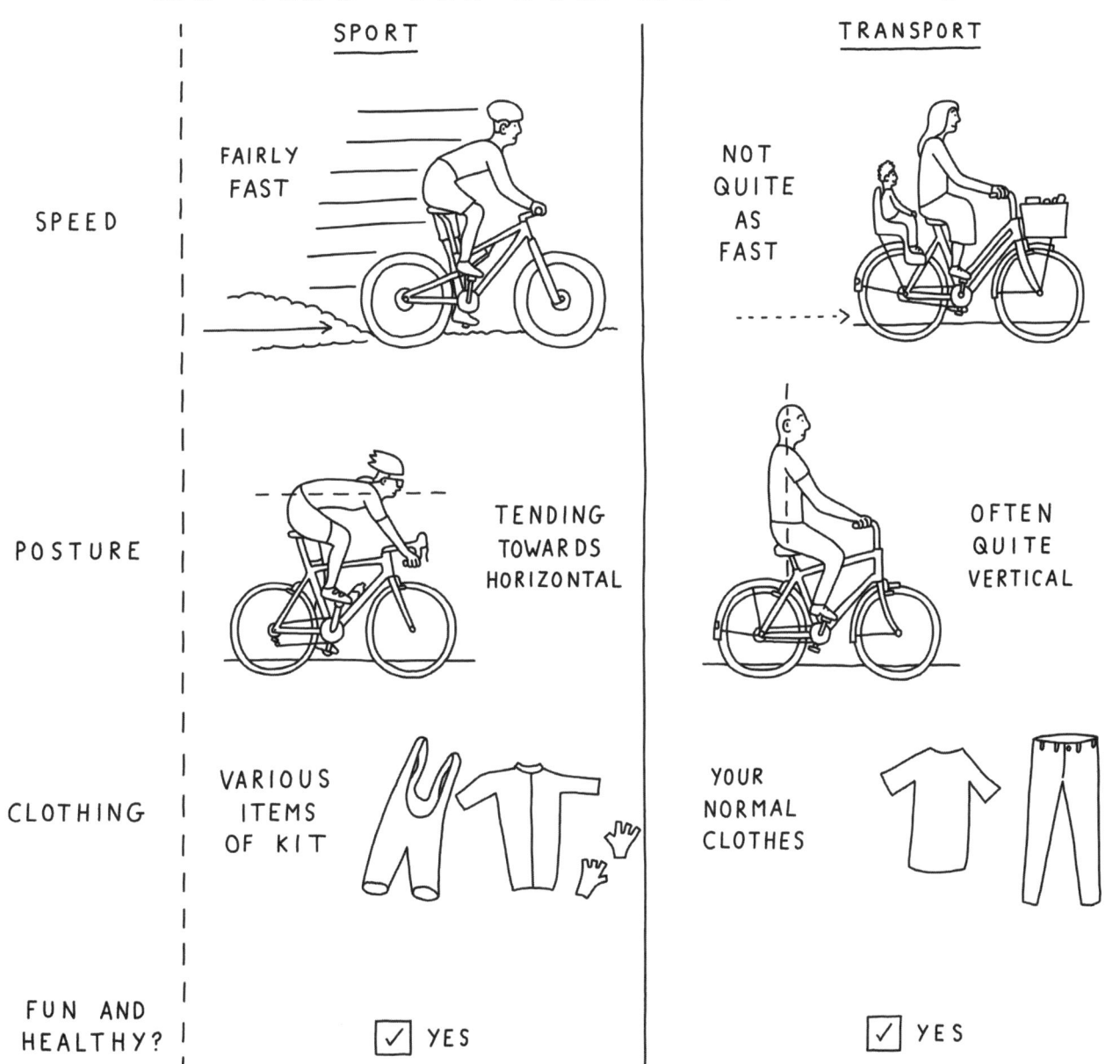

	SPORT	TRANSPORT
SPEED	FAIRLY FAST	NOT QUITE AS FAST
POSTURE	TENDING TOWARDS HORIZONTAL	OFTEN QUITE VERTICAL
CLOTHING	VARIOUS ITEMS OF KIT	YOUR NORMAL CLOTHES
FUN AND HEALTHY?	✓ YES	✓ YES

ENCOURAGING CYCLING

WAYS YOUR CHURCH OR COMMUNITY ORGANISATION CAN WELCOME PEOPLE WHO CYCLE

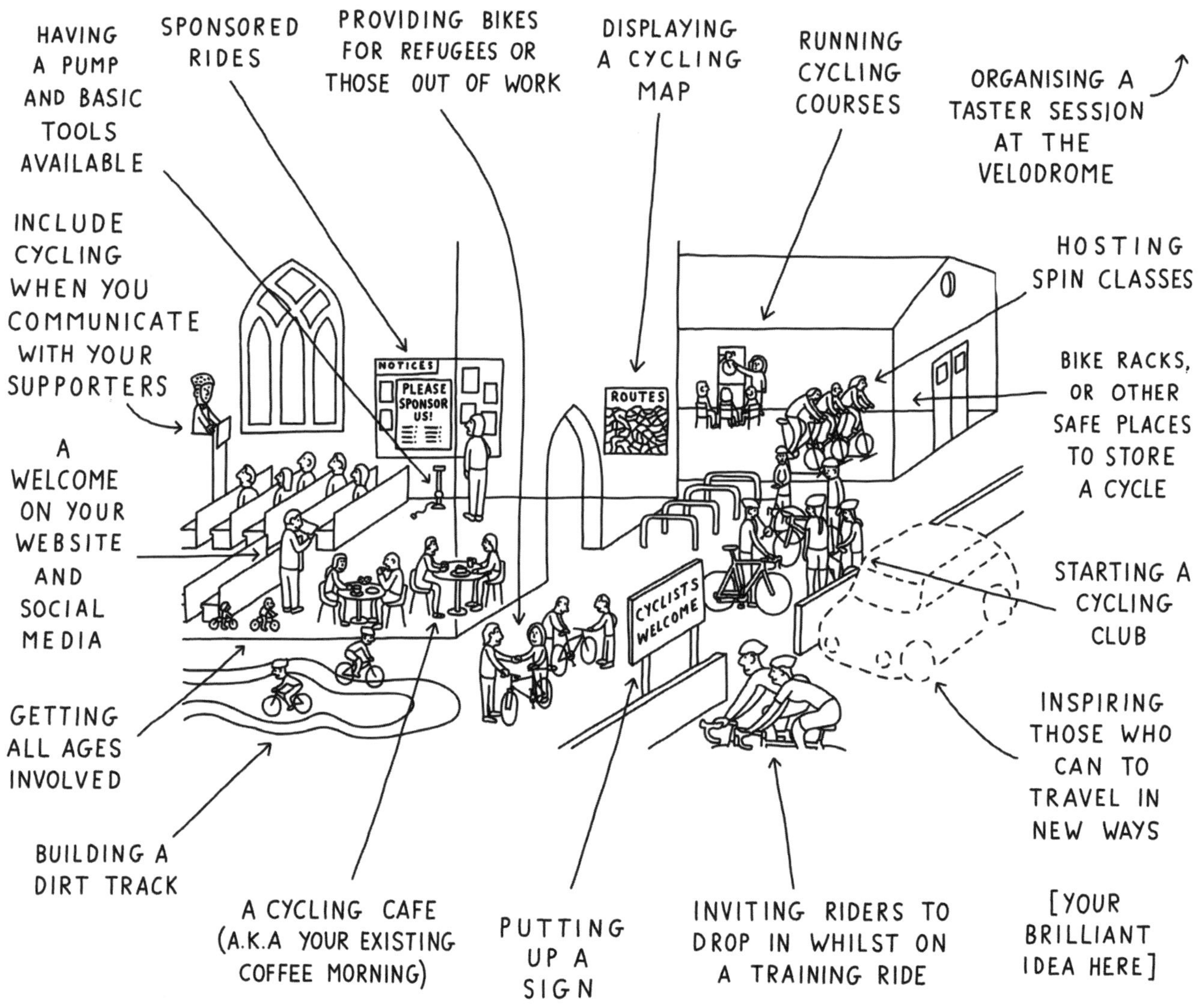

HAVING A PUMP AND BASIC TOOLS AVAILABLE
SPONSORED RIDES
PROVIDING BIKES FOR REFUGEES OR THOSE OUT OF WORK
DISPLAYING A CYCLING MAP
RUNNING CYCLING COURSES
ORGANISING A TASTER SESSION AT THE VELODROME
INCLUDE CYCLING WHEN YOU COMMUNICATE WITH YOUR SUPPORTERS
HOSTING SPIN CLASSES
NOTICES
PLEASE SPONSOR US!
ROUTES
BIKE RACKS, OR OTHER SAFE PLACES TO STORE A CYCLE
A WELCOME ON YOUR WEBSITE AND SOCIAL MEDIA
CYCLISTS WELCOME
STARTING A CYCLING CLUB
GETTING ALL AGES INVOLVED
INSPIRING THOSE WHO CAN TO TRAVEL IN NEW WAYS
BUILDING A DIRT TRACK
A CYCLING CAFE (A.K.A YOUR EXISTING COFFEE MORNING)
PUTTING UP A SIGN
INVITING RIDERS TO DROP IN WHILST ON A TRAINING RIDE
[YOUR BRILLIANT IDEA HERE]

SOCIAL JUSTICE

[QUITE A BIG CAR]

PEOPLE WITH LOTS OF MONEY ARE MORE LIKELY TO OWN A CAR

[LOVELY]

AND LIVE IN A PLACE AWAY FROM BUSY TRAFFIC, NOISE AND POLLUTION

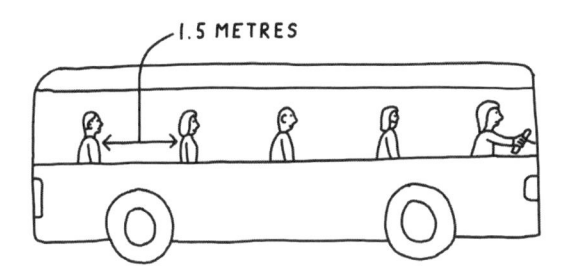

1.5 METRES

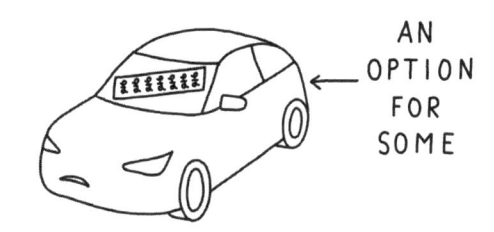

PEOPLE DOING LOWER-PAID JOBS ARE MORE LIKELY TO NEED TO USE PUBLIC TRANSPORT, WHICH MAY BE UNSAFE AT THE CURRENT TIME*

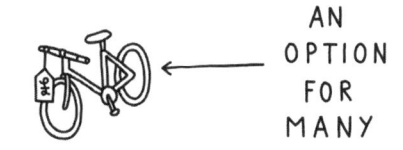

* THE SITUATION - MARCH 2021

AN OPTION FOR SOME

CARS ARE EXPENSIVE

AN OPTION FOR MANY

BIKES COST FAR LESS

ANY SYSTEM WHICH PRIORITISES CARS OVER WALKING, CYCLING AND PUBLIC TRANSPORT FAVOURS THE RICH AND PENALISES THE POOR

WE NEED TO BUILD A TRANSPORT SYSTEM THAT BENEFITS EVERYONE

TRANSPORT HEROES
DURING A PANDEMIC

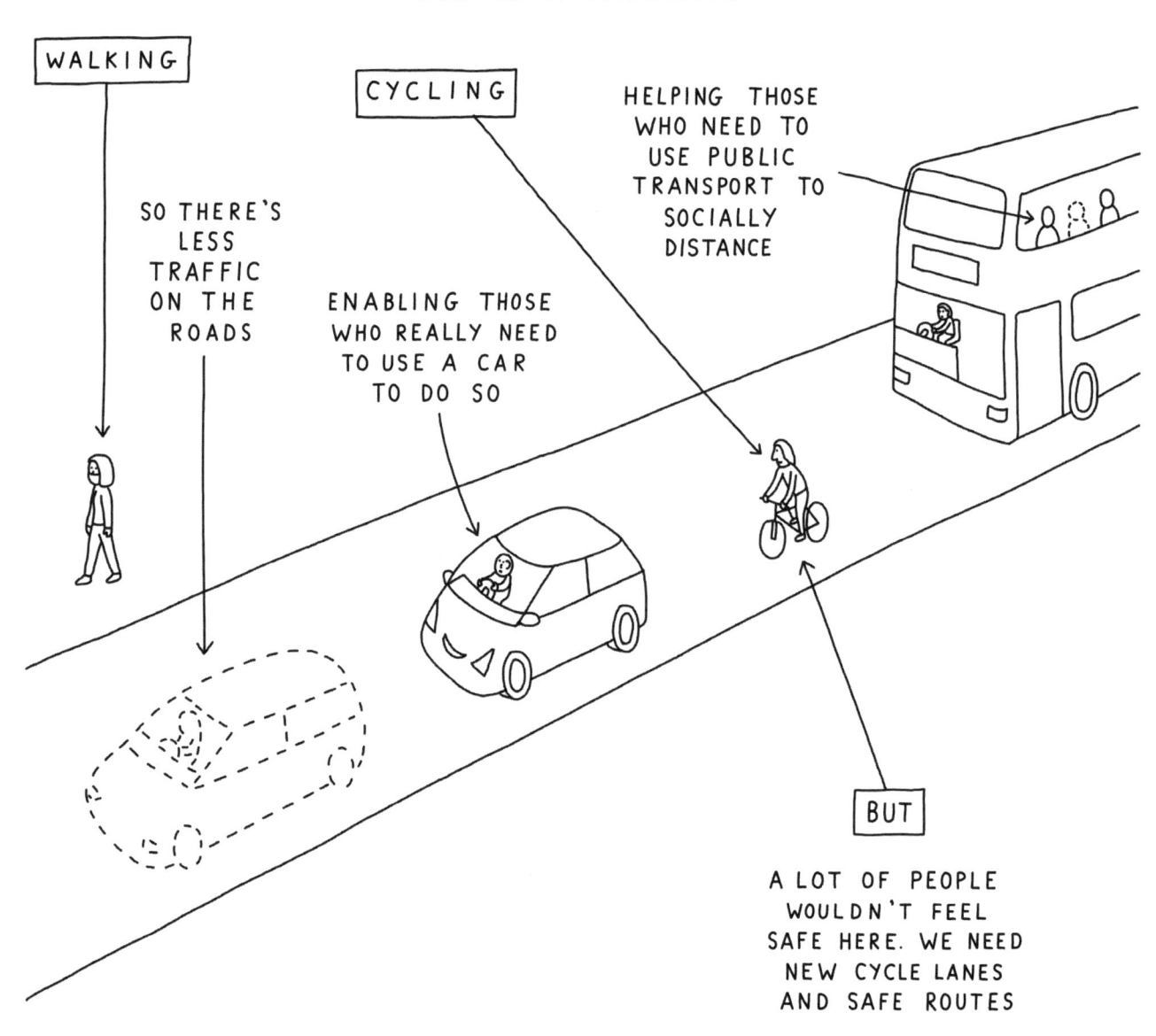

WALKING — so there's less traffic on the roads

CYCLING — enabling those who really need to use a car to do so

Helping those who need to use public transport to socially distance

BUT a lot of people wouldn't feel safe here. We need new cycle lanes and safe routes

SO, WHAT WOULD YOU DO, DAVE?

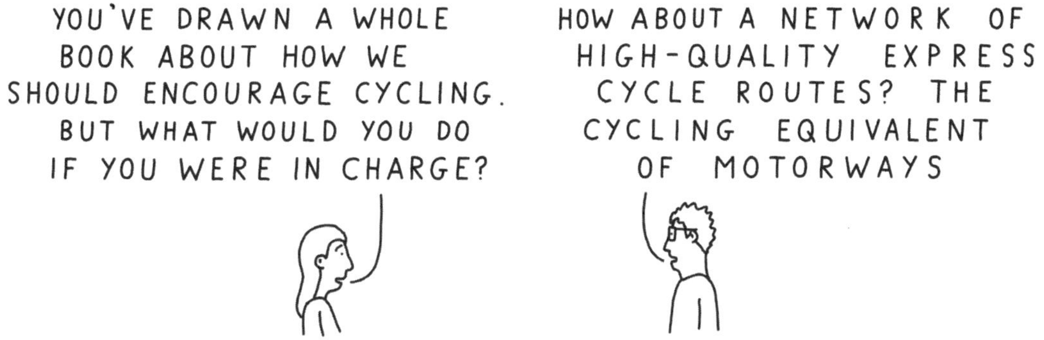
YOU'VE DRAWN A WHOLE BOOK ABOUT HOW WE SHOULD ENCOURAGE CYCLING. BUT WHAT WOULD YOU DO IF YOU WERE IN CHARGE?
HOW ABOUT A NETWORK OF HIGH-QUALITY EXPRESS CYCLE ROUTES? THE CYCLING EQUIVALENT OF MOTORWAYS

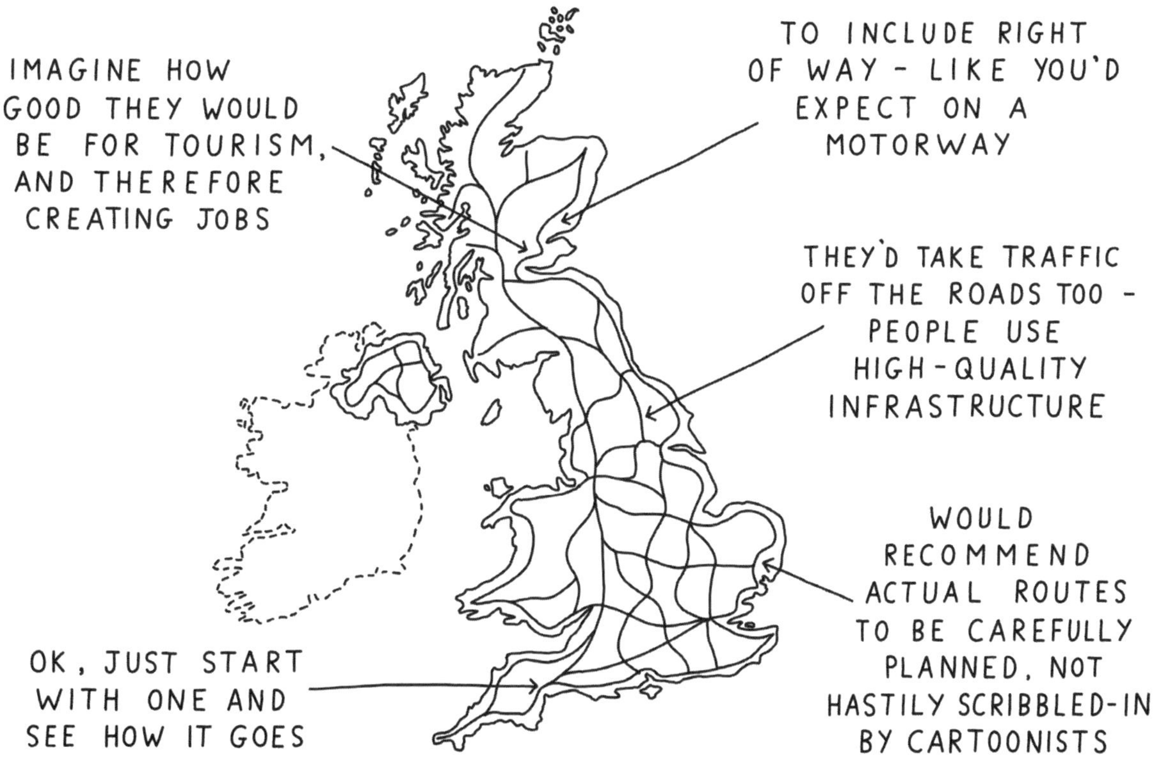
IMAGINE HOW GOOD THEY WOULD BE FOR TOURISM, AND THEREFORE CREATING JOBS
TO INCLUDE RIGHT OF WAY - LIKE YOU'D EXPECT ON A MOTORWAY
THEY'D TAKE TRAFFIC OFF THE ROADS TOO - PEOPLE USE HIGH-QUALITY INFRASTRUCTURE
WOULD RECOMMEND ACTUAL ROUTES TO BE CAREFULLY PLANNED, NOT HASTILY SCRIBBLED-IN BY CARTOONISTS
OK, JUST START WITH ONE AND SEE HOW IT GOES

CYCLE CAMPAIGNING

IDEAS AND STRATEGIES OVERHEARD WHILST EAVESDROPPING AT A MEETING OF EXPERTS

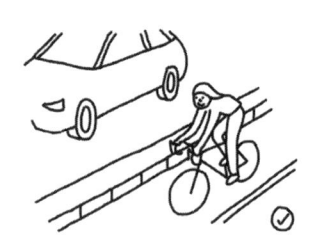

PRAISE GOOD CYCLING INFRASTRUCTURE

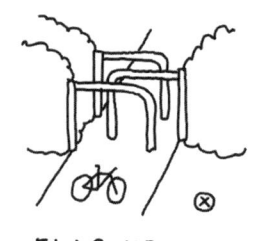

FLAG UP POOR DESIGN

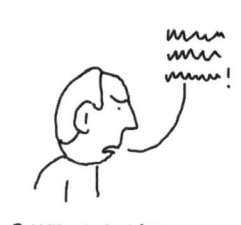

BUT DON'T JUST COMPLAIN →

MAP OF ROUTES WE'D LOVE TO SEE

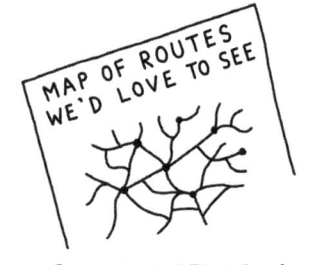

PUT TOGETHER A GOOD PLAN TO HELP YOUR LOCAL AUTHORITY TO GET THE FUNDING

GET TO KNOW THOSE RESPONSIBLE FOR CYCLING WITHIN YOUR LOCAL AUTHORITY (THEY ARE PROBABLY ON YOUR SIDE)

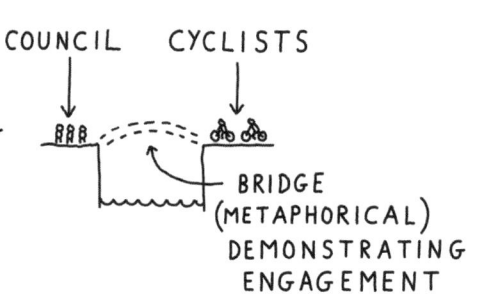

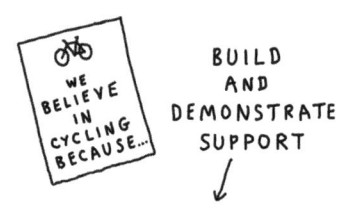

COUNCIL CYCLISTS

BRIDGE (METAPHORICAL) DEMONSTRATING ENGAGEMENT

WE BELIEVE IN CYCLING BECAUSE...

BUILD AND DEMONSTRATE SUPPORT

ONE WAY IS TO CREATE A CYCLING CHARTER

(GOOGLE 'COLCHESTER CYCLING CHARTER' FOR AN EXAMPLE)

JOIN UP WITH OTHERS WHO HAVE THE SAME AIMS

THEN USE THE DIVERSE SKILLS WITHIN YOUR GROUP

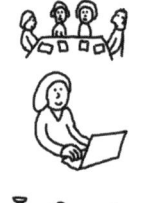

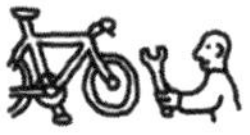

← HOW ABOUT A 'BIKE KITCHEN' (HELPING PEOPLE FIX THE BIKE STUCK IN THEIR GARAGE)?

THE CYCLING WORLD
WHERE WE CAN DO BETTER

REPRESENTATION OF WOMEN AND PEOPLE OF COLOUR

WHO IS ON STAGE AT EVENTS?

WHO IS FEATURED IN MAGAZINES?

MEN'S? WOMEN'S?

BLACK / PINK

DOES A STEP-OVER FRAME MAKE IT A 'WOMEN'S BIKE?' (ANSWER: NO)

WHO ARE CYCLING PRODUCTS MARKETED TO?

KIT THAT FITS ORDINARY PEOPLE GOING FOR A BIKE RIDE

ALL THE HANDY POCKETS. BUT NOT TOO SKIN-TIGHT OR GARISH TO WEAR IN THE PUB

WE'RE NOT ALL BUILT LIKE A RAKE

MOUNTAIN BIKES AND ROAD BIKES NOT BEING THE ONLY BIKES

GREAT BIKES. BUT WHAT ABOUT CARGO BIKES, DUTCH BIKES, FOLDING BIKES, ETC, ETC

CYCLING BEING SEEN AS AN EVERYDAY ACTIVITY RATHER THAN ONLY A SPORT OR FOR 'CYCLISTS'

COMING PAST

THE CITY
HOW IT COULD BE

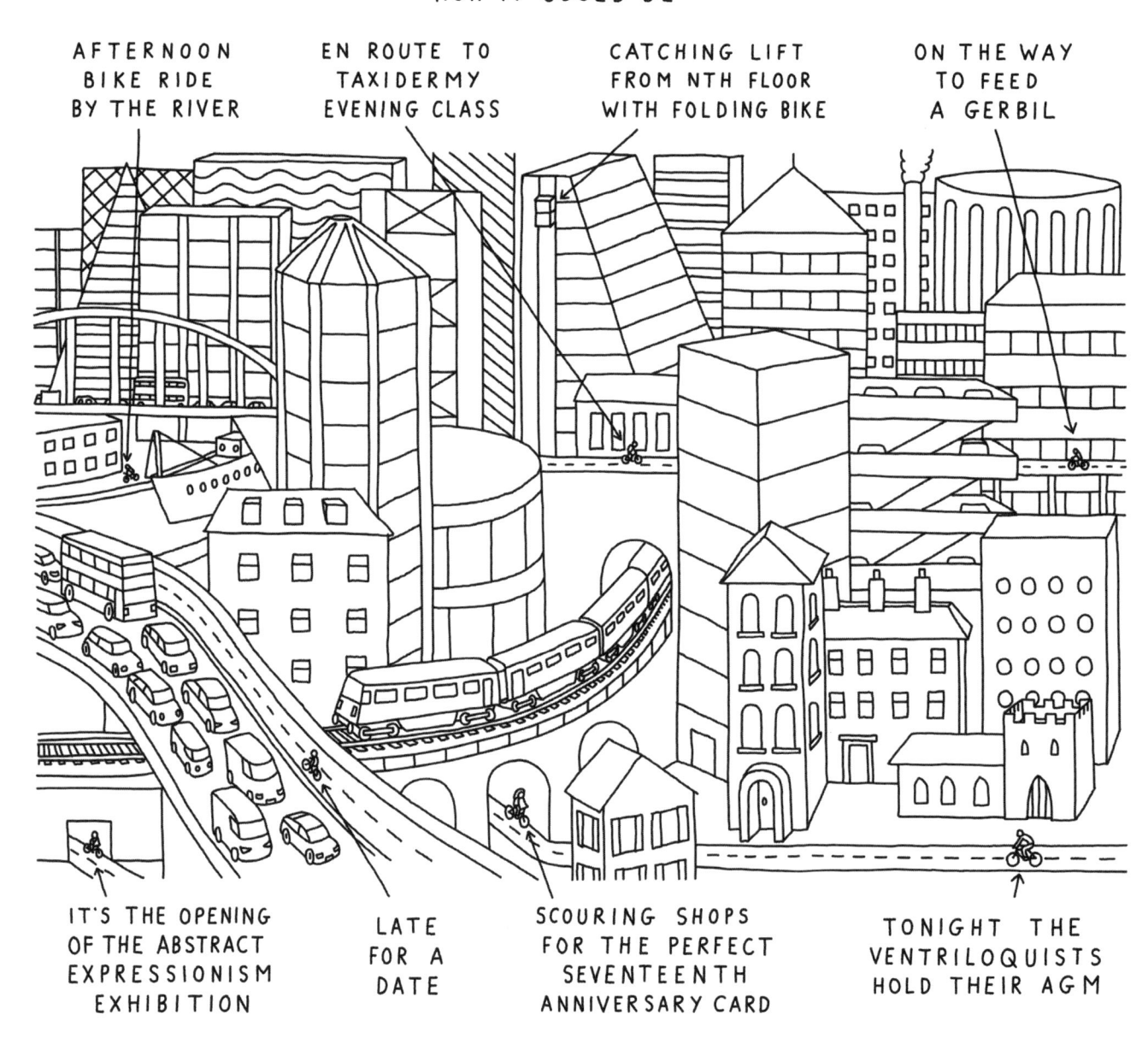

- AFTERNOON BIKE RIDE BY THE RIVER
- EN ROUTE TO TAXIDERMY EVENING CLASS
- CATCHING LIFT FROM NTH FLOOR WITH FOLDING BIKE
- ON THE WAY TO FEED A GERBIL
- IT'S THE OPENING OF THE ABSTRACT EXPRESSIONISM EXHIBITION
- LATE FOR A DATE
- SCOURING SHOPS FOR THE PERFECT SEVENTEENTH ANNIVERSARY CARD
- TONIGHT THE VENTRILOQUISTS HOLD THEIR AGM

THE REVOLUTION

WELCOME TO THE CYCLING REVOLUTION.
ENJOY THE RIDE!

ACKNOWLEDGEMENTS

I started work on *From A to B* in 2019, but most of the book was written during lockdown in 2020 (when I achieved very little else, apart from a little bit of laundry). This wasn't the easiest time to get anything done, and so I'd like to thank everyone who played a part.

A huge thank you to Charlotte Croft at Bloomsbury for recognising the potential in a book of diagrams about cycling as a means of transport, and for guiding the project through what has turned out to be a not entirely straightforward process. Also to Sarah, Zoë and everyone else at Bloomsbury who has worked on the book behind the scenes.

A lot of people have helped me with ideas, and general encouragement. First of all, thank you to my family for their love and support. Also to the members of my highly secret ideas-gathering group, and all those who have supplied suggestions and inspiration in various ways. In no particular order: Alastair Jones, Heather Simmons, Jayne Manfredi, John Cooper, Karen Chalk, Naomi James, Steven Buckley, Tim Hall, Dave Prosser, Steve Tomkins, Matt Hill, Clare Lissaman, Kate Wareham, Ross Wintle, David Preece, Rach Gallant, Trudi Murray, Gary Alderson, Caroline Beckett, Frances Bell, Mark Newitt, Malcolm Mackinnon, Elwin Cockett, Sara Batts-Neale, Katya Tune, Dave Warnock, Julia Wallond, Nigel Brown, Tom Wateracre, Sarah Dean, David Perry, Philip Ritchie, Matt King, Andrew Graystone, Becki Cox, Richard Long, Hannah Leverett, Rosie Rutherford, Elly Mckay-Smith, Ian Sheppard and Clare Causier, and the community at The Fishermen's Chapel in Leigh-on-Sea. A special mention to Bex Lewis, who always encouraged me, and enthusiastically sent me ideas. There will be people I've omitted to mention, for which I apologise.

The vast majority of the cartoons were drawn specifically for this book, but credit needs to go to the following, who commissioned the original versions of some individual drawings: *Guardian Cities* for 'Why we love cycling', 'The urban peloton', 'Cycling in all weathers', 'City cycling', 'Innovations', 'What would make cycling safer?' and 'The shared-use path'; Cycling UK for 'Road safety' and 'Cycle routes'; Landor Links for 'Cycle campaigning'; Landor Links and Duncan Dollimore from Cycling UK for 'Planning'; and The Church of England Diocese of Manchester for 'Encouraging cycling'.

People who have inspired this book: Chris Boardman, for his tireless cycling advocacy, Peter Walker, for the superb 'Bike Nation', and everyone involved in cycle campaigning, locally and nationally, for the work you do in helping us get from A to B safely by bike.

Most of all I'd like to thank Charlotte, my wife, who has helped me with the content at every stage, had to bear the burden of my attempts to complete the book during lockdown, and contributed a huge amount throughout the whole process.

Thank you for buying this book – I hope you enjoy it. Happy cycling!